Fraud Auditing
and Forensic
Accounting

Third Edition

TOMMIE SINGLETON
AARON SINGLETON
JACK BOLOGNA
ROBERT LINDQUIST

WILEY

John Wiley & Sons, Inc.

Copyright © 2006 by John Wiley & Sons, Inc. All rights reserved.

Published by John Wiley & Sons, Inc., Hoboken, New Jersey.

Published simultaneously in Canada.

For general information on our other products and services, or technical support, please contact our Customer Care Department within the United States at 800-762-2974, outside the United States at 317-572-3993, or fax 317-572-4002.

Wiley also publishes its books in a variety of electronic formats. Some content that appears in print may not be available in electronic books.

For more information about Wiley products, visit our Web site at www.wiley.com.

Library of Congress Cataloging-in-Publication Data
Fraud auditing and forensic accounting.— 3rd ed. / Tommie Singleton ... [et al.].
    p. cm.
  Rev. ed. of: Fraud auditing and forensic accounting / G. Jack Bologna, Robert J. Lindquist. 2nd ed. c1995.
  Includes index.
  ISBN-13: 978-0-471-78591-0 (cloth)
  ISBN-10: 0-471-78591-1 (cloth)
  1. White collar crime investigation—United States. 2. Forensic accounting—United States. 3. Fraud investigation—United States. I. Singleton, Tommie. II. Bologna, Jack. Fraud auditing and forensic accounting.
  HV8079.W47F73 2006
  364.16'3—dc22
                              2006007381

Printed in the United States of America

10 9 8 7 6 5 4 3 2 1

Contents

Preface

White-collar crime is rampant, and has been for some time, in the business community of the U.S. economy. Experts have estimated that the costs of white-collar crime averages about 20 times the costs of street crimes each year. The Association of Certified Fraud Examiners (ACFE) estimated that fraud cost the U.S. economy $660 billion in 2004. But white-collar crime has taken a backseat to street crime in terms of media coverage and focus. That is, until Enron, white-collar crimes tended to be overlooked. We hope the hype that has occurred in recent years will continue to bring attention and focus to fraud, and thus help to diminish the costs and occurrences of fraud in the years ahead.

The attention and focus on the major financial fraud scandals led to the passage of the Sarbanes-Oxley Act (SOX) in July 2002 and the adoption of Statement on Auditing Standard (SAS) No. 99, *Consideration of Fraud in a Financial Statement Audit*, in December 2002. This edition brings this book up to date by discussing these and other recent events. We have also extended the discussion about fraud schemes and included more about computer-assisted audit tools (CAATs) and other technological aspects of fraud auditing and forensic accounting.

Primarily, this book deals with fraud of an accounting nature. It deals with fraud from the perspective of how forensic accountants can investigate and document such crimes, how internal and external auditors can detect them, how police and security specialists can investigate them, and how good management practices can help prevent and detect them. Our goal in revising this book was to contribute to the literature of auditing, investigation, and forensics. We hope this edition extends the awareness of the meaning and value of fraud auditing and forensic accounting and contributes to the effectiveness of those in the antifraud profession.

August 2006
Tommie Singleton
Aaron Singleton

Acknowledgments

To add anything of value to the antifraud literature today, one must build on the hard work and intelligent efforts of the pioneers in fraud: Donald Cressey, Edwin Sutherland, Joe Wells, Frank Hartung, Norman Jaspan, Dr. Steve Albrecht, and others. It is also built on the experience and crime-fighting abilities of many whose names are not known but whose experiences have been used to add to the common body of knowledge. For example, Jim Ratley, formerly from the Dallas police department and now with the Association of Certified Fraud Examiners (ACFE), has contributed significantly to the antifraud knowledge.

On a personal note, it was practitioners who helped us to get started. Dr. Tom Buckhoff was both a professor and practitioner. He, more than any other, has taught us about fraud and the antifraud profession, and has given us a personal ongoing education into fraud, much of which came from his personal experiences and investigations. Professionals in our community continued that education, including Ralph Summerford, Mike Mason, and Steve Alexander. These stalwarts of the antifraud practitioner world have continually shared their experiences and knowledge with us.

For us, this foundation of pioneers and experts most assuredly includes Jack Bologna and Robert Lindquist, authors of the first two editions of this book. In 1992, Dr. Singleton began his dissertation at the University of Mississippi on the topic of pioneers in electronic data processing audit. Jack Bologna was one of the fewer than 50 pioneers identified by their peers. Tommie had the privilege of interviewing Jack as part of his dissertation. It was obvious from the interview that Mr. Bologna was extremely capable in the area of fraud and an active member of the antifraud profession. Robert Lindquist has a strong reputation of being a fraud expert and is sought after as an expert witness in fraud cases. His work and efforts are stellar, and he is a well-respected professional in Canada and the United States.

Therefore, we thank all of those pioneers, all of those personal mentors, and all of those seemingly nameless people over the years that have done the real work, but especially we want to thank Jack and Robert. This edition of the book would not have been possible without all of these people, and if it does contribute anything to the antifraud literature, all of the credit goes to them.

Tommie Singleton
Aaron Singleton

CHAPTER 1

Fraud Definitions, Models, and Taxonomies

INTRODUCTION

When bent on exploiting another person, a person's ingenuity in committing fraud may be unlimited. As P. T. Barnum is alleged to have said, "There's a sucker born every minute." He is also alleged to have said, "Trust everyone, but cut the deck."

It is important to understand the definitions, models, and taxonomies of fraud in order to further understand fraud and fraudsters. Therefore, the language of fraud and the antifraud business is a good starting point.

Definition: What Is Fraud?

One person can injure another either by force or through fraud. The use of force to cause bodily injury is frowned on by most organized societies; using fraud to cause financial injury to another does not carry the same degree of stigma. *Fraud* is a word that has many definitions. The more notable ones are:

- *Fraud as a crime. Fraud* is a generic term, and embraces all the multifarious means which human ingenuity can devise, which are resorted to by one individual, to get an advantage over another by false representations. No definite and invariable rule can be laid down as a general proposition in defining fraud, as it includes surprise, trick, cunning and unfair ways by which another is cheated. The only boundaries defining it are those which limit human knavery.[1]

- *Fraud as a tort.* The U.S. Supreme Court in 1887 provided a definition of fraud in the civil sense as:

First: That the defendant has made a representation in regard to a material fact;

Second: That such representation is false;

Third: That such representation was not actually believed by the defendant, *on reasonable grounds, to be true;*

Fourth: That it was made with intent *that it should be acted on;*

Fifth: That it was acted on by complainant to his damage; *and*

Sixth: That in so acting on it the complainant was ignorant of its falsity, and reasonably believed it to be true.

The first of the foregoing requisites excludes such statements as consist merely in an expression of opinion of judgment, honestly entertained; and again excepting in peculiar cases, it excludes statements by the owner and vendor of property in respect of its value. [Emphasis added.][2]

Of the six, the fourth (*intent*) is usually the most difficult to establish in a court case. Guilty parties can use the excuse of an accident or carelessness as the cause of the incident rather than a deliberate intent to steal or commit the fraud, along with a plethora of other viable excuses.

- *Corporate fraud.* Corporate fraud is any fraud perpetrated by, for, or against a business corporation.
- *Management fraud.* Management fraud is the intentional misrepresentation of corporate or unit performance levels perpetrated by employees serving in management roles who seek to benefit from such frauds in terms of promotions, bonuses or other economic incentives, and status symbols.
- *Layperson's definition of* fraud. *Fraud,* as it is commonly understood today, means dishonesty in the form of an intentional deception or a willful misrepresentation of a material fact. Lying, the willful telling of an untruth, and cheating, the gaining of an unfair or unjust advantage over another, could be used to further define the word *fraud* because these two words denote intention or willingness to deceive.

In short, we might say that fraud, intentional deception, lying, and cheating are the opposites of truth, justice, fairness, and equity. Fraud consists of coercing people to act against their own best interests.

Although deception can be intended to coerce people to act against their own self-interest, deception can also be used for one's own defense or survival. Despite that rationale for deception, deception by current standards of behavior is considered mean and culpable. It is considered wrong and evil and can be excused only, if at all, if used for survival. But deception can be intended for a benevolent purpose, too. For example, a doctor might spare a patient from learning that a diagnostic test shows an advanced state of terminal disease. Benevolent deceivers in our society are not looked on as harshly as are those whose intentions and motives are impure. Those who act out of greed, jealousy, spite, and revenge are not so quickly excused or forgiven.

Synonyms: Fraud, Theft, and Embezzlement

Fraud, theft, defalcation, irregularities, white-collar crime, and *embezzlement* are terms that are often used interchangeably. Although they have some common elements, they are not identical in the criminal law sense. For example, in English common law, theft is referred to as *larceny*—the taking and carrying away of the property of another with the intention of permanently depriving the owners of its possession. In larceny, the perpetrator comes into possession of the stolen item illegally. In *embezzlement*, the perpetrator comes into initial possession lawfully, but then converts it to her own use. Embezzlers have a fiduciary duty to care for and to protect the property. In converting it to their own use, they breach that fiduciary duty.

Fraud Auditing, Forensic Auditing, and Financial Auditing

In the lexicon of accounting, terms such as *fraud auditing, forensic accounting, investigative accounting, litigation support,* and *valuation analysis* are not clearly defined. Some distinctions apply between fraud auditing and forensic accounting. Fraud auditing involves a specialized approach and methodology to discern fraud; that is, one audits for evidence of fraud. The purpose is to prove or disprove a fraud exists. Historically, forensic accountants, however, have been called in after evidence or suspicion of fraud has surfaced through an allegation, complaint, or discovery. Fraud

F/A   Forensic accountants are experienced, trained, and knowledgeable in the different processes of fraud investigation: how to interview people (especially the suspect) effectively, how to write reports for court, how to provide expert testimony in court, how the legal system works. The Association of Certified Fraud Examiners (ACFE) refers to this definition of forensic accounting as "fraud examination." In recent years, the broadest of these terms in the antifraud professionals is *forensic accounting,* which typically refers to the incorporation of all the terms involved with investigation, including fraud auditing; that is, fraud auditing is a subset of forensic accounting.

Financial auditing is a wholly different term that needs to be distinguished from forensic and fraud auditing. Financial auditing typically refers to the process of evaluating compliance of financial information with regulatory standards, usually for public companies, by an external, independent entity. Financial audits performed under GAAS (generally accepted auditing standards), required for audits of public companies, must perform fraud-specific procedures. The well-publicized Sarbanes-Oxley Act of 2002 heavily incorporates concepts and procedures to deter and to catch fraud in audits of internal controls over financial reporting. However, the focus of financial audits and financial reporting ultimately is concerned with providing *reasonable* assurance that a *material* misstatement to financial statements has not occurred, regardless of the reason.

Fraud Auditors, Forensic Accountants, and Financial Auditors

Fraud auditors are generally accountants or auditors who, by virtue of their attitudes, attributes, skills, knowledge, and experience, are experts at detecting and documenting frauds in books of account. Their particular attitudes include these beliefs:

- Fraud is possible even in accounting systems in which controls are tight.
- The visible part of a transaction fraud may involve a small amount of money, but the invisible portion can be substantial.
- Red flags of fraud are discernible if one looks long enough and deep enough.
- Fraud perpetrators can come from any level of management or society.

The personal attributes of fraud auditors include self-confidence, persistence, commitment to honesty and fair play, creativity, curiosity, an instinct for what is out of place or what is out of balance, independence, objectivity, good posture and grooming (for courtroom testimony), clear communication, sensitivity to human behavior, common sense, and an ability to fit pieces of a puzzle together without force or contrivance.

The skills fraud auditors require include all of those that are required of financial auditors, plus the knowledge of how to gather evidence of and document fraud losses for criminal, civil, contractual, and insurance purposes; how to interview third-party witnesses; and how to testify as an expert witness.

Fraud auditors must know what a fraud is from a legal and audit perspective, an environmental perspective, a perpetrator's perspective, and a cultural perspective. They also need both general and specific kinds of experience. They should have a fair amount of experience in general auditing and fraud auditing, but should have industry-specific experience as well: for example, banking industry fraud; insurance industry fraud; construction industry fraud; and manufacturing, distribution, and retailing frauds.

Forensic accountants may appear on the crime scene a little later than fraud auditors, but their major contribution is in translating complex financial transactions and numerical data into terms that ordinary laypersons can understand. That is necessary because if the fraud comes to trial, the jury will be made up of ordinary laypersons. Areas of expertise of forensic accountants are not only in accounting and auditing but in criminal investigation, interviewing, report writing, and testifying as expert witnesses. They must be excellent communicators, professional in demeanor, conservative in dress, and well groomed.

Financial auditors traditionally have been seen as, and to an extent have been, numbers-oriented, and their processes have been driven by the audit trail. The discipline of financial auditing has been thought to be almost a checklist of items to complete. In reality, judgment is crucial in financial auditing and has progressively increased in the direction of more dependence on auditor judgment. The Sarbanes-Oxley Act requirements involve auditor judgment to a large degree; auditors are to understand processes significant to financial reporting and to evaluate management's controls (in design and operating effectiveness) over those processes. Additionally, auditors are to consider environmental, including soft, intangible, factors in that evaluation.

Financial auditors have expertise in their knowledge of accounting and financial reporting (GAAP, or generally accepted accounting principles), auditing (GAAS), and how those apply to business transactions. As expressed in the GAAS literature, the most important financial auditing attributes are independence, objectivity, and professional skepticism.

The term *financial auditor* broadly applies to any auditor of financial information or the financial reporting process. The largest classification of financial auditors is those who work for public accounting firms and perform audits of financial statements for public companies. This classification is the most commonly used in this book when referring to financial auditors.

CLASSIC FRAUD RESEARCH

Fraud is a topic much in vogue today. Seminars, symposia, and conferences on that subject abound, sponsored by government agencies, universities, trade groups, professional organizations, chambers of commerce; and business, fraternal, and religious organizations. Most are well attended, particularly because the cost of such crimes to individual businesses and society is substantial, but also because few know much about fraud. Reviewing the literature creates an appreciation for the scope and nature of fraud and builds a foundation for understanding fraud topics.

The current term *fraud* was traditionally referred to as *white-collar crime,* and the two are used synonymously here. The classic works on fraud are *White Collar Crime*, by Edwin H. Sutherland; *Other People's Money*, by Donald R. Cressey; *The Thief in the White Collar*, by Norman Jaspan and Hillel Black; and *Crime, Law, and Society*, by Frank E. Hartung.[3] These authorities essentially tell us:

> *White-collar crime has its genesis in the same general process as other criminal behavior; namely, differential association. The hypothesis of differential association is that criminal behavior is learned in association with those who define such behavior favorably and in isolation from those who define it unfavorably, and that a person in an appropriate situation engages in such criminal behavior if, and only if, the weight of the favorable definitions exceeds the weight of the unfavorable definitions.[4]*

In other words, birds of a feather flock together, or at least reinforce one another's rationalized views and values. But people make their own decisions and, even if subconsciously, in a cost-benefit manner. In order to commit fraud, a rationalization must exist for the individual to decide fraud is worth committing.

> *Trusted persons become trust violators when they conceive of themselves as having a financial problem which is nonshareable, are aware that this problem can be secretly resolved by violation of the position of financial trust, and are able to apply their own conduct in that situation, verbalizations which enable them to adjust their conceptions of themselves as users of the entrusted funds or property.[5]*

Jaspan tried to derive antifraud measures in his research. His book, *The Thief in the White Collar*, is based on his many years of consulting experience on security-related matters, and contains a number of notable and often quoted generalizations. In a nutshell, Jaspan exhorts employers to (1) pay their employees fairly, (2) treat their employees decently, and (3) listen to their employees' problems, if they want to avoid employee fraud, theft, and embezzlement. But to temper that bit of humanism with a little reality, he also suggests that employers ought never to place full trust in either their employees or the security personnel they hire to check on employees.[6] Jaspan, like P. T. Barnum, would *always* cut the deck.

Hartung disagrees with Jaspan's generalizations and focuses on the individual. He argues:

> *It will be noticed that the criminal violator of financial trust and the career delinquent have one thing in common: Their criminality is learned in the process of symbolic communication, dependent upon cultural sources of patterns of thought and action, and for systems of values and vocabularies of motives.*[7]

In reality, both Jaspan and Hartung appear to have been correct. Hartung noted that individuals are inevitably affected by their environment. Although Jaspan might be considered too empathetic to the individual, his suggestions to deter fraud echo the same as modern efforts do: Create an environment with few reasons and with few opportunities to commit fraud.

FRAUD TRIANGLE

Why Is Fraud Committed?

Fraud or intentional deception is a strategy to achieve a personal or organizational goal or to satisfy a human need. However, a goal or need can be satisfied by honest means as well as by dishonest means. So what precipitates, inspires, or motivates one to select dishonest rather than honest means to satisfy goals and needs?

Generally speaking, competitive survival can be a motive for both honest and dishonest behavior. A threat to survival may cause one to choose either dishonest or honest means. When competition is keen and predatory, dishonesty can be rationalized quickly. Deceit, therefore, can become a weapon in any contest for survival. Stated differently, the struggle to survive (economically, socially, or politically) often generates deceitful behavior. The same is true of fraud in business.

"Fraud Triangle"

Of the traditional fraud research, Donald Cressey's research in the 1950s provides the most valuable insight into the question why fraud is committed. The result of this research is most commonly, and succinctly, presented in what is known as the fraud triangle.

Cressey decided to interview fraudsters who were convicted of embezzlement. He interviewed about 200 embezzlers in prison. One of the major conclusions of his efforts was that every fraud had three things in common: (1) pressure (sometimes referred to as motivation, and usually an "unshareable need"); (2) rationalization (of personal ethics); and (3) knowledge and opportunity to commit the crime. These three points are the corners of the fraud triangle (see Exhibit 1.1).

Pressure　　*Pressure* (or incentive, or motivation) refers to something that has happened in the fraudster's personal life that creates a stressful need for funds, and thus motivates him to steal. Usually that motivation centers on some financial strain, but it could be the symptom of other types of pressures. For example, a drug habit or gambling habit could create great financial need in order to sustain the habit and thus create the pressure associated with this aspect of the fraud triangle. Sometimes a fraudster finds motivation in some incentive. For instance, almost all financial statement frauds were motivated by some incentive, usually related to stock prices or performance bonuses or both. Sometimes an insatiable greed causes relatively wealthy people to commit frauds.

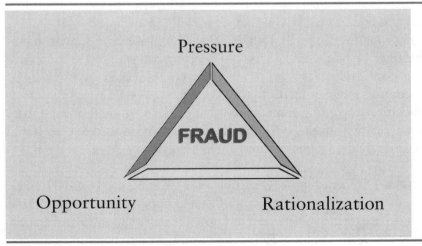

EXHIBIT 1.1　　Fraud Triangle

Beyond the realm of competitive and economic survival, what other motives precipitate fraud? Social and political survival provide incentives, too, in the form of egocentric and ideological motives, especially in financial statement frauds. Sometimes people commit fraud (deception) to aggrandize their egos, put on airs, or assume false status. Sometimes they deceive to survive politically, or have a burning desire for power. They lie about their personal views or pretend to believe when they do not. Or they simply cheat or lie to their political opponents or intentionally misstate their opponents' positions on issues. They commit dirty tricks against opponents.

Motives to commit fraud in business usually are rationalized by the old saying that all is fair in love and war—and in business, which is amoral, anyway. There is one further category of motivation, however. We call it psychotic, because it cannot be explained in terms of rational behavior. In this category are the pathological liar, the professional confidence man, and the kleptomaniac.

Rationalization   Most fraudsters do not have a criminal record. In the ACFE Report to the Nation (RTTN) 2004,[8] 88% of the reported fraudsters had no prior criminal record. In fact, white-collar criminals usually have a personal code of ethics. It is not uncommon for a fraudster to be religious. So how do fraudsters justify actions that are objectively criminal? They simply justify their crime under their circumstances. For instance, many will steal from employers but mentally convince themselves that they will repay it (i.e., "I am just borrowing the money"). Others believe no one is hurt so that makes the theft benign. Still others believe they deserve a raise or better treatment and are simply taking matters into their own hands to administer fair treatment. Many other excuses could serve as a rationalization, including some benevolent ones where the fraudster does not actually keep the stolen funds or assets but uses them for social purposes (e.g., to fund an animal clinic for strays).

Opportunity   According to Cressey's research (i.e., the Fraud Tringle), fraudsters always had the knowledge and opportunity to commit the fraud. The former is reflected in known frauds, and in research studies such as the ACFE RTTNs, that show employees and managers tend to have a long tenure with a company when they commit the fraud. A simple explanation is that employees and managers who have been around for years know quite well where the weaknesses are in the internal controls and have gained sufficient knowledge of how to commit the crime successfully.

But the main factor in opportunity is internal controls. A weakness in or absence of internal controls provides the opportunity for fraudsters to commit their crimes. It is noteworthy that the Treadway Commission (later known as the Committee of Sponsoring Organizations, or COSO) was formed to respond to the savings and loan frauds and scandals of the early 1980s. The committee's conclusion was that the best prevention was strong internal controls, and the result was the COSO model of internal controls, which was incorporated into financial auditing technical literature as SAS No. 78, *Consideration of Internal Control in a Financial Statement Audit*. Then the Sarbanes-Oxley Act (SOX) focused on an annual evaluation of the internal controls by management with an independent opinion of that evaluation by the financial auditors—Section 404 of the act. Again, if the purpose of SOX was to minimize fraud, internal control is the effective way to accomplish that goal. In fact, it could be argued that this aspect of the triangle is the only one that auditors can easily observe or control.

The opportunities to commit fraud are rampant in the presence of loose or lax management and (concomitant) inadequate attention to internal controls. When motivation is coupled with such opportunities, the potential for fraud is increased.

Motivation and Opportunities Fraud

On-the-job fraud, theft, and embezzlement are products of motivation and opportunity. The motivation may be economic need or greed, egocentricity, ideological conflicts, and psychosis. Most on-the-job frauds are committed for economic reasons and often are attributable to alcoholism, drug abuse, gambling, and high lifestyle. Loose or lax controls and a work environment that does not value honesty can provide the opportunity.

Motivations and opportunities are interactive: The greater the economic need, the less weakness in internal controls is needed to accomplish the fraud. The greater the weakness in controls, the level of motivational need necessary to commit a fraud is less.

SCOPE OF FRAUD

How pervasive is business fraud? How likely is it to be discovered either by audit design or by accident? Research in the last 10 years has been able to reveal both the scope of fraud and the most effective means of detecting frauds.

The scope of fraud is such that almost all midsize to large businesses are certain to have a fraud currently being or soon to be perpetrated. Virtually no small business is safe. Nor are not-for-profits or other types of organizations. Research by the ACFE reveals that the estimated level of fraud detected from 1996 to 2004 has been consistent in the U.S. economy—approximately 6% of annual revenues.[9]

Regarding financial frauds, a major study by COSO provides valuable insights. In 1998, COSO released its *Landmark Study on Fraud in Financial Reporting*.[10] The report covered 10 years of the Securities and Exchange Commission (SEC) enforcement cases, analyzing 200 randomly selected cases of alleged financial fraud investigated by the SEC—about two-thirds of the 300 SEC probes into fraud between 1987 and 1997. COSO examined certain key company and management characteristics, and the key findings were interesting: Most fraud among public companies was committed by small firms (well below $100 million in assets), boards of directors were dominated by insiders and inexperienced people, executive officers were identified as associated with financial statement fraud in 83% of the cases, and the average fraud period extended over a period of 23.7 months. The report went on to say: "The relatively small size of fraud companies suggests that the inability or even unwillingness to implement cost-effective internal controls may be a factor affecting the likelihood of financial statement fraud." COSO suggested external auditors focus on the "tone at the top" in evaluating internal control structures.

In 2003, KPMG released its third *Fraud Survey*.[11] In it, KPMG surveyed 459 public companies and government agencies. The report found that fraud is increasing in the number of instances reported since its last survey. Of the respondents, 75% reported losses due to fraud in 2003, as compared to 62% in 1998. Employee fraud was most common category of fraud (60%). The category of financial reporting frauds averaged $257.9 million in costs per organization for the previous year, and the category of medical/insurance frauds averaged $33.7 million. These were the most costly fraud categories in the survey. Of the frauds reported, 36% incurred $1 million or more in costs, up from 21% in 1998. The median loss per incident was $116,000 for all types of fraud (1998). Only 4% of the frauds were discovered during financial statement audits in the 1998 survey, up to 12% in 2003. The most frequent methods of detection were internal controls (77%), internal audit (66%), employee tip (63%), and accident (54%). Obviously, there was some overlap in multiple detection methods.

The ACFE tracks the trend in fraud and statistics on fraud regularly. It has been conducting surveys on occupational fraud and abuse since 1996 and communicating the results to the public via its Report to the Nation. In all three reports (1996, 2002, 2004), the ACFE surveyed hundreds of Certified Fraud Examiners (CFEs), who reported facts on a fraud from the previous year. The results show enormous amounts of fraud each survey. The reported losses due to fraud were about 6% of reported revenues for those entities for each of the three years. Thus one measure of the scope of fraud is about 6% of the U.S. economy, or about 6% of the average firm. According to the most recent ACFE RTTN (2004), that figure would be $660 billion total. Fraud losses have increased by 50% since the first survey in 1996. Financial frauds lasted an average of 25 months before being discovered.

The various ACFE RTTNs have also measured the common methods of detecting fraud. According to the reports, tips and complaints have consistently been the most effective means of detecting frauds, and are a much higher percentage than the second most effective means. Tips and complaints accounted for 39.6% of the initial detection of occupational fraud in the 2004 report. Internal audit was second (23.8%), accident was third (21.3%), internal controls was fourth (18.4%), and external audit was fifth (10.9%).[12]

These research studies and other similar research show that fraud, of various kinds, is widespread. The best detection methods include tips, internal controls, and internal audit. The first two are integral tenets of the Sarbanes-Oxley Act of 2002.

PROFILE OF FRAUDSTERS

Who Commits Fraud?

In view of the last section, one might conclude that fraud is caused mainly by factors external to the individual: economic, competitive, social, and political factors, and poor controls. But how about the individual? Are some people more prone to commit fraud than others? And if so, is that a more serious cause of fraud than the external and internal environmental factors we have talked about? Data from criminology and sociology seem to suggest so.

Let us begin by making a few generalizations about people.

- Some people are honest all of the time.
- Some people (fewer than the above) are dishonest all of the time.
- Most people are honest some of the time.
- Some people are honest most of the time.

Research has been conducted to ask employees whether they are honest at work or not. Forty percent say they would not steal, 30% said they would, and 30% said they might.

Beyond those generalizations about people, what can we say about fraud perpetrators? Gwynn Nettler, in *Lying, Cheating and Stealing*,[13] offers these insights on cheaters and deceivers:

- People who have experienced failure are more likely to cheat.
- People who are disliked and who dislike themselves tend to be more deceitful.
- People who are impulsive, distractible, and unable to postpone gratification are more likely to engage in deceitful crimes.
- People who have a conscience (fear of apprehension and punishment) are more resistant to the temptation to deceive.
- Intelligent people tend to be more honest than ignorant people. Middle- and upper-class people tend to be more honest than lower-class people.
- The easier it is to cheat and steal, the more people will do so.
- Individuals have different needs and therefore different levels at which they will be moved to lie, cheat, or steal.

- Lying, cheating, and stealing increase when people have great pressure to achieve important objectives.
- The struggle to survive generates deceit.

People lie, cheat, and steal on the job in a variety of personal and organizational situations. The ways that follow are but a few:

1. Personal variables

    Aptitudes/abilities

    Attitudes/preferences

    Personal needs/wants

    Values/beliefs

2. Organizational variables

    Nature/scope of the job (meaningful work)

    Tools/training provided

    Reward/recognition system

    Quality of management and supervision

    Clarity of role responsibilities

    Clarity of job-related goals

    Interpersonal trust

    Motivational and ethical climate (ethics and values of superiors and coworkers)

3. External variables

    Degree of competition in the industry

    General economic conditions

    Societal values (ethics of competitors and of social and political role models)

Why Do Employees Lie, Cheat, and Steal on the Job?

These 25 reasons for employee crimes are those most often advanced by authorities in white-collar crime (criminologists, psychologists, sociologists, risk managers, auditors, police, and security professionals):

1. The employee believes he can get away with it.
2. The employee thinks she desperately needs or desires the money or articles stolen.
3. The employee feels frustrated or dissatisfied about some aspect of the job.
4. The employee feels frustrated or dissatisfied about some aspect of his personal life that is not job related.
5. The employee feels abused by the employer and wants to get even.
6. The employee fails to consider the consequences of being caught.
7. The employee thinks: "Everybody else steals, so why not me?"
8. The employee thinks: "They're so big, stealing a little bit won't hurt them."
9. The employee doesn't know how to manage her own money, so is always broke and ready to steal.
10. The employee feels that beating the organization is a challenge and not a matter of economic gain alone.
11. The employee was economically, socially, or culturally deprived during childhood.
12. The employee is compensating for a void felt in his personal life and needs love, affection, and friendship.
13. The employee has no self-control and steals out of compulsion.
14. The employee believes a friend at work has been subjected to humiliation or abuse or has been treated unfairly.
15. The employee is just plain lazy and will not work hard to earn enough to buy what she wants or needs.
16. The organization's internal controls are so lax that everyone is tempted to steal.
17. No one has ever been prosecuted for stealing from the organization.
18. Most employee thieves are caught by accident rather than by audit or design. Therefore, fear of being caught is not a deterrent to theft.
19. Employees are not encouraged to discuss personal or financial problems at work or to seek management's advice and counsel on such matters.
20. Employee theft is a situational phenomenon. Each theft has its own preceding conditions, and each thief has her own motives.
21. Employees steal for any reason the human mind and imagination can conjure up.
22. Employees never go to jail or get harsh prison sentences for stealing, defrauding, or embezzling from their employers.

23. Human beings are weak and prone to sin.
24. Employees today are morally, ethically, and spiritually bankrupt.
25. Employees tend to imitate their bosses. If their bosses steal or cheat, then they are likely to do it also.

To be respected and thus complied with, laws must be rational, fair in application, and enforced quickly and efficiently. Company policies that relate to employee honesty, like criminal laws in general, must be rational, fair, and intended to serve the company's best economic interests. The test of rationality for any company security policy is whether its terms are understandable, whether its punishments or prohibitions are applicable to a real and serious matter, and whether its enforcement is possible in an efficient and legally effective way.

But what specific employee acts are serious enough to be prohibited and/or punished? Any act that could or does result in substantial loss, damage, or destruction of company assets should be prohibited.

The greatest deterrent to criminal behavior is sure and even-handed justice; that means swift detection and apprehension, a speedy and impartial trial, and punishment that fits the crime: loss of civil rights, privileges, property, personal freedom, or social approval. Having said all that, why is it that, despite the dire consequences of criminal behavior, we still see so much of it? Apparently because the rewards gained often exceed the risk of apprehension and punishment; or, stated another way, because the pains inflicted as punishment are not as severe as the pleasures of criminal behavior. The latter seems to be particularly true in cases of economic or white-collar crimes. Many times, if not most, when a fraud is detected, the extent of punishment regarding the perpetrator is to be fired, sometimes without even paying back the fraud losses. So while potential white-collar criminals might believe they might get caught, the ramifications are below some acceptable threshold.

Are white-collar criminals more rational than their blue-collar counterparts? If so, they probably weigh the potential costs (arrest, incarceration, embarrassment, loss of income) against the economic benefit—the monetary gain from their crime. If the benefit outweighs the cost, they opt to commit the crime—not just any crime, but crimes against employers, stockholders, creditors, bankers, customers, insurance carriers, and government regulators.

High-Level and Low-Level Thieves

All thieves steal as a matter of greed or need and as a matter of ease of opportunity. At high levels of organizational life, it is easy to steal because controls can be bypassed or overridden. The sums high-level managers steal, therefore, tend to be greater than the sums low-level personnel steal. For instance, according to the 2004 ACFE RTTN, executives average about $900,000 per fraud, managers about $150,000, and employees about $63,000. The number of incidents of theft, however, is greater at low levels of organizations because of the sheer number of employees found there.

The ACFE RTTN[14] has assessed the profile of fraudsters from the information provided by CFEs in its 2004 survey. The more expensive frauds, in terms of cost/losses, are done by fraudsters who tend to have these traits: (a) have been with the firm a longer time, (b) earn a higher income, (c) are male, (d) are over 60 years of age, (e) well educated {the higher the education, the higher the losses}, (f) operate in collusion rather than alone, and (g) have never been charged with anything criminal. These factors are probably correlated. That is, executives steal larger amounts and they fit this profile. The most frequent frauds, however, tend to point to a slightly different profile: (a) length of service—about the same, (b) income—earns much less, (c) gender—about even between male and female, (d) age—41 to 50, (e) education—high school, (f) operate—alone, (f) criminal record—about the same.

Another source[15] provides a similar profile for a typical fraudster: (a) position—key position, higher up, (b) gender—usually male, (c) age—over 50, (d) marital status—married, and (e) education—highly educated. This profile is similar to the one from the ACFE RTTN, and leads us to this overall conclusion: A white-collar criminal *does not look like a criminal*!

WHO IS VICTIMIZED BY FRAUD MOST OFTEN?

One might think that the most trusting people are also the most gullible and therefore most often the victims of fraud. Using that rationale, we could postulate that organizations with the highest levels of control would be least susceptible to fraud. But organizations that go overboard on controls do not necessarily experience less fraud; and they have the added burden of higher costs.

Controls to protect against fraud by either organization insiders or outside vendors, suppliers, and contractors must be adequate; that is, they must accomplish the goal of control—cost-feasible protection of assets against loss, damage, or destruction. *Cost-feasible protection* means minimal expenditures for maximum protection. Creating an organizational police state would be control overkill. A balanced perspective on controls and security measures is the ideal, and that may require involving employees in creating control policies, plans, and procedures. A balanced perspective weighs the costs and benefits of proposed new controls and security measures. It means that a measure of trust must exist among employees at all levels. Trust breeds loyalty and honesty; distrust can breed disloyalty and perhaps even dishonesty.

Fraud is therefore most prevalent in organizations that have no controls, no trust, no ethical standards, no profits, and no future. Likewise, the more these circumstances exist, the higher the risk of fraud.

FRAUD TAXONOMIES

Most technical books have a glossary at the end. This one provides a taxonomy at the beginning to lay a simple but expanded foundation for what follows in the text. Another benefit of the taxonomy is that it provides a periodic quick review and thus reinforces the lessons learned at the first reading. In essence, the taxonomy summarizes the major principles of fraud auditing and forensic accounting.

General Dichotomies of Frauds

Consumer and Investor Frauds *Fraud,* in a nutshell, is intentional deception, commonly described as lying, cheating, and stealing. Fraud can be perpetrated against customers, creditors, investors, suppliers, bankers, insurers, or government authorities (e.g., tax fraud), stock fraud, and short weights and counts. For our purposes, we will limit coverage to frauds in financial statements and commercial transactions. Consumer fraud has a literature of its own. Our aim is, therefore, to assist accountants and investigators in their efforts to detect and document fraud in books of account.

Criminal and Civil Fraud   A specific act of fraud may be a criminal offense, a civil wrong, or grounds for the rescission of a contract. *Criminal fraud* requires proof of an intentional deception. *Civil fraud* requires that the victim suffer damages. Fraud in the inducement of a contract may vitiate consent and render a contract voidable.

The definition of a criminal fraud according to the ACFE is the one used in this book:

> Criminal fraud *denotes a false representation of a material fact made by one party to another party with the intent to deceive and induce the other party to justifiably rely on the fact to his/her detriment (i.e., his injury or loss).*

Fraud for and against the Company   Fraud can be viewed from yet another perspective. When we think of fraud in a corporate or management context, we can perhaps develop a more meaningful and relevant taxonomy as a framework for fraud auditing.

Corporate frauds can be classified into two broad categories: (1) frauds directed against the company, and (2) frauds that benefit the company. In the former, the company is the victim; in the latter, the company, through the fraudulent actions of its officers, is the intended beneficiary. In that context, we can distinguish between organizational frauds that are intended to benefit the organizational entity and those that are intended to harm the entity.

For example, price fixing, corporate tax evasion, violations of environmental laws, false advertising, and short counts and weights are generally intended to aid the organization's financial performance. Manipulating accounting records to overstate profits is another illustration of a fraud intended to benefit the company but that may benefit management through bonuses based on profitability or stock prices in the market. In frauds *for* the organization, management may be involved in a conspiracy to deceive. Only one person may be involved in a fraud against the organization, such as an accounts payable clerk who fabricates invoices from a nonexistent vendor, has checks issued to that vendor, and converts the checks to his own use.

Frauds for the company are committed mainly by senior managers who wish to enhance the financial position or condition of the company by such ploys as overstating income, sales, or assets or by understating expenses and liabilities. In essence, an intentional misstatement of a financial fact is made, and that can constitute a civil or criminal fraud. But income, for example, may also be intentionally understated to evade taxes, and expenses can be overstated for a similar reason. Frauds for the company by top managers are usually to deceive shareholders, creditors, and regulatory authorities. Similar frauds by lower-level profit-center managers may be to deceive their superiors in the organization, to make them believe the unit is more profitable or productive than it is, and thereby perhaps to earn a higher bonus award or a promotion. In the latter event, despite the fact that the subordinate's overstatement of income, sales, or productivity ostensibly helps the company look better, it is really a fraud *against* the company.

Frauds *against* the company are intended to benefit only the perpetrator, as in the case of theft of corporate assets or embezzlement. The latter specific category of fraud is often referred to as misappropriation of assets. Frauds against the company may also include vendors, suppliers, contractors, and competitors bribing employees. Cases of employee bribery are difficult to discern or discover by audit, because the corporation's accounting records generally are not manipulated, altered, or destroyed. Bribe payments are made under the table or, as lawyers say, "sub rosa." The first hint of bribery may come from an irate vendor whose product is consistently rejected despite its quality, price, and performance. Bribery may also become apparent if the employee begins to live beyond her means, far in excess of salary and family resources.

Several other financial crimes do not fit conveniently into our schema here but also are noteworthy: for example, arson for profit, planned bankruptcy, and fraudulent insurance claims.

Internal and External Fraud   Frauds referred to as corporate or management frauds can be categorized as *internal frauds* to distinguish them from *external fraud* (a category that includes frauds committed by vendors, suppliers, and contractors who might overbill, double bill, or substitute inferior goods). Customers may also play that game by feigning damage or destruction of goods in order to gain credits and allowances.

Corruption in the corporate sense may be practiced by outsiders against insiders, such as purchasing agents, for example. Corruption can also be committed by insiders against buyers from customer firms. Commercial bribery often is accompanied by manipulation of accounting records to cover up its payment and protect the recipients from the tax burden.

Management and Nonmanagement Fraud   Corporate or organizational fraud is not restricted to high-level executives. Organizational fraud touches senior, middle, and first-line management as well as non-management employees. There may be some notable distinctions between the means used and the motivations and opportunities the work environment provides, but fraud is found at all levels of an organization—if one bothers to look for it. Even if internal controls are adequate by professional standards, we should not forget that top managers can override controls with impunity, and often do so. In addition, even the best of internal controls suffers from atrophy, to the degree they depend on human intervention. This effect is measured by "effectiveness" of internal controls, to ensure they are functioning at the level designed and intended, and not at some subordinate level due to slackness on the part of employees responsible for elements of the controls.

Specific Frauds and Categories

As stated earlier, fraud is intentional deception. Its forms are generally referred to as lying and cheating. But theft by guile (larceny by trick, false pretenses, and false tokens) and embezzlement sometimes are included as fraudulent acts. The element of deception is the common ground they all share. But *fraud* and *deception* are abstract terms. They go by many other names as well. For example, in alphabetical order:

Accounts payable fabrication
Accounts receivable lapping
Arson for profit
Bank fraud
Bankruptcy fraud
Benefit claims fraud
Bid rigging
Breach of trust
Breach of fiduciary duty
Business opportunity fraud
Bust out
Cash lapping
Check forgery
Check kiting
Check raising
Collateral forgery
Commercial bribery
Computer fraud
Concealment
Consumer fraud
Conversion
Corporate fraud
Corruption
Counterfeiting
Credit card fraud
Defalcation
Distortion of fact
Double dealing
Duplicity
Electronic Funds Transfer fraud
Embezzlement
Expense account fraud
False advertising
False and misleading statement
False claim
False collateral
False count
False data
False identity
False information
False ownership
False pretenses
False report
False representation
False suggestion
False valuation
False weights and measures
Fictitious person
Fictitious customer
Fictitious employees
Fictitious vendors
Financial fraud
Financial misrepresentation
Forged documents
Forged signatures
Forgery
Franchising fraud
Fraud in execution
Fraud in inducement
Fraudulent concealment
Fraudulent financial statement
Fraudulent representation
Industrial espionage
Infringement of patents
Infringement of copyrights
Infringement of trademarks
Input scam
Insider trading
Insurance fraud
Inventory overstatement
Inventory reclassification fraud
Investor fraud

Kickback
Land fraud
Lapping
Larceny by trick
Loan fraud
Lying
Mail fraud
Management fraud
Material misstatement
Material omission
Misapplication
Misappropriation
Misfeasance
Misrepresentation
Oil and gas scams
Output scams
Over billing

Overstatement of revenue
Padding expenses
Padding government contracts
Payables fraud
Payroll fraud
Performance fraud
Price fixing
Pricing and extension fraud
Procurement fraud
Quality substitution
Restraint of trade
Sales overstatements
Securities fraud
Software piracy
Stock fraud
Subterfuge
Swindling

Tax fraud
Tax shelter scam
Technology theft
Theft of computer time
Theft of proprietary information
Throughput scam
Trade secret theft
Undue influence
Understatement of costs
Understatement of liabilities
Unjust enrichment
Vendor short shipment
Watered stock
Wire fraud
Wire transfer fraud

There are several models for categorizing the numerous possible typologies of fraud schemes. Those models are discussed later and are presented together in Exhibit 1.2.

One way to view the pervasiveness and complexity of fraud might be to design a fraud typology by various groups involved, as in Exhibits 1.2, 1.3, 1.4, and 1.5. An array of fraud characteristics may provide such insight. These lists of fraud perpetrators, victims, and fraud types summarize most frauds, but are far from exhaustive.

To summarize these typologies, our rough guide to classification appears as:

Insider Fraud against the Company

- Cash diversions, conversions, and thefts (front-end frauds)
- Check raising and signature or endorsement forgeries
- Receivables manipulations, such as lapping and fake credit memos
- Payables manipulations, such as raising or fabricating vendor invoices, benefit claims, and expense vouchers, and allowing vendors, suppliers, and contractors to overcharge
- Payroll manipulations, such as adding nonexistent employees or altering time cards
- Inventory manipulations and diversions, such as specious reclassifications of inventories to obsolete, damaged, or sample status, to create a cache from which thefts can be made more easily
- Favors and payments to employees by vendors, suppliers, and contractors

Outsider Fraud against the Company

- Vendor, supplier, and contractor frauds, such as short shipping goods, substituting goods of inferior quality, overbilling, double billing, billing but not delivering or delivering elsewhere
- Vendor, supplier, and contractor corruption of employees
- Customer corruption of employees

EXHIBIT 1.2   Fraud by Corporate Owners and Managers

Victim	Fraud Type
Customers	False advertising
	False weights
	False measures
	False labeling/branding
	Price fixing
	Quality substitution
	Cheap imitations
	Defective products
Stockholders	False financial statements
	False financial forecasts
	False representations
Creditors	False financial statements
	False financial forecasts
	False representations
Competitors	Predatory pricing
	Selling below cost
	Information piracy
	Infringement of patents/copyrights
	Commercial slander
	Libel
	Theft of trade secrets
	Corruption of employees
Bankers	Check kiting
	False application for credit
	False financial statements
Company/Employer	Expense account padding
	Performance fakery
	Overstating revenue
	Overstating assets
	Overstating profits
	Understating expenses
	Understating liabilities
	Theft of assets
	Embezzlement
	Conversion of assets
	Commercial bribery
	Insider trading
	Related party transactions
	Alteration/destruction of records
Insurance Carriers	Fraudulent loss claims
	Arson for profit
	False application for insurance
Government Agencies	False claims
	Contract padding
	Willful failure to file reports/returns

EXHIBIT 1.3   Fraud by Corporate Vendors, Suppliers, and Contractors

Victim	Fraud Type
Customers	Short shipment
Customers	Overbilling
Customers	Double billing
Customers	Substitution of inferior goods
Customers	Corruption of employees

Source: Adapted from Jack Bologna, *Forensic Accounting Review* (1984).

Frauds for the Company

- Smoothing profits (cooking the books) through practices such as inflating sales, profits, and assets; understating expenses, losses, and liabilities; not recording or delaying recording of sales returns; early booking of sales; and inflating ending inventory
- Check kiting
- Price fixing
- Cheating customers by using devices such as short weights, counts, and measures; substituting cheaper materials; and false advertising
- Violating governmental regulations (e.g., Equal Employment Opportunity Act [EEO], Occupation Safety and Health Administration [OSHA], environmental securities, or tax violations standards)
- Corrupting customer personnel
- Political corruption
- Padding costs on government contracts

EXHIBIT 1.4   Fraud by Corporate Customers

Victim	Fraud Type
Vendors	Tag switching
Vendors	Shoplifting
Vendors	Fraudulent checks
Vendors	Fraudulent claims for refunds
Vendors	Fraudulent credit cards
Vendors	Fraudulent credit applications

Source: Adapted from Jack Bologna, *Forensic Accounting Review* (1984).

EXHIBIT 1.5   Fraud by Corporate Employees

Victim	Fraud Type
Employers	False employment applications
Employers	False benefit claims
Employers	False expense claims
Employers	Theft and pilferage
Employers	Performance fakery
Employers	Embezzlement
Employers	Corruption

Source: Adapted from Jack Bologna, *Forensic Accounting Review* (1984).

The ACFE has developed a model for categorizing known frauds that it calls the "fraud tree," which lists about 51 different individual fraud schemes grouped by categories and subcategories. The three main categories are (1) fraudulent statements, (2) asset misappropriation, and (3) corruption. Fraudulent statement fraud schemes typically are done by executives. They are the most expensive frauds but the least frequent ones. They are often driven by motives related to stock prices in the market (e.g., stock bonuses, pressure to keep stock prices trading high or higher, etc.). Asset misappropriation schemes typically are done by employees and include a large number of different schemes. They are the most common by occurrence (frequency) but the least costly per incident. Because they tend to be immaterial, especially individual transactions, they are difficult for financial or internal auditors to discover doing traditional financial and internal audits. Corruption involves a number of schemes, such as bribery and extortion, that usually involve more than one person, even though one might be an unwilling party.

Other notable fraud taxonomies exist. KPMG used a different taxonomy in its fraud surveys. Dr. Steve Albrecht uses another one in his book on fraud.[16] Exhibit 1.6 summarizes these major taxonomies.

EVOLUTION OF A TYPICAL FRAUD

Most frauds follow a similar pattern in the life cycle of the processes or steps. There are differences to consider depending on the fraud. For example, a skimming fraud scheme is "off the books" and therefore

EXHIBIT 1.6   Summary of Models/Typologies/Taxonomies

Source	Fraud Taxonomy
Bologna – Lindquist [2e]	Insider fraud against the company Outsider fraud against the company Frauds for the company
KPMG	Employee fraud Consumer fraud Vendor-related fraud Computer crime Misconduct Medical/insurance fraud Financial reporting fraud
Steve Albrecht	Employee embezzlement Management fraud Investment scams Vendor fraud Customer fraud Miscellaneous fraud
ACFE	Fraudulent statement fraud Asset misappropriation Corruption

requires no real concealment of the fraud. Likewise, the motivation for financial statement frauds is usually very different from that of asset misappropriation frauds. A general evolution of a typical fraud follows.

1. **Motivation/Pressure**   Need
   Greed
   Revenge

2. **Opportunity**
   (control weaknesses)   Access to assets, records, and/or documents that control assets
   No audit trails or separation of duties
   No rotation of duties
   No internal audit function
   No control policies
   No code of ethics

3. **Rationalization (formulation of intent)**

Rationalization of the crime as borrowing, etc., not stealing

4. **Commit the Fraud**

Execute the particular fraud scheme; fraud, theft, embezzlement, etc.

5. **Convert to Cash**

If it is not a cash theft, the fraudster must convert the theft to cash (e.g., theft of inventory, financial fraud to stock to cash, or cashing a check made out to a bogus or real payee)

6. **Conceal the Fraud**

Alter documents and/or records
Forgery
Destruction of records
(For skimming and other off-the-books frauds, no concealment is necessary.)

7. **Red Flags**

Variances detected
Allegations made
Behavior pattern change noted in the fraudster
(If it is an on-the-books scheme, red flags are likely to occur in the accounting records and data. But even off-the-books schemes exhibit the behavioral red flags.)

8. **Audit Initiated**

Detection of fraud or discrepancies detected by some method (tips most common; also internal controls, accident, and internal audit are common methods)
Anomalies identified and determined to be fraudulent in nature

9. Investigation Initiated	Evidence gathered
	Loss of assets confirmed and documented
	Interrogation of third parties, employees with knowledge, and suspect conducted
10a. Disposition: Fraudster Terminated	Employee terminated for cause (often management does not desire to pursue legal disposition for various reasons)
	Insurance claim filed
10b. Disposition: Prosecution Recommended	Criminal prosecution sought
	Civil recovery sought
	Insurance claim filed
11. Trial	Presentation of facts and testimony

Some of these items are covered in this chapter, at least by way of introduction to basic concepts. The remainder of the book focuses on this list, usually in the sequence listed.

ENDNOTES

1. Michigan Criminal Law, Chapter 86, Sec. 1529.
2. *Southern Development Co. v. Silva*, 125 U.S. 247, 8 S.C. Rep. 881, 31 L. Ed. (1887).
3. Edwin H. Sutherland, *White-Collar Crime* (New York: Dryden Press, 1949), p. 234; Donald L. Cressey, *Other People's Money* (New York: Free Press, 1949), p. 30; Norman Jaspan and Hillel Black, *The Thief in the White Collar* (Philadelphia: Lippincott, 1960), p. 37; and Frank E. Hartung, *Crime, Law, and Society* (Detroit: Wayne State University Press, 1965), pp. 125–136.
4. Sutherland, *White-Collar Crime.*
5. Cressey, *Other People's Money.*
6. Jaspan, and Black, *The Thief in the White Collar.*
7. Hartung, *Crime, Law, and Society.*

8. Association of Certified Fraud Examiners (ACFE), *Report to the Nation* (RTTN), 2004.

9. Association of Certified Fraud Examiners (ACFE), *Report to the Nation,* 1996, 2002, and 2004

10. Committee of Sponsoring Organizations (COSO), *Landmark Study on Fraud in Financial Reporting,* 1998.

11. KPMG, *Fraud Survey,* 1994, 1998, and 2003.

12. ACFE, *Report to the Nation:* 1996, 2002, and 2004.

13. Gwynn Nettler, *Lying, Cheating and Stealing* (Cincinnati: Anderson Publishing, 1982).

14. ACFE, *Report to the Nation,* 2004.

15. James A. Hall and Tommie Singleton, *IT Auditing & Assurance* (New York: Southwestern, 2004).

16. W. S. Albrecht and C. Albrecht, *Fraud Examination and Prevention* (New York: Thomson/Southwestern, 2004).

CHAPTER 2

Fundamentals of Fraud Auditing and Forensic Accounting

INTRODUCTION

The Federal Bureau of Investigation estimates that fraud in health insurance alone costs $80 billion each year. The National Insurance Crime Bureau says that 10% of all auto insurance claims, 15% of auto theft claims, and 20% of workers' compensation claims involve some form of fraud. In the credit-card fraud area, Visa International's 1992 cardholder fraud losses were $689 million, up 28% from 1991. The Association of Certified Fraud Examiners (ACFE) reported an estimated $660 billion in losses due to fraud in 2004. Overall, fraud has increased in recent years, causing companies to look for new ways to fight fraudulent activity.

Contrary to what may seem logical, most frauds, embezzlements, and thefts of corporate assets are not discovered in the course of financial audits. The existence of a fraud usually comes to light through (1) an allegation, complaint, or a rumor of fraud brought by a third party (a disgruntled supplier or a fellow employee), (2) an investigator's intuition or general suspicion that something is awry, (3) an exception from an expectation of a person senior to the suspect (an unacceptable condition, profits, sales, costs, assets, or liabilities are too low or too high), or (4) the sudden discovery that something is missing—cash, property, reports, files, documents, or data. Rarely does an auditor know at the outset that a fraud, theft, or embezzlement was committed.

The objective of fraud in the criminal aspect is to determine whether a crime indeed exists. Simply put, a crime occurred if there is a proven loss of something of value to a victim, a perpetrator who caused that loss, and a law that makes that loss a crime. Generally speaking, losses and criminal laws are much easier to determine and to prove than the *causal source* of the loss.

The immediate facts to determine whether a fraud has occurred are whether there is (1) a criminal law, (2) an apparent breach of that law, (3) a perpetrator, and (4) a victim. The six basic steps in the fraud investigation are:

1. Acquire all available details and documents relating to the allegation.
2. Assess the allegation against the available documentation.
3. Assess the corporate environment relative to the person in question.
4. Ask whether a theory of fraud can be developed at this stage. Is there motive and opportunity?
5. Determine whether the available evidence makes sense. Does it meet the test of business reality?
6. Communicate with appropriate parties on the details and status of the fraud.

After performing these steps, two possibilities exist. Either one has identified the fraudster and knows who she is, or one has not. If not, more investigation is necessary. But if one does catch the fraudster, the process becomes critical to what is no longer an investigation but, it is hoped, a prosecution.

Evidence gathered may consist of the testimony of witnesses, documents, items (means and instruments, or fruits of the crime), and possibly the confession of the perpetrator. Experienced fraud investigators know what evidence is needed to prove the crime and how to attain that evidence. Typically, interviewing the alleged, or known, fraudster is done only after competent and sufficient data have been gathered, assessed, and reasoned. Once the prosecution phase begins, evidence must be presented in court—which is where the expert witness skill of a forensic accountant or fraud auditor is valuable. A successful prosecution needs someone who can explain, in layperson's terms, the records, data, documents, financial information, and files supporting the prosecutor's position.

Chapters 4 through 7 provide readers with insight into the mind and behavior patterns of fraud perpetrators, their schemes, and the evidence they leave behind—from which their crimes can be reconstructed. Every fraud has its own unique wrinkles. All thieves do not think alike. They tend to be opportunists. Given a set of circumstances that allow them to steal, they take the easiest way. Elaborate crimes make interesting reading, but they are committed mostly by characters in Agatha Christie novels. In the real world of corporate fraud and financial statement frauds in particular, culprits leave trails and make mistakes. Auditors must learn to look for these telltale signs. While each fraud will be different in some ways, so too frauds will be alike. History repeats itself, at least at the fraud scheme level. History also reveals some timeless characteristics and principles of fraud.

BRIEF HISTORY OF FRAUD AND THE ANTIFRAUD PROFESSION[1]

Fraud auditing literature discloses a common theme: Fraud is endemic and pervasive in certain industries, locales, companies, and occupations at particular points in history. For example, railroad promoters in the 1870s raised more capital from less informed investors than ever before. Their fraud, rather simply, was based on more "water" in their stocks.

According to some, forensic accounting is one of the oldest professions and dates back to the Egyptians. The "eyes and ears" of the king was a person who basically served as a forensic accountant for Pharaoh, watchful over inventories of grain, gold, and other assets. The person had to be trustworthy, responsible, and able to handle a position of influence.

In the United States, fraud began at least as early as the Pilgrims and early settlers. Since early America was largely agricultural, many frauds centered around land schemes. Perhaps the most infamous colonial era land scheme was the purchase of Manhattan Island, bought from the Canarsie Indians from what is now Brooklyn. The land was bought for trinkets worth about $24. In this case, the Indians tricked the white man, as the Canarsie Indians sold land not even connected to Manhattan Island. Land swindles grew as America expanded west and continue to this day to be a major target of fraudsters and con artists. So much so that the phrase "If you believe that, I have some swamp land in Florida I would like to sell you!" has become a colloquialism.

The advent of business organizations created new opportunities for fraud. The earliest corporations were formed in seventeenth-century Europe. Nations chartered new corporations and gave them public missions in exchange for a legal right to exists, separation of ownership from management, and limited liability that protected shareholders from losses of the business entity. One such corporation, the Massachusetts Bay Company, was chartered by Charles I in 1628 and had a mission of colonizing the New World.

The first major corporate fraud is probably the fraud known as the South Sea Bubble.[2] The South Sea Company was formed in 1711 with exclusive trading rights to Spanish South America. The company made its first trading voyage in 1717 and made little actual profit to offset the £10 million of government bonds it had assumed. South Sea then had to borrow £2 million more. Tension between England and Spain led to the capture of South Sea ships by Spain in 1718. In 1719, the company proposed a scheme by which it would take on the entire remaining national debt in Britain, over £30 million, using its own stock at 5% in exchange for government bonds lasting until 1727. Although the Bank of England offered also to assume the debt, Parliament approved the assumption of the debt by the South Sea Company. Its stock rose from £128 in January 1720 to £550 by the end of May that year, in a speculation frenzy.

The company drove the price of the stock up through artificial means; largely taking the form of new subscriptions combined with the circulation of pro-trade-with-Spain stories designed to give the impression that the stock could only go higher. Not only did capital stay in England, but many Dutch investors bought South Sea stock, thus increasing the inflationary pressure.[3]

Other joint-stock companies then joined the market, usually making fraudulent claims about foreign ventures, and were nicknamed "bubbles." In June 1720, the Bubble Act was passed, which required all joint-stock companies to have a royal charter. Partly because it had a royal charter, the South Sea Company shares rocketed to £890 in early June 1720. The price finally reached £1,000 in early August, and a sell-off that began in June began to accelerate. The sell-off was begun largely by directors themselves cashing in on huge stock profits. As the stock price began to decline, the company directors attempted to talk up and prop up the stock (e.g., having agents buy stock) but to no avail—the stockholders had lost confidence and a run started in September. By the end of the month, the stock price dropped to a low of £150.

With investors outraged, and as many of them were aristocrats, Parliament was recalled in December and an investigation began. As part of that investigation, an external auditor, Charles Snell, was hired to examine the books of the South Sea Company. This hiring was the first time in the history of accounting that an outside auditor was brought in to audit books, and marks the beginning of Chartered Accountants in England and thus the beginning of Certified Public Accountants (CPAs) and financial audits as we know them today. Thus CPAs owe their profession, at least to a large extent, *to a fraud*. Cases in more recent history have birthed forensic accountants and fraud auditors: namely, a scandal, the threat of a lawsuit or bankruptcy, and the need to have an expert dig deep into the accounting records. These historical facts are significant among the other frauds of times past, and are why this case is presented.

In 1721, Snell submitted his report. He uncovered widespread corruption and fraud among the directors in particular and among company officials and their friends at Westminster. Unfortunately, some of the key players had already fled the country with the incriminating records in their possession. Those who remained were examined and some estates were confiscated.

At about the same time, France was experiencing an almost identical fraud from a corporation known as the Mississippi Company that had exclusive trading rights to North America in the French-owned Mississippi River area. Using similar tactics of exaggerating the potential profits, the company owner, John Law, was able to cause a frenzied upward spiral of its stock prices, only to see it collapse after the Regent of Orleans dismissed him in 1720. The company sought bankruptcy protection in 1721. Like South Sea, it was a fraud perpetrated by the exaggerations of executive management.

In 1817, the *Meyer v. Sefton* case involved a bankrupt estate. Since the nature of the evidence was such it could not be examined in court, the judge allowed the expert witness who had examined the bankrupt's accounts to testify to his examination. Forensic pioneer Dr. Larry Crumbley considers this accountant to be the first forensic accountant in history and the beginning of forensic accounting as a profession.

In 1920, Charles Ponzi planned to arbitrage postal coupons, buying them from Spain and selling them to the U.S. Postal Service at a profit. In order to raise capital for the scheme, he promised outlandish returns to investors—50% in 90 days. Ponzi paid the first returns with the cash proceeds from those coming in later, then took the proceeds from later entrants to the scheme. He was imprisoned for defrauding 40,000 people of $15 million. To this day, that type of scheme is referred to as a Ponzi scheme.

In the 1920s, Samuel Insull was involved in a fraud scheme similar to the railroad and South Sea Bubble schemes, but it occurred in the electric utility business. Insull sold millions of dollars of common stock in electric utility companies to unwary investors. The stock was greatly overpriced in terms of the utilities' real assets. When the stock market collapsed in 1929, it was apparent that Insull's holding company was insolvent and had been for some time.

Some researchers, such as Dr. Dale Flesher and Dr. Tonya Flesher, have presented sound arguments that the Securities Act of 1933 and the Securities Exchange Act of 1934 are a direct result of the Kreuger fraud rather than the stock market crash of 1929. Kreuger & Toll, a multibillion-dollar conglomerate, was a huge fraud built on shell companies and *unaudited financial statements*. Kreuger & Toll securities were among the most widely held in the United States. When the company went under in 1932, investors lost millions in the largest bankruptcy of its time. Therefore, the argument goes, the existence of these legislative acts requiring financial audits of all companies with listed securities and the Securities and Exchange Commission (SEC) is the result of a major financial fraud. The acts of 1933 and 1934 essentially created the demand for financial auditors and CPAs that exists to this day.

During the 1950s, more doctors were involved in more income tax frauds than ever before or since. Food franchisers, in the late 1960s, are another example of the fraud phenomenon. Some fast-food franchisers sold unwary small investors on untested restaurant concepts at overvalued prices. These half-baked concepts led to the bankruptcy of many of the franchisees. During the Watergate era of the early 1970s, more politicians were involved in corruption and fraud against taxpayers, and more corporations were involved in political and commercial bribery than ever before.

A major savings and loan scandal hit hard in the early 1980s, preceding the energy and telecommunication companies' frauds in the 1990s. The latter led the seeming explosion of fraud around the last half of the 1990s and the early 2000s. During this period, high-dollar frauds reached all types of industries. For example, Waste Management in trash services, Enron in energy, WorldCom in telecommunications, Adelphia in media, Fannie Mae in government, and HealthSouth in health services all occurred during this time. Several of these frauds were among the *largest ever,* and they occurred during a short period of time.

Although the cost of the WorldCom fraud was far greater, the most notable fraud, as far as impact on the business community, is probably Enron. In 2001, Enron filed bankruptcy after disclosing major discrepancies in revenues and liabilities in its financial reports. The audit firm Arthur Andersen came to an end as a result of the ramifications of the Enron scandal by 2002. In 2002, the U.S. Congress passed the Sarbanes-Oxley Act (SOX) due to that fraud and others, such as WorldCom. Perhaps nothing has brought more attention to fraud audits and forensic accounting than the Enron scandal and SOX.

Are all of these events merely historical flukes? Did media attention create them? Perhaps. Media attention may have created the original public awareness, but the frauds and corruption were there all the time, and there exists no real way of measuring or comparing them. Part of the problem during the period of time when such large frauds occurred was the mind-set of the auditors, which has since turned around completely. Nothing is taken for granted anymore, and the financial well-being of the general public is again the ultimate concern. Suspicion fell on industries, professions, and various areas of government. The undivided attention of auditors, regulators, management, and employees then led to wholesale charges of fraud, theft, and corruption.

The fraud environment can be and is often viewed as a pendulum, swinging from one extreme to the other with little time in between at the proper balancing point. After 2002, the pendulum was close to an extreme end, one that entailed ultra-conservatism on the part of companies, and auditors as well, and the stiffest requirements and enforcement by regulators and legislators. This cycle (pendulum swing) is a natural result of human nature, business cycles, and the nature of legislation and regulation. The cycle can certainly be influenced and controlled to some extent, but it will never cease.

REVIEW OF TECHNICAL LITERATURE

The technical literature begins with criminal and regulatory statutes involving business. For example, such literature includes the Sherman Antitrust Act (1890), the Internal Revenue Act (1913), the Securities Act of 1933 and Securities Exchange Act of 1934, Health Insurance Portability and Accountability Act of 1996 (HIPAA), and Gramm-Leach-Bliley Act of 1999 (GLBA), to name a few. Other applicable laws are related to mail fraud, fraud by wire, and the Federal Trade Commission (FTC). More federal laws that have contributed to the growth of fraud auditing include the Labor-Management Reporting and Disclosure Act, the Welfare-Pension Fund Act, Employee Retirement Income Security Act (ERISA), and the Foreign Corrupt Practices Act.

The savings and loans scandals of the early 1980s led to the Treadway Commission, which carried on its work as the Committee of Sponsoring Organizations (COSO), which is still functioning today. According to Treadway Commission findings, the best thing to prevent scandals, such as the savings and loan ones, was for companies to have a strong set of internal controls. The model developed by the group has come to be known as the COSO Model of Internal Controls. It focuses on five key areas of internal controls:

1. Risk assessment
2. Control environment
3. Information and communication
4. Monitoring
5. Control activities

In the 1990s, the AICPA adopted the COSO model as SAS No. 78, *Consideration of Internal Control in a Financial Statement Audit*. In the late 1990s and early 2000s, a strong global economy met an increase in fraud in public companies and a lack of effective oversight. The result was a serious shock to the economy and to society as a whole. Public concern over fraud, in general, erupted to new and seemingly endless heights. Although concern over fraud has decreased some (a natural pendulum effect), the mentality toward fraud has clearly changed and for the better. Another positive effect is how these changes have created a greater awareness of the need to further develop the discipline of fraud auditing. However, billions of dollars were lost, creating a serious "black eye" for the financial audit profession, and a wave of legislation resulted.

The latest round of legislation passed in the fight against fraud includes SOX, GLBA, and HIPAA. In the current environment, there is an extremely heightened expectation for businesses, auditors, investigators, and regulators to stop fraud. In order to control fraud, the response spurred by legislation must equal or exceed the energy exerted by fraudsters, which appears to have pervasively infiltrated society.

The Sarbanes-Oxley Act in particular has greatly affected the awareness of and attention to fraud. The AICPA's Statement on Standard No. 99 (SAS 99), *Consideration of Fraud in a Financial Statement Audit*, codified and complemented SOX's tenets, or "best practices" in antifraud. The Public Company Oversight Board (PCAOB), created by SOX and responsible for overseeing standards and enforcement, is setting its own standards affecting internal controls and fraud audits. The bottom line is, management has to accept responsibility for fraud per SOX and financial auditors have to be active in detecting fraud to comply with SAS No. 99.

SAS 99 has two basic requirements for financial statement audits. One is for auditors to exercise "professional skepticism"; that is, auditors are to be constantly mindful of the potential for fraud. The other is that fraud assessment must be included in audit steps from planning to reporting findings. Importantly, SAS 99 notes that evaluating audit evidence and adjusting the audit is a continual process. The audit team must identify, assess, and respond to fraud risks. Subsequently, the audit team must evaluate the findings of the audit tests and report to "an appropriate level of management" (usually the audit committee). Documentation must exist for all of these audit steps.

Section 404 of SOX requires management to evaluate the effectiveness of internal controls over financial reporting and to report on their evaluation in the annual report. This section also forces management to state their responsibility for internal controls. The internal control evaluation report and certain financial reports have to be signed by the chief executive officer and chief financial officer, providing a legally enforceable claim. More important, management's report on internal controls is evaluated by the financial (external) auditors who opine on that report.

SOX also brought about these changes of note:

- More independent boards of directors (especially the audit committee)
- Increased involvement of the audit committee (especially oversight of management and antifraud programs)
- More financial expertise on the audit committee
- More independent reporting lines (external and internal auditors report directly to the audit committee)

PCAOB Audit Standards No. 2 (AS 2) and No. 3 (AS 3) both address fraud. PCAOB guidance is superior to the audit guidance provided by the AICPA (SASs), although PCAOB has mostly accepted SAS guidance to date. AS 2 adopts many SAS 99 requirements. As part of that adoption, AS 2 (via SAS 99) notes that the audit of internal control and the financial statement audit are connected and requires the nature, timing, and extent of financial statement audit procedures to be adjusted according to the results of the internal control audit. Results here certainly include any findings regarding fraud. Importantly, AS 2 references the COSO Internal Control model with regard to managing fraud risk.

Sarbanes-Oxley, SAS 99, and AS 2 have much more depth than can be summarized here, but these regulations and technical standards have stimulated similar legislation and standards abroad. Yet the need for fraud-auditing talents is not related solely to comply with new governmental regulations.

AUDITOR'S MIND-SET

The argument for mind-set does not quite hold for many of the financial frauds around the turn of the millennium. Of those, most were caught by whistleblowers or the financial collapse of the entity. In some cases, too many people, including auditors, regulators, and company employees, knew, and someone eventually had the ethics and the courage to report the fraud. After the initial attention to these large frauds, those same entities (auditors, regulators, company management, etc.) felt pressure to uncover any frauds and did, continuing the fraud wave.

Fraud auditing, forensic accounting, and/or fraud investigation (i.e., forensic accounting) put things together rather than taking them apart, as is the case in classic financial auditing or the modern method of systems analysis. The process of forensic accounting is also sometimes more intuitive than deductive, although both intuition and deduction play important parts. Financial auditing is more procedural in many regards and is not intended to work as effectively in detecting frauds as the tenets of fraud auditing and forensic accounting.

Mind-set, not methodology, is probably going to be the best detection of frauds from Enron forward—not a mind-set of paranoia, which trusts no one and sees evil everywhere, but a mind-set trained or experienced to identify the signs of fraud, the most effective means of detecting frauds, and the natural tendency to question the *substance* of the matter. The term *professional skepticism* is often used in this regard and applies to financial, fraud, and forensic accounting. In addition to skepticism, fraud auditors should recognize that:

- Fraud can be detected as well as discovered by accident or tip.[4]
- Financial audit methodologies and techniques are not really designed to detect fraud but rather designed to detect material financial misstatements.
- Fraud detection is more of an art than a science. It requires innovative and creative thinking as well as the rigors of science.
- Determination, persistence, and self-confidence are more important attributes for a fraud auditor than intelligence. Logic and problem solving and detective skills are critical success factors for fraud auditors and forensic accountants.

WHAT IS FORENSIC ACCOUNTING?

In this book, the term *forensic accounting* refers to the comprehensive view of fraud investigation. It includes the audit of accounting records to prove or disprove a fraud. It includes the interview process of all related parties to a fraud, when applicable. And it includes the act of serving as an expert witness, when applicable.

Forensic Accounting Defined

Although relatively new to the accounting profession, the role of a forensic expert in other professions has been in place for some time. *Webster's Dictionary* defines the word *forensic* as "belonging to, used in, or suitable to courts of judicature or to public discussions and debate." Accordingly, the term *forensic* in the accounting profession deals with the relation and application of financial facts to legal problems. Forensic accounting evidence is oriented to a court of law.

The involvement of the forensic accountant is almost always reactive; this distinguishes forensic accountants from fraud auditors, who tend to be actively involved in prevention and detection in a corporate or regulatory environment. Forensic accountants are trained to react to complaints arising in criminal matters, statements of claim arising in civil litigation, and rumors and inquiries arising in corporate investigations. The investigative findings of the forensic accountant will impact an individual and/or a company in terms of their freedom or a financial award or loss. The ACFE refers to this person as a fraud examiner.

The forensic accountant draws on various resources to obtain relevant financial evidence and to interpret and to present this evidence in a manner that will assist both parties. Ideally, forensic accounting should allow two parties to more quickly and efficiently resolve the complaint, statement of claim, rumor, or inquiry, or at least reduce the financial element as an area of ongoing debate. Objectivity and independence of the forensic auditor are paramount for these purposes.

Who Needs Forensic Accounting?

The increased business complexities in a litigious environment have enhanced the need for this discipline. It is possible to summarize the range of application into these general areas:

- *Corporate investigations.* Companies react to concerns that arise through a number of sources that might suggest possible wrongdoing within and without the corporate environment. From the anonymous phone call or e-mail from disgruntled employees and third parties, these problems must be addressed quickly and effectively to permit the company to continue to pursue its objectives. More specifically, the forensic accountant assists in addressing allegations ranging from kickbacks and wrongful dismissals to internal situations involving allegations of management or employee wrongdoing. At times, a forensic accountant can meet with those persons affected by the allegations, rumors, or inquiries; they may view the accountant as an independent and objective party, and thus be more willing to engage in discussion.

- *Litigation support.* Litigation support includes assisting counsel in investigating and assessing the integrity and amount relating to such areas as loss of profits, construction claims, product liability, shareholder disputes, bankruptcies, and breach of contract. Obviously, litigation support is initiated by an attorney responding to some kind of legal action.

- *Criminal matters.* Efforts to prevent white-collar crime have consistently used accountants and auditors in attempts to sort out, assess, and report on financial transactions related to allegations against individuals and companies in a variety of situations, such as arson, scams, fraud (e.g., kickbacks or embezzlement), vendor frauds, customer frauds, investment scams, and stock market manipulations. In criminal matters, accountants and auditors as expert witnesses are increasingly important in court cases.

- *Insurance claims.* The preparation and assessment of insurance claims on behalf of the insured and insurers may require the assistance of a forensic accountant to assess both the integrity and the quantum of a claim. The more significant areas relate to the calculation of loss arising from business interruption, fidelity bond, and personal injury matters. Whereas certain of these cases require financial projections, many need historical analysis and other accounting and auditing-oriented services.

- *Government.* Forensic accountants can assist governments to achieve regulatory compliance by ensuring that companies follow the appropriate legislation. Grant and subsidy investigations and public inquiries form a part of this service to government.

To generalize the type of situation that requires a forensic accountant, one is needed when there is a potential perceived loss, real financial loss, or risk of loss.

What Should a Forensic Accountant Know and Be Able to Do?

Many of the aspects of forensic accounting fall outside the traditional education, training, and experience of auditors and accountants. These skills, abilities, and/or knowledge are necessary to serve as an effective forensic accountant:

- *Ability to identify frauds with minimal initial information.* Many times, the fraud investigation begins with minimal knowledge of the specifics of a potential fraud. The forensic accountant needs to be able to identify the possible scheme (i.e., fraud theory approach), the possible manner it was perpetrated, and potentially effective procedures to prove or disprove the potential fraud (i.e., the "theory").

- *Identification of financial issues.* When forensic accountants are presented with a situation generated by a complaint, allegation, rumor, inquiry, or statement of claim, it is important that they clearly identify the financial issues significant to the matter quickly. They base these decisions on experience and knowledge, and any resulting recommendations must reflect both common sense and business reality. For example, if documents are needed from a foreign jurisdiction, although the most obvious recommendation would be to obtain these records, it is usually not practical to do so. Other alternatives must be considered.

- *Knowledge of investigative techniques.* When the issues have been identified, it is imperative that further information and documentation be acquired to obtain further evidence to assist in either supporting or refuting the allegation or claim. It is a question of knowing not only where the relevant financial documentation exists but also the intricacies of generally accepted accounting principles (GAAP), financial statement disclosure, and systems of internal control, and being aware of the human element involved in frauds.

- *Knowledge of evidence.* The forensic accountant must understand what constitutes evidence, the meaning of "best" and "primary" evidence, and the form that various accounting summaries can take to consolidate the financial evidence in a way that is acceptable to the courts. It is imperative that a forensic accountant understand the rules of evidence in court and how to conduct the investigation from the beginning as if all evidence will make it to a court of law. Otherwise, evidence could be compromised and found inadmissible if it does get to court.

■ *Interpretation of financial information.* It is unusual for a transaction or a series of events to have only one interpretation. The forensic accountant must be extremely conscious of a natural bias that can exist in the interpretation process. It is important that transactions be viewed from all aspects to ensure that the ultimate interpretation of the available information fits with common sense and the test of business reality. A proper interpretation of information can be assured only when one has looked behind and beyond the transaction in question without any scope limitations. In particular, a forensic accountant who is called as an expert witness must be aware of alternative accounting or financial formulas, rules, and interpretations.

■ *Presentation of findings.* The forensic accountant must have the ability to clearly communicate the findings resulting from the investigation in a fashion understandable to the layperson. The presentation can be oral or written and can include the appropriate demonstrative aids. The role of forensic accountants in the witness box is the final test of the findings in a public forum. By its nature, however, accounting and financial information is difficult for the average layperson to comprehend. Therefore, the forensic accountant as an expert witness must have above-average communication skills in distilling financial information in a manner that the average citizen can understand, comprehend, and assess to reach a sound conclusion.

■ *Investigative skills.* Forensic accountants usually apply investigative skills at the appropriate time during the course of their investigations. For example, in dealing with criminal matters, the primary concern is to develop evidence around motive, opportunity, and benefit. Of equal concern is that the benefit of doubt is given to the other side to ensure that proper interpretations are given to the transactions. Other concerns, such as the question of method of operation and the issue of economic risk, must also be addressed.

Similarly, investigative skills are needed in litigation support. The forensic accountant must ensure that: a proper foundation exists for the calculation of future lost profits; all assumptions incorporated into the work product are recognized and identified; he understands his limitations as an expert; and the issue of mitigation of damages is considered.

■ *Investigative mentality.* Along with their accounting knowledge, forensic accountants develop an investigative mentality that allows them to go beyond the bounds set out in either GAAP or generally accepted auditing standards (GAAS). These three tenets in forensic accounting are driven by the necessity to prove *intent* in court in order to prove there was a *fraud.* The investigative mentality develops in the search for best evidence, for competent and sufficient evidence, for *forensic evidence.* For example:

  ● *Scope is not restricted as a result of materiality.* Often, especially in the early stages of a management/employee fraud, the transactions are small and accordingly are more easily conveyed to the court to show a pattern of conduct that is deceitful. As the dollar value of the transactions and their complexity increase, the ability to convey the essence of the transaction is hampered, and the forensic accountant's task is made more difficult.

  ● For the most part, the *use of sampling* is not acceptable in establishing evidence.

  ● The important difference affecting scope is the critical principle of *the assumption of integrity* of management and documentation, especially in corporate investigation and matters of white-collar crime.

In a recent case of secret commissions involving a purchasing agent for a large retail distributor and a major vendor, it was determined that the vendor was selling product to the purchasing agent's company through a company owned by their wives. At the time there was some concern as to how the plaintiff could overcome the documented evidence that placed ownership and control of the company with the wives. Bearing in mind alternative sources of information, the working papers of the accountant for the company were obtained, and an organization description confirmed that the shareholders were indeed the wives but the executive decision makers were their husbands. Thus, the best evidence no longer made it necessary to imply, notwithstanding ownership, that control rested with the husbands.

The investigative mentality is best developed by continued experience in the witness box. It is through this process that the forensic accountant's eyes are opened, because counsel for the opposing side raises issues and possibilities the accountant may not have considered up to that point. Repeated experience as a forensic witness creates a greater awareness of what is relevant and must be considered, so the witness can present financial evidence independently and objectively to reflect the reality of the situation.

Interview Skills   Throughout the course of seeking evidence and information, the forensic accountant becomes involved in the interviewing process. This process is another art to master. There are many things about the interview process, and even what order to interview parties of interest, that should be learned. Most important, the forensic accountant must be prepared to handle a confession in a way that ensures that the evidence is admissible in a court of law.

When a questionnaire was circulated among the staff members of Peat Marwick Lindquist Holmes, a Toronto-based firm of chartered accountants responsible for the forensic and investigative accounting practice, responses were insightful and should be of interest to the reader.

Q1: How would you distinguish forensic accounting, fraud auditing, and investigative auditing from financial auditing?

A. The distinction is related to one's goals. Financial auditing attempts to enable the auditor to render an opinion as to whether a set of transactions is presented fairly in accordance with GAAP. The financial statements upon which the opinion is rendered are always the representations of management. The auditor is primarily concerned with qualitative values (hence the concept of materiality comes into play) and generally is not concerned about whether the financial statements communicate the policies, intentions, or goals of management.

Forensic accounting, fraud auditing, and investigative auditing measure financial transactions in relation to various other authorities, such as the Criminal Code, an insurance contract, institutional policies, or other guidelines for conduct or reporting. The report is prepared by the accountant/auditor rather than by the client or subject and does not include an opinion on the findings. In the investigation, one does not reject evidence as being immaterial; indeed, the smallest item can be the largest clue to the truth.

Finally, where qualitative values are obviously an issue, even more important is the determination of the context—the mind and intentions of the criminal, the integrity of an insurance "accident," or the reasons for a particular occurrence. However, in one important respect, these different practices must be identical. That is, the auditor/accountant must be skilled and experienced, and must maintain independence and objectivity.

B. *Forensic accounting* is a general term used to describe any financial investigation that can result in a legal consequence. Fraud auditing is a specialized discipline within forensic accounting, which investigates a particular criminal activity, namely fraud. Investigative auditing involves reviewing financial documentation for a specific purpose, which could relate to litigation support and insurance claims as well as criminal matters.

The objective of financial auditing is to provide the auditor with a degree of assurance in giving an opinion with respect to a company's financial statements. The materiality level of an investigative auditing engagement is much lower and more focused than that of the normal financial auditing engagement.

Q2: How would you define what you do as a forensic accountant?

A. I think of myself as one who seeks out the truth.

B. I would define my forensic accounting responsibilities as follows: (1) Investigation and analysis of financial documentation; (2) communication of the findings from my investigation in the form of a report, accounting schedule, and document briefs; (3) coordination of and assistance in further investigation, including the possibility of appearing in court as an expert witness.

C. My role is that of an objective observer or expert. The final report that is issued as a result of my work will be used to negotiate some sort of settlement, be it financial or be it imprisonment. My role as a forensic accountant extends beyond the particular financial circumstances and seems to be one of an objective individual who provides the buffer between, in civil instances, the client and counsel, and, in criminal instances, the investigator and the prosecutor. Therefore, I am considered an integral member of the team of professionals assigned to any given case. Related to the specific work that I do, it has been described to me, and I agree, that the makeup of a given forensic accountant is one-third business person, one-third investigator, and one-third accountant.

Q3: What qualities of mind and/or body should a forensic accountant possess?

A. Creativity: the ability to step out of what would otherwise be a normal business situation and consider alternative interpretations that might not necessarily make business sense; curiosity: the desire to find out what has taken place in a given set of circumstances; perseverance: the ability to push forward even when the circumstances don't appear to substantiate the particular instance being investigated or when the documentation is very onerous and presents a needle-in-a-haystack scenario; common sense: the ability to maintain a "real-world" perspective; business sense: the ability to understand how businesses actually operate, not how business transactions are recorded; confidence: the ability to believe both in yourself and in your findings so that you can persevere when faced with cross-examination.

B. As with any other pursuit, a healthy mind in a healthy body is a solid foundation. Beyond that, one should have generous proportions of common sense, inquisitiveness, skepticism, and an ability to avoid the natural tendency to prejudice—that is, to be fair and independent. In addition, because forensic work ultimately can lead to court appearances, good posture, grooming, vocal projection, and stamina can all be valuable attributes.

C. The foremost quality a forensic accountant requires is independence, because a forensic accountant is often forced to balance conflicting opinions about the same piece of documentation. The second major quality is an intense sense of curiosity coupled with a sense of order—a desire to put the puzzle back together.

D. Common sense/street smarts; sensitivity/understanding of human behavior; analytical!; logical/clear; ability to simplify complexities and delete jargon; not be prone to lose the forest for the trees; ability to identify and assess alternative explanations and interpretations; ability to quickly assess cost-benefit of pursuing alternative avenues of investigation and reporting contents/formats.

E. The forensic accountant needs to be calm, cool, and collected; have good business judgment; and have a mind that can deal logically with esoteric issues and precise matters. A forensic accountant involved in litigation must be physically fit to withstand the long days and long nights of investigation and preparation for trial and the trial itself. Forensic accountants need to have a pleasant appearance and demeanor so that they will not be offensive when in the witness box.

Q4: What skills are most important to the successful practice of forensic accounting?

A. Solid technical accounting and financial skills—the basis of your "expertise"; ability to quickly prioritize issues and map out a "game plan"—good judgment; ability to communicate well—both verbally and in writing—is necessary to obtaining information, directing your staff, presenting your findings, and achieving your desired results. Even the best-planned and executed assignment can fail if you are unable to clearly and concisely present your findings.

B. A forensic accountant needs to be precise, pay attention to detail, and be a broad thinker; that is, not suffer from tunnel vision.

C. When looking at a given forensic accounting engagement, there are two major areas that come to mind in the completion of a given case. First, there is the investigative aspect, and second, the communication aspect. I feel that investigative skills would include areas such as the ability to assimilate large volumes of information, general organization and administrative skills, use the microcomputer or understand the abilities of the microcomputer, and interpersonal skills. Communication skills would include the ability to write a comprehensive report understandably.

D. Communications skills: oral/written; interpersonal skills; listening skills; ability to synthesize/integrate; ability to identify/prioritize objectives/issues.

STEPS IN FRAUD INVESTIGATION

Perhaps a brief overview of a fraud investigation is the best way to convey the principles of forensic accounting. In terms of organizational fraud, the objective is to determine whether a fraud has occurred or is occurring and to determine who the fraudster is. In litigation support, the objective is determined by the client.

It is important to note that the *last step* in the process of the investigation is to *approach the suspect*. That can happen intentionally and accidentally. The intentional approach should be easy enough to avoid, but the accidental requires some extra effort. When an auditor comes across an anomaly (document, accounting transaction, or other evidence of something that "should not be" or a red flag associated with known frauds, or a violation of internal controls), before approaching someone for an explanation, *first* he should ascertain the probability that the reason for the anomaly is *not fraud*. The reason for this caution is often when an auditor unwittingly has evidence of a fraud in hand, she goes to a party responsible for the fraud and asks for an explanation for the anomaly. At this point, the investigation at best has been severely hampered and at worst has been compromised for obtaining a confession or conviction in court.

For example, an internal auditor notices on performance reports that actual expenses are exactly twice the budget. That is classified, in our terminology, as an anomaly ("should not be"). The natural inclination is to go to the person responsible for authorizing checks in that business unit and ask for an explanation. However, if that person is using an authorized maker fraud scheme combined with forged endorsement, he could be cutting two checks for a single invoice— one for the vendor, and one for the fraudster to forge an endorsement and convert to cash. If the auditor does approach that person, either he will come up with a viable excuse, or the auditor could unknowingly offer one. In a real case, the fraudster remained silent, and the auditor said, "You must have paid the vendor twice," to which she replied, "Yes. That is what I did." The fraudster then had the opportunity to replace the stolen funds without getting caught. Had the auditor *assumed* it could be fraud, then he would have had the opportunity to gather evidence to determine whether it was error or fraud, and possibly would have found the fraud. But by going to the fraudster, he gave her an undetectable exit strategy to the fraud. In other cases, fraudsters confronted by accident have suddenly retired, burned the business building (to destroy accounting records), or done other things that frustrated any appropriate conclusion to the fraud.

Steps in Investigating a Fraud

The first step is the initialization of the investigation. If it is an organizational fraud, most often that is a tip or an accidental discovery of a fraud. *Predication* is necessary to initiate the fraud investigation. Predication is the set of circumstances that would lead the prudent, reasonable, and professionally trained individual to believe that a fraud has occurred, is occurring, or will occur. In litigation support, however, predication is a call from a lawyer.

If the specific fraud is not known, or if there is limited information on the fraud, then the next step would be the fraud theory approach. In this approach, the forensic accountant, probably in a brainstorming setting, would propose the most likely fraud scheme (if not previously known), and the manner in which that fraud scheme could have been perpetrated on the victim organization. This latter substep is often necessary even in litigation support. Obviously, the forensic accountant needs to be familiar with fraud schemes and red flags associated with each (see Chapters 4 and 5). The theory then serves as the basis for developing a fraud investigation plan.

Using the theory, the forensic accountant develops a plan to gather sufficient and competent evidence (i.e., forensic evidence). This step is where the fraud auditor is particularly applicable (see Chapters 4 through 10 for various concepts in gathering evidence). In this step, an examination is made of accounting records, transactions, documents, and data (if applicable) to obtain sufficient evidence to prove or disprove that the fraud identified earlier has occurred. Issues of importance include custody of evidence and other legal matters (see Chapter 13).

After gathering accounting evidence, the forensic accountant will attempt to gather evidence from eyewitnesses, using interviews. This process goes from people the greatest distance from the fraud (not involved but possible knowledgeable), to an ever-narrowing circle of people close to the fraud (firsthand knowledge), to the *last step* of *interviewing the suspect.*

Finally, the forensic accountant writes up the findings in a report to the party who him. If the case goes to court, this report, or a similar one, may be necessary during the trial. But regardless, if the case goes to trial, the forensic accountant's work will have to be presented in an effective manner to the judge or jury (see Chapters 11 through 13).

Axioms

Some caveats, or axioms, about fraud are important to remember throughout the steps in determining whether fraud has occurred:

- Believe fraud by its nature is clandestine, hidden.
- Reverse proof. That is, preclude all other explanations for the circumstances and evidence that exist.
- Avoid opinions of guilt or innocence.

WHAT IS FRAUD AUDITING?

Fraud auditing is creating an environment that encourages the detection and prevention of frauds in commercial transactions. In the broadest sense, it is an awareness of many components of fraud, such as the human element, organizational behavior, knowledge of fraud, evidence and standards of proof, an awareness of the potentiality for fraud, and an appreciation of the so-called red flags. Some of the functions of a fraud auditor follow.

In short, fraud auditing is the process of detecting, preventing, and correcting fraudulent activities. While completely eliminating fraud is the goal, it is simply not feasible. The concept of reasonableness is applicable here, and this concept is often associated with the fraud-related fields of financial accounting and auditing. Fraud auditors should be able to prevent a reasonably preventable fraud.

Accounting-type frauds usually are accompanied by the modification, alteration, destruction, or counterfeiting of accounting evidence. But accounting records can be either intentionally or accidentally modified, altered, and destroyed, as by human error or omission. The first objective for the fraud auditor, then, is to determine whether a discrepancy in accounting records is attributable to human error. If so, there may be no actual fraud. If the discrepancy (missing records, destroyed records, modified records, counterfeit records, errors, omissions) cannot be attributed to accidental or human error, further investigation should follow at an appropriate level.

What Should a Fraud Auditor Know and Be Able to Do?

More broadly, fraud auditing focuses on creating an environment that encourages the detection, prevention, and correction of intended or executed fraud. The main thrust of this book is to provide auditors, investigators, and other persons in the fraud environment with the ability to establish and influence forces that effectively counter attempts at fraud. Ability comes from insight, knowledge, and experience in viewing fraud as an economic, social, and organizational phenomenon.

Setting the Tone   Fraud auditors should set the tone and the standard, including demonstrating the highest standards of ethical conduct. This goal means that the fraud auditor within a company should have in place, and communicated to all employees, an effective corporate code of conduct, which should also include conflict-of-interest policy guidelines signed by employees to provide a clear understanding of the intent of management and the level of expectations. There should also be in agreements, especially with vendors, a clause allowing the company to inspect the records of related parties in the normal course of business.

Effective Corporate Governance   SOX, in many ways, is an attempt to mandate good corporate governance tenets, or best practices, for publicly traded companies. Fraud auditors need to be familiar with best practices of corporate governance as they relate to fraud. Closely aligned to "tone at the top" is the need for fraud auditors to assist the board in ensuring the entity is reasonably vigilant regarding fraud detection and prevention. Of particular importance would be the audit committee of the board of directors having oversight of a strong antifraud program or set of programs. Therefore, fraud auditors should be able to contribute to an effective fraud program as a part of overall corporate governance.

Common Body of Knowledge   Fraud auditors should know the aspects of the common body of knowledge regarding fraud. That knowledge includes: fraud schemes, red flags and the ones associated with specific frauds, the fraud triangle, fraud research, emerging fraud issues, steps in a fraud investigation, legal aspects of fraud (especially evidence), fraud professional organizations, fraud certifications, sociobehavioral characteristics of white-collar criminals, and the other things covered in this book. The fraud auditor, of course, needs to be able to apply that knowledge in the fraud environment.

Ripe circumstances for fraud are (1) conditions in the environment, such as social values, prevailing moral and ethical standards, and economic, competitive, political, and social conditions; and (2) motives in the mental dispositions of individuals who are most likely to commit a crime. That is when the three legs of the fraud triangle come together.

Although the motive for a crime is not a necessary element of proof in sustaining a conviction (whereas criminal intent is), motivation is important to the investigator and the auditor because it tends to identify the more likely suspects when the actual culprit is unknown. The motive also helps to construct a theory of the case; that is, the who, what, when, where, how, and why of the crime. So motivation should not be discounted. It can narrow the search for the culprit and substantially aid in reconstructing the crime.

As a general rule, motives can be separated into five major categories:

1. Psychotic (e.g., mentally impaired)
2. Economic (e.g., Cressey's "unshareable need," personal financial pressures)
3. Egocentric (e.g., power, ego)
4. Ideological (e.g., to provide for an animal shelter, to meet social needs)
5. Emotional (e.g., challenge, revenge, greed)

Of the five motivations, economic motivation is the most common. The individual wants or needs money or wealth. Fraud psychology is its own field, but the average fraud auditor should know something of it. Psychotic motivation can impair a successful criminal prosecution when an insanity plea is made. Egocentric motivation means the individual wants more prestige, more recognition, higher social or political status, or even a job promotion. Ideological motivation means that the individuals feel that their cause or values are morally superior to those of the victim, or they feel exploited, abused, or discriminated against by the victim.

Motives should be viewed from another perspective as well; a series of emotions may also serve as motives—motives such as jealousy, spite, revenge, anger, greed, bigotry, hatred, pride, covetousness, gluttony, and sloth; or fears of ridicule, rejection, poverty, sickness, pain, death, failure, loss, and even uncertainty. Clearly a competent investigator must know people and their motivations—their needs, wants, demands, and desires; their values, beliefs, and attitudes; and their individual peculiarities.

Skills Set   Inevitably, accounting and investigative (legal) skills cross over and are inextricably tied together in the context of a forensic audit. Although auditors and investigators exhibit similar skills in some ways, when separated they demonstrate different abilities. As for accounting skills, an effective fraud auditor should be able to do these things competently:

- Establish accounting, audit, and internal control (when, where, and how fraud is most likely to occur in books of account and in financial statements).
- Conduct a review of internal controls.
- Assess the strengths and weaknesses of those controls.
- Design scenarios of potential fraud losses based on identified weaknesses in internal controls.
- Know how to identify questionable and exceptional transactions (too high, too low, too often, too rare, too much, too little, odd times, odd places, odd people).
- Identify questionable and exceptional account balances and variations.
- Distinguish between simple human errors and omissions in entries and fraudulent entries (intentional error, such as recurring small errors versus unintentional random error and ignorance).
- Know how to follow the flow of documents that support transactions.
- Follow the flow of funds into and out of an organization's account.
- Search for underlying support documents for questionable transactions.
- Review such documents for peculiarities like fake billings; destruction of data; improper account classification; irregularities in financial data; and substitution of copies for original documents.

A couple of notes with regard to these skills should be made. One of these is the "toos" and the "odds" method for identifying possibly fraudulent transactions. Transactions are suspect if they are too high, too low, too often, too rare, too close, at odd times, in odd places, and so forth. A good example of the "too close" idea is the common check fraud perpetrated at a high dollar amount that bypasses the usually necessary high-level approval by paying the amount with multiple checks just under the threshold for (extra) approval. A midlevel accounts payable manager may be able to solely sign checks only for $1,000 and under, but can get $1,998 without additional approval with just two checks.

Beyond these skills that also relate to investigation, fraud and especially forensic auditors should be reasonably able to:

- Verify compliance with regulatory, legal, and evidential matters (how to discern, detect, and document such frauds).
- Gather and preserve evidence to corroborate asset losses, fraudulent transactions, and financial statements.
- Document and report a fraud loss for criminal, civil, or insurance claims.
- Be aware of management, administrative, and organizational policies, procedures, and practices.
- Review documents related to legal and general business functions.
- Test the organization's motivational and ethical climate.

The skills of a criminal investigator are in some respects similar to those of an auditor. An auditor and a detective both seek the truth: the auditor with respect to the proper accounting of business transactions and the detective/investigator with respect to the proper, legal behavior of citizens. Both should have inquisitive minds and challenge things that appear to be "wrong," knowing that many times, the opposite of what one would logically expect is the logical place to start.

Auditing for fraud is as much of an intuitive process as it is a formal, analytic methodology. It is as much of an art as it is a science. As a consequence, it is difficult to teach and more difficult to learn. Skill depends on the right mind-set (thinking like a thief, probing for weaknesses) and practice. But it is not technique that one should master; rather, it is mental disposition: doggedness and persistence. One seeks relevant information without assumption, organizes it in some meaningful way, and then sees the pattern it creates. One goes behind and beyond those transactions to reconstruct what may have led to them and what has followed from them.

Investigative Intuition   Laypersons call this gift investigative intuition. Investigators call it professional judgment—judgment derived from knowledge, education, training, acquired skills, and experience. No one is wholly born with it, although certainly some are born more capable and some learn better. Intuition is learned mainly by trial and error. It is not a formula, and it cannot actually be taught.

The hunch of an amateur may not be worth much, based as it is on naiveté. The hunch of a trained investigator is worth much more, because it is based on experience, knowledge, and training. Even when auditors or investigators say they have discovered a fraud in accounting records by accident, it may be no accident; their trained eyes and ears can discern the truth. Police detectives also attribute some of their investigative insights to accident, chance, or good luck. But there again, their breakthroughs are not simply random events; they are brought about by their concentration and focus on the issue at hand. It is not black magic or fortuitous circumstances.

The authors would like to counter the feigned humility of some investigators and auditors by proposing that "accidental" discoveries of crimes by investigators and frauds by auditors usually are attributable not to pure chance but to know-how. Unfortunately, not all investigators or auditors have such know-how. The investigative mentality comes with age, training, self-discipline, experience, and a mind-set that understands that crime and fraud are possible in any environment, at any time, by anyone, *if the circumstances are ripe.*

Applicable Laws and Regulations   Fraud auditors should be familiar with applicable legislation, standards, and other requirements. That includes criminal and regulatory statutes involving business (see the "Review of Technical Literature" section in this chapter for details), These laws, together with the increase in fraud in public companies, waste and abuse in government contracting, and the current public concern over white-collar crime, create a greater need for further development of the discipline of fraud auditing.

Who Needs Fraud Auditors?

The need for fraud-auditing talent is not related solely to compliance with new governmental regulations. In the private sector, fraud-auditing skills are also useful in most cases of financial crime, such as embezzlement; misrepresentations of financial facts; arson for profit; bankruptcy fraud; investment frauds of all manner and description; bank fraud; kickbacks and commercial bribery; computer frauds; electronic funds transfer (EFT) systems frauds; and credit card frauds; and scams and shams by vendors, suppliers, contractors, and customers.

In the United States, the largest body of trained and experienced fraud auditors comes from government audit and investigative agencies like the Internal Revenue Service (IRS), Federal Bureau of Investigation (FBI), Government Accounting Office (GAO), and the SEC. Police authorities on the state and local levels have few audit resources at their disposal; as a consequence, their ability to investigate certain white-collar crimes is limited. There is a need for fraud auditing in both public and private sectors of the economy.

Public accounting firms and other organizations in the private sector are developing fraud audit expertise. Although relatively few public accountants and internal auditors are specifically trained and experienced in this discipline, their numbers are rapidly increasing. In fact, in today's environment, it is hard to think of a firm that does *not* need fraud auditors.

Principles of Fraud Audits

Many principles of fraud audits should be understood by all auditors. They are:

- Fraud auditing is different from financial auditing. It is more a mind-set than a methodology.
- Fraud auditors have different approaches from financial auditors. Fraud auditors mostly focus on exceptions, oddities, accounting irregularities, and patterns of conduct. Financial auditors mostly focus on the audit trail and material misstatements.

- Fraud auditing is learned primarily from experience, not from audit textbooks or last year's work papers. Learning to be a fraud auditor means learning to think like a thief: "Where are the weakest links in this chain of internal controls?" "How can I steal on my job and get away with it?"
- From an audit perspective, fraud is intentionally misrepresenting financial facts of a material nature. From a fraud-audit perspective, fraud is an intentional misrepresentation of material financial facts.
- Frauds are committed for economic, egocentric, ideological, emotional, and psychotic reasons. Of the five, the economic motive is the most common.
- Fraud tends to encompass a theory structured around motive, opportunity, and rationalization (the "fraud triangle").
- Fraud in a computerized accounting environment can be committed at any state of processing—input, throughput, or output. Input frauds (entering false and fraudulent data) are the most common.
- The most common fraudulent schemes by lower-level employees involve disbursements (payables, payroll, and benefit and expense claims).
- The most common fraudulent schemes by higher-level managers involve "profit smoothing" (deferring expenses, booking sales too early, overstating inventory).
- Accounting-type frauds are caused more often by absence of controls than by loose controls.
- Fraud incidents may not be growing exponentially, but fraud losses are growing fairly rapidly ($400 billion in 1996 to $660 billion in 2004.[5]
- Accounting frauds are discovered more often by reactive measures than by proactive ones. (Tips and accident make up over 60% of frauds detected.) Only about 10% of frauds are detected by financial auditors, and only about 24% of frauds are detected by internal audit, which is the highest of any proactive measures.
- Fraud prevention is a matter of adequate controls and a work environment that places a high value on personal honesty and fair dealing.

Financial Audit versus Fraud Audit

Many in the public, and some in the U.S. Congress, have questioned why financial auditors do not detect more fraud. The general public believes that a financial auditor would detect a fraud if one were being perpetrated during the financial auditor's audit. For instance, both the KPMG Fraud Survey and the ACFE Report to the Nation show only about 10% of frauds are detected by financial auditors. The truth, however, is that the procedures for financial audits are designed to detect material misstatements, not immaterial frauds. While it is true that many of the financial statements and frauds could have, perhaps should have, been detected by financial auditors, the vast majority of frauds could not be detected with the generally accepted audit standards (GAAS) of financial audits. Reasons include the dependence of financial auditors on a sample and the auditors' reliance on examining the audit trail versus examining the events and activities behind the documents. The latter is simply cost-prohibitive.

Before the Enron scandal, and the subsequent passage of SOX and adoption of SAS No. 99, catching a fraudulent transaction in a financial audit was basically a crapshoot. Financial audit procedures were based on uncovering material deviations in financial data and significant variances from acceptable accounting and auditing standards. But since SOX and SAS No. 99, things have changed. Financial auditors are much more involved in detecting fraud, even immaterial ones.

Still, there are some basic differences today between the procedures of fraud auditors and those of financial auditors. Fraud auditors look behind and beyond the transactions and audit trail to focus on the substance of the transactions instead. The questions the fraud auditor has uppermost in mind are not how the accounting system and internal controls stack up against applicable standards but rather:

- Where are the weakest links in this system's chain of controls?
- What deviations from conventional good accounting practices are possible in this system?
- How are off-line transactions handled, and who can authorize such transactions?
- What would be the simplest way to compromise this system?

- What control features in this system can be bypassed by higher authorities?
- What is the nature of the work environment?

Another difference is the current status of technical guidance combined with research on frauds. Frauds can be divided into three main categories: (1) financial frauds, (2) asset misappropriations, and (3) corruption (ACFE fraud tree). Financial frauds are typically perpetrated by executive management and average millions of dollars in losses. According to a recent KPMG Fraud Survey, that average is about $258 million. Generally speaking, therefore, financial frauds are likely to be material, and thus financial audit procedures have the potential to detect them—because they would be a material misstatement, due to a material fraud. However, those who might be responsible for fraud audits internal to the firm could be constrained or thwarted in detecting the fraud, because executives are in a position to hide the fraud or misdirect fraud auditors' efforts. Cynthia Cooper argues that at WorldCom she was thwarted from doing her job as internal auditor, but she eventually did uncover the financial fraud being perpetrated there.

Two types of financial frauds deserve special attention. Management override of controls and collusion, the coordination of multiple persons toward a common objective, are frauds that are *always possible* (in *any* internal control environment) and are the *absolute hardest frauds to prevent*. Moreover, these frauds are difficult to detect, especially collusion. Fraud auditors and financial auditors need to be conscious of these frauds. To counter these frauds to the extent possible, the control environment must:

- Incorporate and promote a solid segregation of duties.
- Address and limit conflicts of interests.
- Utilize a strong ethical culture.
- Monitor and review constantly.

People who have access to corporate assets and knowledge of the internal and accounting controls, or who hold management roles in which they can override such controls, are in the best position to commit financial frauds against their companies. The threat of fraud is greatest at the senior management level because access to assets and authority to bypass controls is greatest at that level. But financial fraud is also possible among personnel with accounting, finance, data processing, and property-handling responsibilities. They too may have access to accounting records and can use that knowledge and authority to compromise controls and to access corporate assets.

Asset misappropriation in most forms, especially physical asset misappropriation, actually exhibits opposite characteristics of the average financial fraud. It is often immaterial, as in construction, where materials are stolen pervasively throughout the industry. Because of the clandestine nature of fraud combined with the procedures of financial audits, it is not likely that financial auditors will detect such fraud during their audits. Fraud auditors, however, do have procedures and techniques designed to detect these kinds of frauds, given an adequate opportunity to apply them.

Also, from an accounting and audit standpoint, fraud is an intentional misrepresentation of a material fact in the books of account and ultimately the financial statements. The misrepresentation may be directed against such organizational outsiders as shareholders or creditors, or against the organization itself by covering up or disguising embezzlement, incompetence, misapplication of funds, and theft or improper use of organizational assets by officers, employees, and agents. Fraud may also be directed against an organization by outsiders (vendors, suppliers, contractors, consultants, and customers) through overbilling, double billing, substituting inferior materials, or misrepresenting the quality and value of goods purchased or the credit standing of customers. Such outsiders may also be guilty of corrupting insiders (commercial bribery). Frauds of this kind (asset misappropriation) occur most often when these conditions exist:

- Internal controls are absent, weak, or loosely enforced.
- Employees are hired without due consideration for their honesty and integrity.
- Employees are poorly managed, exploited, abused, or placed under stress to accomplish financial goals and objectives.
- Management models are themselves corrupt, inefficient, or incompetent.
- A trusted employee has an unresolvable personal problem, usually of a financial nature, brought on by family medical needs, or alcoholism, drug abuse, excessive gambling, or expensive tastes.

- The industry of which the company is a part is naturally susceptible to or has a tradition of corruption.
- The company has fallen on bad times—it is losing money or market share, or its products or services are becoming passé.

Thinking Like a Fraud Auditor

Investigating fraud requires the combined skills of a well-trained auditor and a criminal investigator. However, finding these skill sets in one person is rare. Part of the mission of this book is to better acquaint auditors with criminal-investigative rules, principles, techniques, and methods and to provide criminal investigators with some knowledge of accounting and auditing rules, principles, techniques, and methods. The result is, it is hoped, an ability to think more like a fraud auditor.

Fraud auditors and detectives tend to be "thinker" types, in the sense that they deal with situations requiring objectivity on their part. Personal feelings and personal biases are inappropriate for making sound decisions and drawing logical conclusions and inferences. Fraud auditors enjoy thinking and learning. They enjoy solving problems, especially challenging ones.

Intuition is crucial in the fraud auditing process. Accountants and investigators sometimes equate intuition with professional judgment— judgment derived from knowledge, education, training, acquired skills, and experience. It is not knowing the answer, but knowing the questions. It is not a formula, and is difficult at best to teach.

In circumstances in which evidence is sparse, fraud auditors can theorize about the facts and play on hunches. They are sensitive to nonverbal cues, are spontaneous in solving problems, and can refine and rework a problem with a variety of approaches until it is solved. The hunch of a trained investigator is generally worth much more than that of the inexperienced investigator, because it is based on experience, knowledge, and training. Then again, inexperienced fraud auditors might be more open and more perceptive.

The knack of intuition can be acquired if one retains an open, objective, and inquisitive mind—not necessarily an analytical mind but one that can synthesize data and put it all together in some sort of scenario of what may have happened. Good intuition often can be mistakenly attributed to accident, chance, or good luck, but breakthroughs are not simply random events. Rather, the break occurs because the auditor's intuition was pushed and bent in the right direction.

Mystery stories generally are exercises in deductive logic, and most laypersons believe crimes can be detected and proven that way. Some can be. But crime or fraud discernment generally involves applying inductive as well as deductive logic. A recurring theme in most mystery stories is the solution of crimes through a brilliant flash of insight at some point in the investigation. Some minor or oddball thing happened or was found or observed that ultimately led to the crime's solution. A minor fact becomes the major fact in unraveling the crime or identifying the killer.

The process called deduction is more like synthesis. It was not a missing piece in a jigsaw puzzle that solved the crime but a missing link in the chain of evidence that brought the insight to the fore. It can be described as seeing the whole and the hole at once. The union of time, space, and energy caused the flash. That is intuition. But this knack of seeing the hole and the whole all at once comes with experience and the right mind-set. Mind-set is a predisposition to believe in the things one sees, feels, tastes, touches, smells, and experiences— to believe in one's own competence.

Good investigators are open to their senses, open to suggestions, open to oddities. Great investigators do not have a sixth sense but are able to create a synergy in seeing the "big picture" from their five senses to notice the sameness and differences that matter in solving the fraud. Sherlock Holmes had this talent for seeing the simple oddity: the dog that did not bark.

The most accepted scientific methods for deriving truth involve using deductive and inductive reasoning. In deductive reasoning, one proceeds from the general to the specific, whereas in inductive reasoning, one proceeds from the specific to the general. Inductive reasoning involves an empirical approach to truth, taking a sample of the whole and predicting a probable outcome based on that sample. In deductive reasoning, one makes clinical observations; conducts physical examinations and interrogations; eliminates the extraneous; and draws inferences to arrive at certain generalizations or conclusions.

Financial auditors tend to use the inductive approach, whereas investigators tend to use the deductive approach. Fraud auditors may have to use both approaches in developing their investigative mentality.

In summary, fraud involves so many variables in terms of fraud types, defrauder types, victim types, crime methods, techniques, tools, means, and instruments that any effort to unify them into a comprehensive theory of causation or solution seems impossible. This fact is why intuition, experience, and training are so vital to fraud auditing. Thinking like a fraud auditor means being perceptive, using inductive logic based on perception, and knowing how fraud plays into audits and criminal investigations.

Training for Fraud Auditors

Fraud auditing is a relatively new field in private sector accounting. The public sector has had fraud auditing expertise for some time—at least since the Federal Income Tax Law was passed in 1913. Since that time, a host of federal regulatory agencies have been created with the power to review certain business organizations' records (e.g., the SEC, Federal Trade Commission, Comptroller of the Currency, Federal Deposit Insurance Corporation, Wage and Hour Division of the Labor Department, etc.).

Up to the time of Enron, there were few young accountants in the field of fraud auditing. Those in this specialized field tended to be experienced in financial auditing, either in public accounting or fraud auditing in government agencies, before they ventured into private practice. But beginning with 2000, training for fraud auditors has changed. For instance, prior to 2000, there were very few courses in fraud auditing, and no degree with 18 hours or more of fraud education. Now there are a few college degree programs in fraud auditing or forensic accounting, and the number of these courses or degrees is growing rapidly.

Also, many professional associations now provide fraud auditing training. The ACFE offers many seminars and training, featuring its week-long course known as fraud boot camp. The American College of Forensic Examiners Institute (ACFEI) is another organization that provides continuing education and seminars specifically on fraud. The Institute of Internal Auditors (IIA) provides periodic specialized training and conferences on fraud auditing, as does the Information Systems Audit and Control Association (ISACA) and the AICPA. In fact, it is hard to find an accounting or auditing professional organization that does not offer training for fraud auditors today.

Subjects that could be or should be covered by training for fraud auditors include:

- Criminal, civil versus contractual fraud
- Financial frauds versus asset misappropriation fraud schemes
- Material versus immaterial misrepresentation
- Error versus irregularity and fraud
- Identification of anomalies
- Conspiracies or collusion versus individually perpetrated fraud
- Fraud principles, such as the fraud triangle
- Fraud schemes, categorizations (e.g., ACFE fraud tree)
- Red flags associated with specific frauds
- Profile of white-collar criminal
- Fraud research
- Criminal justice theories
- White-collar crime theories and principles
- Interviewing skills
- Legal ramifications of evidence and expert testimony
- Fraud committed for the company versus against the company
- Insider versus outsider frauds
- Insiders in collusion with outsiders (i.e., customers, suppliers, competitors, contractors)
- High-level versus low-level employee perpetrated frauds
- Long- versus short-term performance criteria
- Fraud in high- versus low-trust organizations
- Internal versus external auditor's liability for detecting fraud
- Statement versus transaction frauds
- Overstated versus understated profits, revenues, assets, losses, expenses, and liabilities
- Diversion versus conversion of assets
- Fake debits versus fake credits
- Receipts versus disbursement frauds
- Fabrication of accounts payable versus accounts receivable frauds
- Front-end frauds (skimming receipts) versus rear-end frauds (disposing of assets)

- On-book versus off-book frauds
- Concealment, destruction, and alteration of records
- Premature booking of sales versus delayed recording of expenses
- Fraud auditing versus forensic accounting
- Fraud auditing versus financial auditing
- Columbo versus Perry Mason
- Thinking like a thief versus acting like a thief
- Fraud in manual versus computerized accounting systems
- Input versus output versus throughput frauds
- Altering input versus destroying or suppressing throughput
- Compromising controls versus compromising personnel
- Psychosocial characteristics of thieves versus embezzlers
- Greed versus need as motivations for fraud
- Motivation versus opportunity as inducements to commit fraud
- Detection versus prevention of fraud
- Allegation of fraud versus discrepancy detection
- Risk prevention versus risk transfer versus risk assumption
- High-risk industries, companies, occupations, personalities
- Thinking like a thief
- Designing fraud scenarios
- Thinking creatively (right-brain) as well as logically (left-brain)
- Assessing the strengths and weaknesses of internal controls
- Testing for compliance with control policies and procedures
- Monitoring ratios and trends of key account categories (including sales to cost of sales, inventory, receivables, freight out, and commissions)
- Monitoring variances, exceptions, and oddities in accounting transactions and account balances—debit balances in payables, credit balances in receivables, out-of-cycle and out-of-pattern transactions, and so on
- Following the flow of funds and supporting documents through the system and beyond
- Locating hidden assets
- Inspecting support documents for authenticity
- Reconstructing transactions from outside sources when support documents are missing or destroyed
- Determining the net worth and living expenses of suspects
- Gathering and preserving evidence of accounting frauds; documents, correspondence, testimony, and so on

- Documenting losses from fraud, theft, and embezzlement for criminal, civil, and insurance purposes
- Estimating related damages from such losses
- Testifying as an expert witness in accounting matters
- Deterring fraud in books of account—creating awareness of the risk of fraud, establishing personnel policies, ethical codes, and loss prevention programs, conducting audits

Attitude, mind-set, and demeanor outcomes deal heavily with personal values and beliefs. Students of fraud auditing, after completing studies, for example, should assume they are just beginning an adventure in a field of high interest and excitement in which they can match wits with other accountants, lawyers, members of the media, and some of the most ingenious criminal minds in the world—white-collar criminals.

The fraud auditor's mind-set suggests that fraud is possible in any organization. It is simply a matter of motive, opportunity, and the integrity of employees and managers. Therefore, if fraud is possible, it should be looked for; that is, audit programs should make sufficient provision for the review of internal controls and the testing of compliance therewith. In this regard, a high priority should be given to personal and professional values, such attributes as truth, honesty, accountability, fairness, and independence, in conducting fraud audits.

ANTIFRAUD PROFESSIONAL ORGANIZATIONS AND CERTIFICATIONS

The Association of Certified Fraud Examiners (ACFE) was founded in 1988 by Joe Wells and others. It was the dream of Donald Cressey and Edwin Sutherland, two pioneers in white-collar crime, that was made a reality by Wells and his friends. The ACFE is a global, professional organization dedicated to fighting fraud and white-collar crime, with over 30,000 members in over 100 countries. Since its inception, the ACFE has been a major resource for fraud information and training. The Certified Fraud Examiner (CFE) program is an internationally recognized accrediting process for individuals who possess the specialized skills required to detect, investigate, and deter fraud. Some have said that the ACFE is the premier financial sleuthing organization in the world today.

Another antifraud organization is the American College of Forensic Examiners Institute (ACFEI). The ACFEI is an independent, scientific, and professional society that is multidisciplinary in its scope, covering a large number of forensic-related disciplines or areas including forensic accounting. The ACFEI's purpose is the continued advancement of forensic examination and consultation across the many professional fields of its membership. The ACFEI has elevated standards through education, and training.

One of the ACFEI certifications is the Certified Forensic Accounting (Cr.FA). The role of the forensic accountant necessitates specialized training and skills that are not typically part of an accountant's formal education. Forensic accountants are professionals who use a unique blend of education and experience to apply accounting, auditing, and investigative skills to uncover truth, form legal opinions, and assist in investigations. Forensic accountants may be involved in both litigation support (providing assistance on a given case, primarily related to the calculation or estimation of economic damages and related issues) and investigative accounting (looking into illegal activities). Thus the Cr.FA program provides advanced education and training to cover the wide range of skills, abilities, and knowledge necessary in forensic engagements. As of January 1, 2006, a person must be a CPA to acquire the Cr.FA certification.

SUMMARY

Fraud auditing is not easy. The work is often frustrating and grueling. The fraud accountant will be surrounded with data, documents, reports, analyses, observations, and interview notes; and times, dates, places, people, procedures, and policies to remember. The pace of the audit and the working environment is generally very busy. To the inexperienced observer, the status of the audit may even seem chaotic. Often the fraud auditor does not know what to look for, or even why, other than that something looks suspicious or out of place. Being overly organized when doing fraud audit work may be a handicap. One needs a lot of freedom and space to let one's imagination run wild. One needs to poke holes into everything, including pet theories and biases.

Fraud auditors cannot accept anything anyone says as the gospel truth. They must not assume that any document is what it purports to be. When conflicts between statements of witnesses occur, fraud auditors must not take sides or prejudge their veracity. They must keep an open mind. The proof of fraud is rarely when and what one thought when one first began the audit. Preconceptions are dangerous. They invariably lead one down the wrong path.

Fraud auditors must not assume that the victim knows or understands what happened, either. Building one's own theory based on the victim's preconceptions is equally dangerous. But one must not discourage the victim or the victim's personnel from talking. They probably have an answer or two that will help in the long run, an answer that they do not believe is relevant or significant at the time.

Good fraud auditors and investigators truly are a breed apart from their colleagues in auditing and law enforcement, but they differ in personality, communication style, lifestyle, and beliefs and values. Effective fraud auditors tend to be like the fictional television character Columbo, and investigators tend to be like Perry Mason.

- Mason: the articulate, clinically cold, calculating, brilliant, logical, deductive reasoner whose eternal questions are: Who did it? and Why?
- Columbo: the stumbling, bumbling, cigar-chomping, eternally curious fool whose persistence and doggedness on such questions as what, where, when, how many, how few, and how often always seem to end up proving the why and who issues too.

In simple, psychological terms, Mason is a left-brain thinker: logical, sequential, orderly, linear, deductive, analytical, and intellectual. Columbo, however, is a right-brain thinker: intuitive, creative, emotional, holistic, artistic, and inductive. In short, Mason analyzes, Columbo synthesizes. Mason takes it apart and Columbo puts it all together. Mason is the brilliant pathologist and Columbo is the phenomenologist. The questions they ask are What happened? versus Why did it happen? Neither of those questions or types of thinkers is necessarily better than the other, as long as they serve the purpose. The differences are ultimately unimportant, so long as the fraud investigation is successful.

ENDNOTES

1. Some of the information in this section comes from Dr. Robert E. Jensen's Web site at Trinity University, www.trinity.edu/rjensen/415wp/AmericanHistoryOfFraud.htm, last accessed January 13, 2006.
2. The South Sea Bubble story was taken from the online free encyclopedia known as Wikipedia: http://en.wikipedia.org/wiki/The_South_Sea_Company.
3. http://www.ca.edu//~dmcneil/bubble.html.
4. According to the ACFE 2004 *Report to the Nation,* the number-one method of detection is tip and the number-three method is accident.
5. Association of Certified Fraud Examiners (ACFE), *Report to the Nation* (RTTN), 1996, 2002, 2004.

CHAPTER **3**

Auditor Liability for Detecting Fraud

INTRODUCTION

Financial auditors who audit public companies are the most common group of auditors and the group most often discussed in terms of auditor liability. While internal, fraud, and outsourced/consulting auditors face similar issues and share the same liability in some cases, differences do exist. The requirements for audits of public companies are mandated at a higher level by federal laws and legally enforceable regulatory standards. In this chapter, financial auditors conducting audits of public companies (also known as external or independent auditors or public accountants), or organizations otherwise subject to the regulations discussed, are the principal focus of discussion.

Auditor liability has never been a crystal-clear issue to the public, regulators, or even auditors themselves. Some of the more notable reasons are the amount of judgment and expertise involved in accounting and auditing, public misconceptions, political influence, constantly changing requirements, the substantive and sampling nature of audits, and other environmental factors. Lawmakers and regulators have tried to establish liability definitively in practical terms, but the task is not an easy one. Financial auditors (internal and external) may still be in doubt as to the extent of their legal and professional responsibility for fraud detection when conducting financial audits. Numerous laws and regulatory standards have been put in place in a relatively short period of time and are still maturing. Auditors implementing these requirements will adjust, learn, and become more proficient over time, but now they are still learning both how recent regulations work in practice and the boundaries of their liability.

The general public, as opposed to financial auditors, does not seem to have any doubts about auditor liability, nor do the courts. There is a growing public perception that auditors, by the nature of their education, intuition, and work experience, can and should be able to sniff out fraud wherever and whenever it exists in financial records and/or data. That standard is far higher than anyone in the audit professions has ever advocated or thought reasonably possible. No auditor could ever live up to such a strict standard of care. Nor could any auditor afford the premiums for professional liability insurance if the public's perception of the standard became a legal reality.

The public's perception of auditor responsibility for fraud detection is highly unrealistic and contributes to what is commonly known as the expectations gap. The expectations gap is the difference between what the public *thinks* a financial audit is and what financial audits *really are*. Part of the gap stems from a lack of transparency on the part of auditors and audit regulators, who need to educate the public better about the process and content of financial audits, accounting principles and rules, and financial reporting and disclosures.

The public's part of the gap is mostly out of uneducated misconceptions. Few people know that financial statement audits are aimed at providing reasonable assurance as to whether a material misstatement in the financial statement exists or not and whether financial transactions are recorded and financials statements are presented in conformity with generally accepted accounting principles (GAAP) or not. That language is nearly synonymous with the financial audit "opinions" issued for financial statement audits mandated by generally accepted auditing standards (GAAS) as promulgated by the American Institute of Certified Public Accountants (AICPA). In addition, GAAS states that the "The auditor has a responsibility to plan and perform the audit to obtain reasonable assurance about whether the financial statements are free of material misstatement, whether caused by error or fraud."[1]

The public simply *assumes* that fraud should be caught in a financial audit. Although that is not a false statement, it is not a true one either. Outside of the aforementioned misconception about the purpose of financial statements, the process and procedures within a financial audit are also misunderstood. Financial auditors, to some extent, rely on management's (or otherwise the entity's) representations; it is impractical and would be unreasonable for auditors to try to *absolutely, perfectly, unquestionably* determine whether financial statements were accurate and in compliance with regulations. Also, financial audits occur mostly after the end of the period being audited (although notably the trend is for more audit work to be done within the period). As with other crimes, the more time that goes by after a fraud has been committed, the harder it is to catch. Audit procedures traditionally have not directly targeted fraud, although that is changing. The changes mainly stem from two new regulations.

Increased Auditor Liability

Growing concern and expectation of the public and Congress culminated in the advent of the Sarbanes-Oxley Act of 2002 (SOX) and the adoption of Statement on Auditing Standard (SAS) No. 99, *Consideration of Fraud in a Financial Statement Audit.* Since those documents were put in place, even more attention has been brought on the issue of auditors detecting fraud, and of course more technical guidance has been provided for financial auditors. SOX addresses the financial auditor's responsibility to detect fraud in direct and indirect tenets.

Indirectly, for example, the Public Companies Accounting Oversight Board (PCAOB) was created in reaction to public and congressional perception that large financial frauds had happened while being audited by a large financial audit firms that were not performing their professional duties appropriately and that were not being properly regulated by the AICPA. These aspects of SOX and PCAOB lead us to believe that the PCAOB's creation was a simultaneous reaction with SOX:

- The PCAOB answers directly to the Securities and Exchange Commission (SEC). Prior to the passage of SOX, the Financial Accounting Standards Board (FASB) and the American Institute of Certified Public Accountants (AICPA) were delegated authority under the SEC, but did not report directly to the SEC.
- An examination of the quality of audits of SEC firms now is performed periodically not only by peers (other public accounting firms in a peer review) but also by the PCAOB.
- In order to conduct financial audits of SEC companies, a financial audit firm must be registered with the PCAOB.

■ The members of the PCAOB are not all CPAs; two of them cannot be CPAs or former CPAs. All members of the FASB, the practical authority for accounting standards, have been CPAs or former CPAs.

All of these aspects point to two main regulatory changes: a tighter link of control between the law and the entities under the law and independent supervision and monitoring.

SOX and SAS No. 99 have increased the expectation that auditors will detect fraud; auditor liability has also increased. By definition, auditors are now held liable for SOX and SAS No. 99 requirements, both of which explicitly or implicitly imply that auditors must consider fraud and must perform specific procedures to detect fraud. SOX and SAS No. 99 are much more complex than summarized here; for now, it is important to know they were largely formed due to an inability to control and to hold auditors liable for fraud. Both SOX and SAS No. 99 will be covered in greater detail later in this chapter and in subsequent chapters.

What, then, is the financial auditor's legal standard of care and what is her responsibility for detecting fraud? How is auditor liability enforceable and to what degree? Reviewing literature on, understanding past efforts in relation to, and knowing the most recent changes to auditor liability can best answer those questions.

Brief History of Auditors' Liability for Detecting Fraud

SEC Acts of 1933 and 1934   Auditors had been sued before the stock market crash of 1929, the Securities Act of 1933, and the Securities Exchange Act of 1934. However, the SEC acts added more responsibility and liability to the independent financial auditor and, more important, established a public perception of accountability. The acts were most likely influenced more by a fraud than by the stock market crash of 1929.

By the time of that stock market crash, external auditing had become a somewhat standardized profession, but not a particularly large one. Since bankers were the primary users of financial statements, the only companies needing audits were those that depended on banks for capital. Companies that depended on stockholder financing were not required to have audits. Consequently, often even companies listed on the New York Stock Exchange did not issue audited financial statements. That situation would change because of Ivar Kreuger—one of the greatest swindlers the world has ever seen.

The most widely held securities in the United States (and the world) during the 1920s were the stocks and bonds of Kreuger & Toll, Inc., a Swedish match conglomerate. The company was founded and headed by Ivar Kreuger, supposedly the richest man in the world. Kreuger's securities were popular because they sold in small denominations and paid high dividends and interest (often 20% annually). Financial reporting as we know it today was in its infancy; stockholders based their investment decisions solely on dividend payments. Kreuger's dividends were paid, however, out of capital, not profits. Kreuger was essentially operating a giant pyramid scheme, which was hidden from the investing public by Kreuger's insistence that financial statements not be audited. He advocated that financial secrecy was paramount to corporate success. In Kreuger's defense, some amount of secrecy was needed because he was often dealing with foreign kings and dictators about government monopolies and taxes on wooden matches. Subsequently it was discovered that many of his companies' assets were in the form of intangible monopolies.

The stock market crash of 1929 made it more difficult for Kreuger to sell new securities to fuel his pyramid scheme, and he committed suicide in March 1932. Within three weeks, his companies were in bankruptcy as it became apparent that there were few assets to support the unaudited financial statements that had been issued over the years. The bankruptcy was the largest on record up to that time and resulted in numerous changes in financial reporting.

Newspaper articles kept U.S. citizens aware of the extent of Kreuger's fraud; meanwhile, Congress had been and was considering the passage of the federal securities laws. Thus, the timing of the bankruptcy and the corresponding media coverage made it politically expedient to pass laws that would make similar schemes difficult in the future. A single event, the demise of Ivar Kreuger's fraud scheme, had shaken investors' confidence and provided the media event of the decade.

The passage of the Securities Act of 1933 and the issuance by the New York Stock Exchange of rules mandating audits of listed companies can both be attributed to the Ivar Kreuger case. Even a movement toward uniformity in accounting principles can be laid at

Kreuger's feet. Auditors thus owe much of their livelihood to the fraud perpetrated by Ivar Kreuger. In fact, some might say that Kreuger did more good than harm for the financial community, since because of him the auditing profession saw improvements to financial reporting thereafter. A person of his ilk was needed to show the world that auditors are necessary and can make a contribution to a regulated securities market.

Kreuger's fraud and the reactionary SEC acts illustrate an important point relevant to discussion of fraud and auditor liability issues: History repeats itself and moves in cycles. These cycles are similar to the concept of business cycles: growth, climax, recession, trough, and back to growth. With regard to auditor liability for fraud, one can definitively see these cycles occurring over the past 70 years. There have been (including now) periods of time when heightened awareness to auditor liability, usually because of large and/or numerous frauds, necessitates swift and numerous changes. (As mentioned, the early 1980s had the savings and loan scandals, the early 1990s had numerous auditor litigations, and the early 2000s experienced an abysmal amount of fraud and auditor litigation.) Afterward, a period of gradual, slow decrease in the attention given to fraud will ensue until fraud becomes rampant again, more changes are needed, and the cycle begins once more.

The term *pendulum swing* is often used to refer to this cycle. Auditors should consider this cyclical phenomenon with regard to their liability. As an example, compare the Financial Fraud Detection and Disclosure Act of 1986 and SOX as discussed below. Although occurring over 15 years apart, the similarities in purpose and content are striking.

Auditor Responsibility

In *United States v. Arthur Young & Co.* (March 21, 1984), the Supreme Court tried to define *professionalism* in the accounting profession in the loftiest terms. In a unanimous decision the Court stated:

> By clarifying the public reports that collectively depict a corporation's financial status, the independent auditor assumes a public responsibility transcending any employment relationship with the

client. The independent public accountant performing his special function owes ultimate allegiance to the corporation's creditors and stockholders, *as well as to the investing public. This "public watchdog" function demands that the accountant maintain* total independence from the client at all times *and requires* complete fidelity to the public trust. *To insulate from disclosure a certified public accountant's interpretations of the client's financial statements would be to ignore the significance of the accountant's role as a* disinterested analyst charged with public obligations. *[Emphasis added.]*

The Court continued:

It is therefore not enough that financial statements be accurate; the public must also perceive them as being accurate. Public faith *in the reliability of a corporation's financial statement depends upon the* public perception *of the outside auditor as an independent professional. [Emphasis added.]*

The Court recognized the effect of the public's perception on financial audits and auditors. It also emphasized the importance of independence in the arrangement between the auditor and the audited entity. Most important, the Court notes that *even if* the auditor did his job, if the public believes that the auditor or the financial statements are corrupt, the auditor has not fulfilled his primary duty, which is to the public.

The Auditing Standards division of the AICPA summarized auditors' responsibilities regarding fraud and illegal acts under GAAS:

The auditor's responsibility to detect and report fraud is set out in Statement on Auditing Standards (SAS) No. 16, The Auditor's Responsibility for the Detection of Errors or Irregularities (1977) and SAS No. 17, Illegal Acts by Clients (1977). The standards were developed as a direct result of problems in the business community in the mid-1970s. The disclosure of client frauds, such as Equity Funding, and questionable payments, primarily in foreign countries, stirred the profession to adopt more specific standards in the area of client misconduct.

SAS No. 16 established an affirmative requirement for auditors; the auditor is required to plan the examination to search for material errors and irregularities and to carry out the search with due skill and care. The auditor's responsibility with regard to illegal acts is less distinct; because auditors are not lawyers trained to recognize illegal acts, they are not expected to search for illegal acts but rather to be aware that some matters that come to their attention during the examination might suggest that illegal acts have occurred. If auditors discover an error, irregularity, or illegal act, they are required to report it to management and, depending on its significance, possibly to the board of directors or its audit committee. Auditors are also required to assess the effect on the financial statements and, if material, to insist on adjustment or additional disclosure in the statements or to qualify the audit report.

SAS No. 16 recognizes that although there is an affirmative responsibility to search for material errors and irregularities, there is a chance that they will not be found. Auditors test selectively; that is, they usually sample accounts rather than examining 100% of accounts. Thus, if the sample does not identify a fraudulent transaction, the auditor will be less likely to suspect one in the unsampled portion of the financial statements. Auditors, of course, control this sampling risk, but to eliminate it would require them to examine all of the entity's transactions for the year, which would result in astronomical audit costs and still would not necessarily detect cleverly forged or unrecorded transactions.

Foreign Corrupt Practices Act of 1977

The Foreign Corrupt Practices Act of 1977 (FCPA) not only prohibited illegal payments but also addressed issues related to fraud, such as internal controls. Specifically, the FCPA required SEC registrants to establish and maintain financial books, records, and accounts. It also required the establishment of internal accounting controls sufficient to meet these objectives:

- Transactions are executed in accordance with management's general or specific authorization.
- Transactions are recorded as necessary to prepare financial statements (i.e., generally accepted accounting principles) and to maintain accountability.

- Access to assets is permitted only in accordance with management authorization.
- The recorded assets are compared with existing assets at reasonable intervals.

After the passage of the FCPA, many corporations established internal and information technology (electronic data processing, or EDP) audit functions or bolstered the staffs of these organizational units only to discover no decrease in the number of defalcations—frauds, thefts, and embezzlements—by corporate users. Researchers tested the hypothesis that an increase in the perceived aggressiveness by internal and external auditors in detecting corporate irregularities would function as a deterrent.[2] Their study concludes that managers contemplating acts of management fraud are not deterred by the presence of internal and external auditors; neither does an increase in the perceived aggressiveness of the internal or external auditor significantly decrease the occurrence of corporate irregularities. Thus these tenets may benefit the corporation only in terms of asset misappropriation and corruption, but not fraudulent statements (see Chapter 1).

Legal Liability

One source for insight on the financial auditor's standard of care and responsibility for fraud detection is *American Jurisprudence*. Under the general heading "Accountants," that volume offers this:

> *It is generally recognized that a public accountant may be held liable on principles of negligence, to one with whom he is in privity, or with whom he has a direct contractual relation, for damages which naturally and proximately result from his failure to employ the degree of knowledge, skill, and judgment usually possessed by members of that profession in the particular locality.*

But Section 17, page 366, reads:

> *An accountant is not an insurer of the effectiveness of his audit to discover the defalcations of frauds of employees but may be found liable for fraudulent or negligent failure to discover such defalcations*

because of lack of compliance with proper accounting procedures and accepted accounting practices or by his contract in the light of circumstances of the particular case. . . . And the employer may be precluded from recovery because of his own negligence when it has contributed to the accountant's failure to perform his contract and to report the truth.[3]

The second excerpt gives auditors a breather. Obviously they should not be held liable for not detecting fraud when their clients deceive them.

In 1984 the Institute of Internal Auditors (IIA) issued its *Statement on Internal Auditing Standards*, which deals with deterrence, detection, investigation, and reporting of fraud. The statement makes a number of interesting points in its foreword and summary. To quote from the foreword:

Fraud is a significant and sensitive management concern. This concern has grown dramatically in recent years due to a substantial increase in the number and the size of the fraud uncovered. The tremendous expansion in the use of computers and the amount of publicity accorded computer-related frauds intensifies this concern. The issue of the internal auditor's responsibilities for deterrence, detection, investigation, and reporting on fraud has been a matter of much debate and controversy. Some of the controversy can be attributed to the vast differences in internal auditing's charter from country to country and from organization to organization. Another cause of the controversy may be unrealistic—nevertheless increasing—expectations of the internal auditor's ability to deter and/or detect fraud in some circumstances.[4]

The IIA's current *International Standards for the Professional Practice of Internal Auditing* (SPPIA) states, "The internal auditor should have sufficient knowledge to identify the indicators of fraud but is not expected to have the expertise of a person whose primary responsibility is detecting and investigating fraud."[5] Internal auditors also have the opportunity to evaluate fraud risks and controls and to recommend action to mitigate risks and improve controls. Specifically, the IIA Standards require internal auditors to assess risks facing their organizations. This risk assessment is to serve as the basis from which audit plans are devised and against which internal controls are tested. The IIA Standards require the audit plan to be presented to and approved by the audit committee (or board of directors where no audit committee exists). The work completed as a result of the audit plan provides assurance on which management's assertion about controls can be made.

Financial Fraud Detection and Disclosure Act of 1986

The public furor in the United States about the liability of external auditors for detection of fraud continued through the 1980s. In fact, the pressure for imposing more stringent requirements on public accountants for fraud detection appears to grow with each passing day. In the United States, the Financial Fraud Detection and Disclosure Act of 1986 was one manifestation of the public's concern. The congressional history and details of that bill follow.

> *The regulatory system established by the federal security laws is based on the concept of complete and fair disclosure of important information to investors and other users of corporate financial reports. This regularity system is administered by federal agencies, such as the Securities and Exchange Commission (SEC), working in concert with private, independent auditor firms, which check corporate financial records and certify the reports given to the public. Over the past several years, numerous cases of massive financial fraud have occurred where the independent auditors failed to either detect or to report the fraudulent activities at the companies being audited. These include E.F. Hutton, United American Bank, General Dynamics, E.S.M. Government Securities, Inc., Home State Savings and Loan of Ohio, American Savings and Loan of Florida, Saxon Industries, San Marino Savings and Loan of California, and many others. The costs of these frauds have been enormous both financially and in terms of public confidence in the soundness of the nation's economic system. The AICPA, a private trade organization, establishes GAAS, which are used by independent auditors and accepted by the SEC. Under present GAAS rules, independent auditors do not include as part of their audit significant procedures to detect management fraud, and their consideration of fraud is restricted to its material impact on a corporation's financial statements. In a large corporation, financial fraud amounting to millions or even hundreds of millions [of dollars] could go unreported because such amounts would not be considered material to the total financial condition of the corporation.*

Even when actual fraud and illegal acts are discovered, the GAAS rules only say that the auditor should inform the company's management and consider resigning from the audit account. There is no requirement that auditors report fraud or illegal acts to the appropriate government authorities. In addition, auditors rely on the internal control systems of a corporation, but do not issue an opinion regarding the adequacy of management's internal controls. Thus, financial fraud has occurred in many corporations which have been allowed to operate with substandard or nonexistent internal controls because the independent auditor did not report on the adequacy of internal controls.

The AICPA and the SEC were criticized on this issue ten years ago by the Senate Subcommittee on Reports, Accounting and Management. That subcommittee's final unanimous report stated that auditors should look for illegal acts and report them to government authorities. The AICPA appointed its own study group, the Cohen Commission, which failed to recommend active detection and reporting of illegal acts. The SEC and the AICPA did nothing further until the Subcommittee on Oversight and Investigations began its accounting hearings on February 20, 1986.

At the March 6, 1985 hearing, Chairman Dingell was joined by other members in expressing his concern about an audit rule that merely suggested that the auditor, as the public watchdog, only consider leaving the premises if he or she found a criminal, instead of reporting the criminal to the proper authorities. In response, the AICPA established a new group, the Treadway Commission, to further study the issue. Neither private accounting organizations nor the SEC have the authority to grant independent auditors immunity from legal action that could arise as a result of fraud detection and disclosure responsibilities, so legislation is the only way to fully protect auditors performing their duties in good faith.

Chairman William Seidman of the Federal Deposit Insurance Corporation, who formerly headed a large audit firm, agreed with Chairman Dingall and Congressman Wyden at the Subcommittee's April 28, 1986, hearing that auditors should look for fraud and report it to regulators.[6]

The Financial Fraud Detection and Disclosure Act of 1986 amends the federal securities laws to provide reasonable assurance that fraudulent activities at companies covered by these laws will be discovered and reported to the proper authorities. The act does not apply to small businesses or other companies that are exempt from the securities laws. The act was necessary now because the SEC and the accounting profession lacked the authority to provide full legal protection for auditors who report fraudulent activities.

The act strengthened the regulatory system of federal agencies working with private audit firms by establishing clear standards for the detection and reporting of financial fraud as well as the tools necessary to meet those standards and fully protect auditors performing their duties. The act did not create a new federal agency or regulatory burden but instead assured that audits conducted under the existing system would meet the legitimate concerns of Congress and the public that major companies were not operating fraudulently. The incremental audit costs of meeting the standards established by the act were minuscule when compared with the lost billions of dollars resulting from frauds and the decline of public confidence in the integrity of the nation's economic system. The act has several basic provisions:

- The act requires that auditors include specific and substantive procedures for detecting financial fraud as part of the audit plan. Current audit standards regard fraud detection as incidental to the financial audit. Therefore, many auditors either fail to recognize indications of fraudulent activities or else convince themselves that such activities are not within the scope of the audit and that they have no responsibility to act on such matters.
- The act requires that auditors evaluate the internal control systems established by corporate managers in order for auditors to determine whether those internal controls assure that corporate assets are being handled properly and lawfully. Existing audit standards on reviewing internal controls were not strong enough in this regard.
- The act requires auditors to issue a written report that: (1) gives the auditors' opinion regarding the adequacy of internal control systems; (2) identifies any weaknesses in those systems; and (3) states that the audit was conducted in a manner that provides reasonable assurance that fraudulent activities have been detected and reported. The auditors' written report is the place where auditors give opinions on the results of the audit. Current standards did not require that auditors issue an opinion on fraud detection or the adequacy of internal controls.
- The act requires that the individuals actually responsible for the audit sign the audit opinion on behalf of the firm conducting

the audit. Existing audit opinions bore only the name of the audit firm conducting the audit, even though the firms auditing most SEC registrants were giant organizations with hundreds of partners and thousands of staff. This provision in the act is a no-cost, common sense way to enhance personal accountability to help ensure that the audit was conducted properly. It also provided personal recognition for the individuals doing good work and enabled the public and regulatory authorities to determine if auditors identified with problem audits were being made responsible for other audit engagements. The practice of individuals signing work product personally on behalf of their firm is commonplace in the legal profession and others.

- The act requires public disclosure of known or suspected fraudulent activities and gives auditors a responsibility for assuring such disclosure. Current standards do not provide adequate disclosure of fraudulent activities, and auditors had no responsibility for assuring disclosure. Under existing rules, the corporate managers who are often involved in the fraud were given sole responsibility for reporting to the public. The act requires disclosure of activities that, in an auditor's view, may be fraudulent so that users of financial reports and corporate managers will be able to take appropriate actions without the delay inherent in complete legal proceedings to reach conclusions that satisfy every requirement of law and evidence. In most cases losses are magnified and irrevocable by the time legal proceedings are completed. This provision meets the requirement of the securities laws to give fair and complete disclosure of important information to the public in a timely manner, so that the financial markets will operate efficiently.

- The act requires that auditors report known or suspected illegal activities to the appropriate government, regulatory, or enforcement authorities. Existing standards required only that auditors report such activities to corporate management (who may be involved) and then consider resigning the audit engagement if the corporate managers do not take appropriate action. Auditors are employed to be the public watchdog, and the public was not served by the existing standard, which only suggests that the watchdog leave the premises if she finds a criminal. This provision also improves the efficiency of government regulatory and enforcement authorities by giving them the information that can be found only through the work of on-site auditors.

- Finally, the act provides complete legal protection for auditors who perform their duties under the act in good faith. Although the public expects auditors to report known or suspected fraudulent activities, auditors could suffer legal liability for honest reporting of their findings. This provision is consistent with the legal protection given to officials acting in good faith on the public's behalf in other areas. While the act attempted to establish clear standards to meet the public's expectations of auditors, it also attempted to protect the people who will implement its provisions.[7]

Treadway Commission, COSO, SAS NO. 78, and PCAOB Standard No. 2

In the early 1980s, the number of savings and loan (S&L) scandals and frauds stirred the U.S. Congress and audit profession to action. Once again the public asked questions about the financial auditors who audited these companies and gave them "clean" audit opinions while the fraud was going on. A committee was formed to analyze the frauds and what could be done to mitigate them, chaired by James C. Treadway, Jr. (Executive Vice President and General Counsel, Paine Webber, and a former commissioner of the SEC). It became known as the Treadway Commission.

The commission recommended that companies (specifically publicly traded companies) should employ better internal controls. Based on those recommendations, the work continued under the Committee of Sponsoring Organizations (COSO), which was sponsored by the American Accounting Association (AAA), the AICPA, the Institute of Management Accountants (IMA), the IIA, and the Financial Executives International (FEI). COSO developed a model for internal controls that has become known as the COSO Model.

The COSO model defines internal control as "a process, effected by an entity's board of directors, management, and other personnel, designed to provide reasonable assurance regarding the achievement of objectives in the following categories: effectiveness and efficiency of operations, reliability of financial reporting, and compliance with applicable laws and regulations." The COSO model emphasizes that the internal control system is a tool of, but not a substitute for, management and that controls should be built into, rather than built onto, operating activities. Although the report defines internal control as a process, it recommends evaluating the effectiveness of internal control as of a point in time.

The COSO Model focuses on five areas of internal controls: risk assessment, the control environment, information and communication, monitoring, and control activities. Generally speaking, the latter had been the focus of internal controls up to then.

COSO's internal control environment covers factors such as integrity and ethical values of management, competence of personnel, management philosophy and operating style, how authority and responsibilities are assigned, and the guidance provided by the board of directors.

Under risk assessment, COSO addresses the risk of failing to meet financial reporting objectives, failing to meet compliance, and failing to meet operational objectives. COSO suggests that the entity identify external and internal risks to the entity and to individual activities. The cost-benefit consideration is a part of the COSO Model, as is the dynamic nature of risk assessment. The COSO Model considers management's analysis of risk and its ability to override and adjust the internal control system.

Information systems are covered in the information and communication segment of the COSO Model. This area covers the need to capture pertinent internal and external information, the potential of strategic and integrated systems, and the need for data quality. The communication subsection discusses conveying internal control matters and gathering competitive, economic, and legislative information.

COSO discusses the monitoring aspect by recognizing the need for management to monitor the entire internal control system through the internal control system itself and through special evaluations directed at specific areas or activities. It uses an internal perspective for monitoring, and covers internal controls in broad terms.

Control activities and procedures are discussed as used throughout the entity in the COSO Model. COSO uses only one classification scheme for information systems (IS) control procedures. COSO emphasizes the desirability of integrating control activities with risk assessment.

After its introduction in the early 1990s, the COSO Model was widely adopted by the accounting and business world. In 1992, the AICPA adopted the COSO Model officially by incorporating it into the auditing technical literature as SAS No. 78, *Consideration of Internal Controls in a Financial Statement Audit*. SAS No. 78 revised SAS No. 55, *Consideration of Internal Control in a Financial Statement Audit*, and makes the COSO model part of external audit standards.

RECENT DEVELOPMENTS IN AUDITOR LIABILITY

SEC—Round II: Arthur Levitt (Late 1990s)

When Arthur Levitt was chairman of the SEC (July 1993 to February 2001), he advocated changes in audit standards and financial statements. In particular, he wanted to see financial auditors more independent by reducing the number of additional services that a financial audit firm could supply to a SEC client, to decrease conflicts of interest he perceived to exist when large consulting and other services contracts are coupled with financial audit fees.

After a lot of lobbying, Levitt and the SEC changed the original independence rules to a set more acceptable to the auditing profession, and they were finally adopted in the late 1990s. Then the Enron scandal hit. Arthur Andersen had consulting fees of about $25 million and audit fees of about $27 million the last year before the fraud was exposed. This anecdotal evidence of the need for more stringent independence rules led to the inclusion of such in the Sarbanes-Oxley Act. After Enron, Levitt stated that his greatest regret while he was at the SEC was in not following his original plans to implement stronger independence rules.

Research on SEC Fraud Cases: 2001

In 2001, Mark Beasley and his coauthors examined 45 SEC enforcement actions against auditors from 1987 to 1997. The researchers studied all of the cases to determine why the financial auditors had been charged with violations. The most common problem with the auditors was lack of due professional care (71%), with inappropriate level of professional skepticism (60%) and overreliance on inquiry as a form of audit evidence (40%) as the next two most common problems. Two additional problems were failure to corroborate management's explanations that were inconsistent or refuted by other evidence (36%) and assuming internal controls exist when they may not (24%).

The research suggests two things about financial auditors and liability: (1) the liability of financial auditors was still a concern despite all of scandals and standards, and (2) the liability pertains to the mundane and clearly delineated aspects of financial audits (due professional care, professional skepticism); it appears that the predominant causes of SEC enforcements against CPAs is not the mysterious aspects of financial audits and fraud, or the deceitfulness of client management. Lack of due professional care (following technical literature) was by far the most common cause of audit failure and the resulting SEC enforcement action.[8]

Sarbanes-Oxley Act and SAS No. 99

In 1997, the AICPA adopted SAS No. 82, *Consideration of Fraud in a Financial Statement Audit*. The next year, the AICPA established a task force to revise it. After the scandals at Enron and WorldCom, things moved rapidly at the AICPA and the U.S. Congress.

In June 2002, Congress was working on a bill to address the issues in the Enron scandal. Arthur Levitt and others had provided input to Congress in developing a reform bill that was sponsored by Senator Paul S. Sarbanes and Representative Michael G. Oxley. After the WorldCom fraud was exposed in June that year, Congress moved the bill up to debate after the July 4 recess. On July 30, 2002, Congress passed the Sarbanes-Oxley Act of 2002 (SOX). All of the prior standards or regulations pale in comparison to the effects of the passage of SOX.

Related to fraud and auditor liability, some of the major points in SOX are:

- Financial audit firms are prohibited from providing certain services in conjunction with financial audit fees (i.e., independence—similar to Levitt's original proposal at the SEC).

- A more independent board (PCAOB) was established to issue auditing standards for SEC companies (at least two of the five-member board are from the public—that is, these two members are *not* CPAs or former CPAs).
- PCAOB was given oversight of financial auditors for SEC companies (to "police" those who should or should not be auditing SEC companies).
- Section 404: Management is required to assess the effectiveness of the system of internal controls within 90 days of the audit report date and *must* identify any material control weaknesses; concomitantly, the financial auditors must opine on that evaluation. This new requirement could be seen as more exposure or liability for the financial auditors.
- The financial auditor is to be hired and have its audit fees set by the audit committee.
- Financial auditors must be rotated.

After the Sarbanes-Oxley Act was passed, PCAOB was responsible for audit technical literature. PCAOB's first standard was to officially adopt all previous standards set by the FASB and its predecessors. The second standard was to provide guidance on compliance with Section 404, management's evaluation of internal controls and the independent financial auditor's opinion of that evaluation. The standard recommends the COSO Model for evaluating internal controls. Thus no other model has been more widely adopted and employed in an antifraud context than the COSO Model.

In 2002, the AICPA adopted SAS No. 99, *Consideration of Fraud in a Financial Statement Audit*, which superceded SAS No. 82. The most significant differences between SAS No. 99 and its predecessor are the process itself and the auditor's responsibility for immaterial frauds.

The process itself is changed in several ways, but perhaps the most notable is the brainstorming required in the planning stage. Auditors are required to brainstorm the specific fraud schemes that might be perpetrated and the level of risk for each. Accordingly, the high risks must be addressed in the audit procedures themselves. Second, the auditor basically assumes that a revenue recognition (financial statement) fraud is going on. The AICPA argues that the risk assessment process as a whole is very different, including many more elements than previously required.

Under SAS No. 99, financial auditors must do the following regarding financial audits and their responsibility for fraud:

- Understand the characteristic causes and signs of fraud.
- Assess the risks of a material financial statement misstatement due to fraud.
- Plan and perform the audit to obtain reasonable assurance about whether the financial statements are free of material misstatement, whether caused by error or fraud.
- Exercise due care in planning, performing, evaluating, and documenting the results of audit procedures and instances of fraud.
- Possess the proper degree of professional skepticism, assuming neither dishonesty nor unquestioned honesty of management.
- Assign significant engagement responsibilities to audit personnel with the experience and training indicated as needed by the risk assessment (i.e., personnel experienced in antifraud).
- Report all instances of fraud to the appropriate level of management.
- Insist that financial statements affected by a material fraud be modified to reverse the affects of the fraud or provide a qualified opinion.
- Inform the company's audit committee of fraud, except those that are clearly inconsequential.

In those instances where a misstatement is or may be the result of fraud, and the effect is either material or cannot be determined, the auditor is required to take certain specific steps:

- Attempt to obtain additional evidence.
- Consider the implications for other aspects of the audit.
- Discuss the matter and the approach for further investigation with an appropriate level of management that is at least one level above those involved and with senior management and the audit committee, if appropriate.
- Consult legal counsel.

In those instances where a misstatement is or may be the result of fraud, and the effect is either material or cannot be determined, SAS No. 99 suggests that the auditor *should*:

- Consider consulting legal counsel.
- Consider the need for a separate fraud audit.

There certainly appears to be a significant trickle-down effect in the business world from SOX. If SOX is a compilation of "best practices," as most experts contend, then it should apply to more than SEC companies—it should apply to all organizations. More of the SOX tenets are being incorporated into non–public company auditing standards or requirements. For example, Congress passed a law that the Tennessee Valley Authority (TVA)—a government entity— *must* comply with SOX requirements. Since TVA distributes electricity to hundreds of suppliers, all of them have been subjected to a one-time SOX Section 404 audit, and the larger ones *must* conduct one every year, just as SOX requires for SEC companies.

Conclusion

Authorities in business management insist that the audit function, both internal and external, is a visible deterrent to fraud and accounting irregularities. This assumption is predicated on a theory held by law enforcement authorities, who suggest that the visible presence of a uniformed police officer or marked police car on regular patrol deters crime.

The history of auditors and liability to detect fraud reveal at least one general pattern: The public expects auditors to find fraud, especially large financial statement frauds. It also reveals the paradox for financial auditors of having executive management both customer and suspect for fraud. Therefore, what is the best strategy for auditors to take?

- Depend on the federal government: SEC, PACOB, and U.S. Congress?
- Depend on better antifraud education and training: more and better auditors and auditing?
- Depend on SOX Section 404: more and better internal controls?
- Rely on more honest senior managers?
- All of the above?

The time is past for auditors to perform damage assessment and control. It is time for risk reduction and risk prevention. Regulations mandate a risk-based approach, and audits are conducted using this approach. However, improvements can be made, and there are obvious and serious risks and perils out there regarding fraud and auditor liability. In well over 100 cases of public companies and regulated financial institutions in the United States, stockholders, creditors, or regulatory authorities have alleged that audit failures by major public accounting firms occurred during the past 25 years. Each one represents a significant enough risk to threaten the very existence of the audit firm; the demise of Big Five financial audit firm Arthur Andersen, with over 100,000 global employees, could have been prevented by a handful of key persons who caused damage to hundreds of thousands of employees, investors, creditors, and other stakeholders.

SUMMARY

The business and financial environment is changing rapidly, and the audit profession must change and adapt more rapidly than it has done in the past if it is to continue to play a useful role in society and maintain public confidence. Education of the public and exercising due professional care will help the audit profession close the gap.

ENDNOTES

1. "Generally Accepted Accounting Standards," *AICPA Professional Standards,* Vol. 1, AU Sec. 110 (New York: American Institute of Certified Public Accountants, November, 1972, pp. 322–323. [Sources include SAS No. 78 and SAS No. 82.]
2. Wilfred C. Uecker, Arthur P. Brief, and William R. Kinney, Jr., "Perception of the Internal and External Auditor as a Deterrent to Corporate Irregularities," *The Accounting Review* (July 1981), pp. 465–478.
3. *American Jurisprudence,* 2d ed., Vol. 1, Sec. 15 (Rochester, NY: The Lawyers Cooperative Publishing, 1962), pp. 365–366.
4. Institute of Internal Auditors (IIA), "Statement on Internal Auditing Standards," Altamonte Springs, FL: 1984.

5. Institute of Internal Auditors (IIA), "International Standaards for the Professional Practice of Internal Auditing," Altamonte Springs, FL: September 2004. Section 1210.A2, Proficiency and Due Professional Care.
6. *Financial Fraud Detection and Disclosure Act,* H.R. Doc. No. 4886, 99th Cong. 2d Sess., 1986.
7. *Ibid.*
8. Mark S. Beasley, Joseph V. Carcello, and Dana R. Hermanson, "Top 10 Audit Deficiencies," *Journal of Accountancy* 191, No. 4 (April 2001), pp. 23–29. [NOTE: Some overlap of problems was identified and therefore the percentages do not add up to 100%.]

CHAPTER 4

Fraud Schemes

INTRODUCTION

In order to prevent fraud, detect fraud, or investigate fraud, one needs to understand as many fraud schemes as possible. In Chapter 1, various taxonomies were presented to classify frauds. The authors believe the best taxonomy for fraud auditors and forensic accounting is the one used by the Association of Certified Fraud Examiners (ACFE). There are several reasons for this choice.

First, the ACFE is emerging as the primary antifraud organization. Its only purpose is the antifraud profession, whereas the American Institute of Certified Public Accountants (AICPA), Institute of Internal Auditors (IIA), and Information Systems Audit and Control Association (ISACA) have different primary objectives. Other groups have a similar goal, but none has the sole purpose of fighting fraud for fraud auditors and forensic accountants. As such, the ACFE's model serves as the de facto standard one for the antifraud profession.

Second, the ACFE taxonomy has been stable over time. There are about 51 individual fraud schemes classified in the ACFE fraud tree. That number has not changed over the years. Fraudsters find different or even new ways to carry out frauds, but most often it is one of the old-fashioned fraud schemes used by perpetrators (e.g., the Internet and other technologies open up new ways to perpetrate some of the frauds not new schemes).

Third, the ACFE taxonomy has a limited number of schemes, as do all of the other taxonomies discussed in Chapter 1. That is, there is not an unlimited number of schemes to consider. There are only about 51. And even then, about 20 of those make up over 80% of all the frauds committed. Thus the study of the most common fraud schemes better enables a fraud auditor or forensic accountant to detect or prevent the vast majority of potential fraud schemes. While this trait is not unique to the ACFE taxonomy, it is worth pointing out for purposes of understanding the ongoing analysis of fraud schemes.

Fourth, there is little overlap in the ACFE fraud tree, especially when compared to the other taxonomies. Many taxonomies are categorized by vendor, customer, employee, and consumer. Yet some frauds involve both a vendor and an employee (e.g., kickbacks), so there is an overlap in classifying a single fraud. The authors believe there is less overlap in the ACFE taxonomy than in any of the others in classifying a single fraud occurrence.

Last, the ACFE model has unique characteristics for it's three major categories that make it easy to apply to fraud audits, investigations, fraud prevention programs, and so on. (See Exhibit 4.1). These unique characteristics and descriptors assist in customizing and tailoring fraud audits or controls for the antifraud environment.

EXHIBIT 4.1   ACFE Fraud Tree: Unique Characteristics of Each Category

Descriptors	Financial Fraud	Asset Misappropriation	Corruption
Fraudster	Executive management	Employees	2 parties
Size of the fraud	Largest: $1–258 million	Smallest: $93,000	Medium: $250,000
Frequency of fraud	Least often: 7.9%	Most often: 92.7%	Medium: 30%
Motivation	Stock prices, bonuses	Personal pressures	Challenge, business
Materiality	Likely	Unlikely	Depends
Benefactors	Company and fraudster	Fraudster (against company)	Fraudster
Size of victim company	Large	Small	Depends

ACFE FRAUD TREE

The ACFE model for categorizing known frauds is referred to as the fraud tree (see Exhibit 4.2). It categorizes the individual fraud schemes into a classification model of categories, subcategories, and microcategories. The three main (top-level) categories are (1) financial statement fraud, (2) asset misappropriation, and (3) corruption. These major categories are unique in their characteristics (see Exhibit 4.1). That is, the characteristics that describe or define a financial statement fraud are very different from those that describe an asset misappropriation, when using the same descriptors. Why is that important? A thorough knowledge of the categories and their specific characteristics is crucial in the success of designing and conducting fraud audits as well as fraud prevention and detection programs.

The ACFE *Report to the Nation* (RTTN) provides statistics on frauds periodically since 1996. The 2004 RTTN will be used in providing statistics for the analysis of descriptors in the fraud tree.[1]

Scheme Category Characteristics

Fraudster In the financial statement frauds, the fraudster tends to be executive management, usually the chief executive officer (CEO), chief financial officer (CFO), or some other C-level manager. The fraudster for asset misappropriation, however, is usually an employee—albeit one in a key position, and one considered trustworthy. In corruption schemes, the fraudster could be anyone but always involves at least two parties, even if one is an unwilling participant (e.g., extortion). Obviously, these are very different groups of people. Chapter 1 discusses the profile of a fraudster in more detail.

Size of the Fraud The fraud category with the highest average loss is financial statement frauds. The average financial statement fraud is between $1 million and $257.9 million depending on the survey and year. The 2004 RTTN statistics show the average financial statement fraud at $1 million but it was higher in years past. (In the 2002 RTTN, it was $4.25 million.)

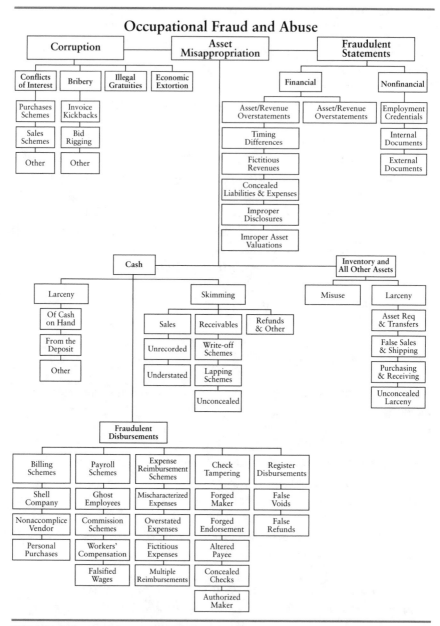

EXHIBIT 4.2   ACFE Fraud Tree

KPMG also conducts periodic fraud surveys of hundreds of businesses and government agencies. In its 2003 Fraud Survey KPMG reported the average financial statement fraud was $257.9 million.[2] By comparison, the average fraud in the asset misappropriation category is only $93,000. The average corruption fraud is $250,000.

Frequency of Fraud   The category with the most frequent *occurrences* of fraud is asset misappropriation. Over 92% of all frauds are classified in this category. Financial frauds, by comparison, made up only 7.9% of all frauds by occurrence. Corruption made up 30.1% of frauds. The fact these percentages add up to more than 100% is noteworthy. If a fraudster manages to hide a fraud for some period of time, it is not unusual for him then to add another fraud to his nefarious affairs. Sometimes bold fraudsters start their crime with more than one type of fraud. Either way, it should be noted some fraudsters not only occasionally conduct more than one fraud, but those frauds cross categories.

Motivation   In Chapter 2, in the section entitled "What Fraud Auditors Should Know and Be Able to Do," there is a list of known motivations: psychotic, economic, egocentric, ideological, and emotional. These motivations tend to be associated with only one or two of these categories. Certain motivators are associated with financial statement frauds, and different motivators tend to be associated with asset misappropriation frauds. Such associations are extremely valuable in conducting fraud audits and fraud investigations, and they are *very* valuable in designing antifraud programs for management or the board.

Financial statement frauds tend to be motivated by *egocentric* motives. They also tend to be motivated by stock prices, directly or indirectly. For example, the first financial fraud recorded in accounting history was the South Sea Bubble scandal in England around 1720. In Chapter 2, this scandal is discussed in more detail. The motive behind the fictitious profits was the market price of its stock. Three hundred years later the motive behind financial statement fraud is basically unchanged, all the way up to and including Enron,

WorldCom, and others of the last decade. Stock option bonuses are a double motive: First keep the stock price up to get the bonus, and second get/keep the stock price high so the options, or existing stock held, will be as valuable as possible. Performance bonuses, pressure from stockholders, and other pressures are indirectly linked back to stock price as well.

Asset misappropriation frauds, however, are usually motivated by *economic* pressures. White-collar crime researcher Donald Cressey called this type of motivation an "unshareable need." For example, high debt, such as large balances on credit cards, and an inability to make further payments on debt bring considerable economic pressure. This pressure could also be driven by a gambling, drug, or alcohol habit whose fuel (cash) needs replenishing. Fraudsters sometimes persuade themselves to commit an asset misappropriation fraud because of *emotional* motives, such as the challenge to beat the system or being disgruntled with management or the company.

Corruption frauds could be motivated by the same kinds of things as asset misappropriation is. However, corruption frauds often are driven by business motives (*economic*), such as the *bribery* scheme to gain access to otherwise inaccessible markets.

Materiality The fraud categories are also different in the area of materiality. Financial frauds often will be considered material to the organization. They are invariably in the millions, and occasionally billions (e.g., Enron and WorldCom), of dollars. Asset misappropriation, however, is *most likely to be immaterial to the financial statements*. Corruption could be material, especially for frauds above the average cost of corruption frauds, which is $250,000. It could also be immaterial, depending on the size of the organization, and whether it is below the average cost.

Benefactors Financial statement frauds are perpetrated on behalf of the company, although usually because such frauds are necessary in order for the fraudster to benefit as well. In Chapter 1, this type of fraud is referred to as *frauds for the company*. Asset misappropriation and corruption, on the contrary, benefit the fraudster and are classified in Chapter 1 as *insider fraud against the company*. Corruption can also benefit the company in some schemes, such as some briberies.

Size of Victim Company Because financial statement fraud usually is motivated by stock prices or something directly related to stock prices, the companies victimized by financial statement fraud tend to be publicly traded ones, which tend to be larger companies. Such companies tend to have more resources to apply to internal controls, internal audit, and antifraud programs and therefore have a smaller risk associated with asset misappropriations, which are intrinsically harder to control.

The opposite is true regarding asset misappropriation and victim organizations. Because these organizations tend to be small, they have either scarce resources to attend to prevention and detection of fraud or simply are unable to focus on it (do not care, are unaware of the risks, etc.). Often a company of this size has only one accountant and cannot justify proper segregation of duties. *"An insufficient or absent segregation of duties is almost always associated with asset misappropriation schemes."*

The ACFE 2004 RTTN confirms this supposition. Organizations were divided into sizes: 1 to 99, 100 to 999, 1,000 to 9,999, and 10,000 or more employees. The largest average fraud by size was in the over 10,000 employee range, at $105,500 (possibly because they had the most financial statement frauds, which are the largest amounts per fraud). The second highest was the 100 and below employee range, at $98,000. If that number were used as a ratio of average fraud cost per average number of employees, the smallest organizations have a staggeringly higher ratio than the others, over 13 times higher than the second highest ratio! See Exhibit 4.3 for a comparison.

EXHIBIT 4.3   Average Cost of Fraud per Employee

Number of Employees[a]	Average Fraud	Fraud$/ Employee
<100	$98,000	$1,960/emp.
100–999	$78,500	$143/emp.
1,000–9,999	$87,500	$16/emp.
10,000+	$105,500	$10/emp.

[a] For average number of employees, we took the mean of the size, except for 10,000+, where we used 11,000.

Fraud Tree and Who Audits Whom   Using Exhibit 4.1 and the preceding discussion, it seems intuitive as to which group of auditors should be considered primarily responsible for which types of frauds. This section discusses this issue in generalities, or what appears to be the natural association of each category. By no means are these associations absolute. For example, an effective antifraud program for a large publicly traded company would most likely include all three major fraud scheme categories and most likely be charged to the internal audit function by the audit committee.

Financial Statement Fraud: Financial Auditors   The auditor group most likely to be most responsible for financial statement fraud is financial auditors. That is true for at least three reasons.

First, the amount of a financial statement fraud in total tends to lead to a material misstatement of the financial reports. The goal of financial audits is to ensure that the financial statements fairly present the financial health of an entity in all material respects. Financial audit procedures, therefore, are designed to detect material misstatements. And financial statement frauds often are material with respect to the financial reports. In addition, financial auditors must comply with SAS No. 99, *Consideration of Fraud in the Financial Statement Audit,* and be able to detect a fraud that causes a material misstatement of the financials. Likewise, because asset misappropriation and corruption tend to be immaterial, it is unrealistic to expect financial auditors to detect them. That caveat is compounded by the fact fraud audits are significantly different from financial audits. According to the ACFE 2004 RTTN, less than 11% of frauds are detected by financial auditors. The 2003 KMPG Fraud Survey also has less than 11% of frauds being detected by financial auditors, and that survey was done by a financial audit firm.

Second, financial statement audits are designed to detect material misstatements in the financial reports. The majority of frauds are immaterial, but financial statement frauds are almost always material. Procedures to detect fraud are very different from procedures used in financial audits to detect material misstatements. In general, financial audit procedures are not designed to detect fraud, though some fraud-specific procedures are required, namely SAS No. 99 procedures. However, since financial audit procedures are designed to detect material misstatements, and since the vast majority of financial statement frauds are material, and since financial audits are by nature concerned with financial statements, then financial auditors are naturally a prime defence against financial statement frauds.

Third, because executive management is involved with financial statement fraud, the internal auditors can be fooled or pressured into complicity. Management can override controls, but executive management can *really* override controls. The CFO *can* simply direct subordinates to cook the books. Executive management can cajole internal auditors and/or CFOs into becoming co-conspirators.

Internal audit can be fooled or circumvented. For instance, Cynthia Cooper (chief audit executive for WorldCom) tells how she was locked out of the corporate computers and circumvented, with reports and transactions being generated clandestinely without her ability to see, review, or question them. She says she clandestinely came back to work late at night and finally was able to gather evidence of the fraud. Other internal auditors from some of the most recent and infamous financial scandals have confessed privately to the authors that they were deliberately kept away from the real set of books, activities, and knowledge that would have disclosed the fraud, and it was the CEO or CFO who was behind that effort. A fraudster executive who is perpetrating a financial statement fraud can frustrate the best-intentioned internal auditor. But the independent external auditor should be in a better position to detect the financial statement fraud, especially if it is material.

Asset Misappropriation: Internal Auditors The auditor group most likely to be most responsible for asset misappropriation fraud is internal auditors. As stated, because asset misappropriation schemes tend to be immaterial, especially individual transactions, they are difficult for financial auditors to discover doing traditional financial audits. They are also difficult for internal auditors to detect during *traditional* internal audits, for the same reasons.

However, it is more reasonable to expect internal audit to develop and execute antifraud programs and fraud audits than financial auditors. Effective antifraud programs are of necessity ongoing programs. Obviously, the internal audit function is the only reasonable group of auditors to oversee a continuous program. Those programs usually are initiated and overseen by either the audit committee or the CEO/CFO or both. Therefore, it makes sense for the internal audit function to execute those programs and report back to the audit committee and/or CEO/CFO.

Corruption: Possibly Either   Corruption frauds tend to be larger than asset misappropriation. If it becomes material, then clearly the financial auditors should have some responsibility, especially under SAS No. 99. These frauds also sometimes involve laws and regulations (e.g., bribery, kickbacks on government contracts, and extortion could be illegal acts). Because of the legal aspect of certain corruption schemes, either compliance audits by internal audit or, if the fraud is material, financial audits by external auditors could be involved.

Thus sometimes the primary responsibility lies with external audit and sometimes with internal audit. Most likely, internal audit functions involved with antifraud programs or fraud audits will be concerned primarily with asset misappropriation, but they may be interested in, or be charged with, corruption and financial statement fraud, in particular if the program is initiated by the audit committee.

FINANCIAL STATEMENT SCHEMES

The category of financial statement schemes is broken down into two subcategories: financial and nonfinancial. The latter is fairly insignificant in terms of frequency, so this discussion is limited to the financial schemes. These six schemes are addressed in SAS No. 99, *Consideration of Fraud in a Financial Statement Audit*, as well. Most of the financial statement scandals involve some kind of revenue manipulation scheme, which is why SAS No. 99 stresses that financial auditors should *assume* this kind of fraud may be occurring in the client's books and deliberately look for this type of fraud *throughout* the audit process.

The most common financial statement fraud scheme is related to revenue overstatement. In some cases, companies simply invent revenues. (A credit to Revenue and debit to Accounts Receivable produces miracles on the balance sheet and income statement.) There are five schemes under this subcategory in the fraud tree.

Timing Differences (Improper Treatment of Sales)

There are a variety of ways to perpetrate a timing differences scheme to exaggerate revenues for the current fiscal period. One way is to push excess inventory to salespeople or consignment whereupon the inventory is treated as a sale, knowing full well that much of it will be returned—but in a subsequent period. This method is known as channel stuffing. Sales also can be booked in other violations of generally accepted accounting principles (GAAP) (e.g., early revenue recognition). For instance, a three-year contract to provide services across the period can all be booked as revenue in the current year to inflate profits for the next set of financials, at the expense of future financials, and obviously not in compliance with GAAP and the matching principle.

Enron used a similar method in its special purpose entities (SPEs) to account for all of the revenue from long-term agreements in the current year. In another fraud, the CFO for a bankrupt company (as a result of a financial statement fraud) admitted in his deposition that many sales were booked before they were actually consummated. His reason: "If you knew in your heart it was a sale, then we booked it."

Fictitious Revenues

Fictitious revenues are created simply by recording sales that never occurred. They can involve real or fake customers. The end result is an increase in revenues and profits, and usually assets (the other side of the fictitious accounting entry).

For example, the infamous Equity Funding scandal used a fictitious revenues scheme to inflate both revenues and accounts receivable. Equity Funding was an insurance company, to be specific, a reinsurer. To create fictitious revenues, the CEO simply created phony insurance policies. After seven years, the fraud was finally exposed in 1973 by a recently fired and disgruntled employee. At that time, $2 billion of the $3 billion in Receivables was phony.

Concealed Liabilities (Improper Recording of Liabilities)

One way to perpetrate this fraud scheme is to simply postpone the recording of liabilities in the 12th month of the fiscal year so that the current year will have less expenses, and record that liability in the first month of the next fiscal year. It is precisely because of this possibility that financial auditors perform subsequent-period substantive tests—looking for invoices that are dated the year under audit but posted in the first month of the subsequent year.

Another way is to move those liabilities somewhere else. If the company is large and has subsidiaries, this objective can be accomplished by moving the liability to a subsidiary, especially if that company is either not audited or audited by a different audit firm (an intentional decision to hide the fraud). This scheme probably is used often by companies. That assumption is based on the fact it is difficult to detect in audits. However, if it is occurring, there should be changes in certain ratios: EPS, Debt/Equity, etc.

The fraudsters at Parmalat used this method of hiding liabilities to perpetrate a financial statement fraud of over $1.3 billion, moving liabilities to subsidiaries in the Caribbean, far from corporate headquarters in Italy, and to companies audited by a different financial audit firm. The executives at Parmalat also invented assets and forged documents to back up entries for them, which illustrates the complexity of many frauds: The fraudster begins perhaps with a single fraud scheme but sometimes expands to multiple schemes. Adelphia used the same fraud method, moving liabilities to off–balance sheet affiliates.

Finally, a simple failure to record liabilities accomplishes the same purpose. Without the liability, there is no additional expense, no reduction in assets, or no decrease in equity that normally occurs.

Inadequate Disclosures

One principle of fraud is that it is always clandestine. The fraudster will attempt to cover up for frauds in the books. (This is not necessary for off-the-book schemes.) This cover-up extends to disclosures.

While Enron was technically GAAP compliant in disclosing SPEs in the financial statements and annual report, it was fraudulent in handling the associated revenues, and it was clandestine in its disclosures. Enron did make disclosures regarding the SPEs, as required, but they were so obfuscated that even financial experts could not read them and understand exactly the financial ramifications of those SPEs, which is what was intended. Also, Andrew Fastow, Chief Financial Officer (CFO), reportedly hid his association with the SPEs from the board to further obfuscate their disclosure. Other methods include omission in disclosures of liability, significant events, and management fraud. An inadequate disclosure can be a way to hide evidence of a fraud.

Improper Asset Valuation

By inflating the amounts of assets (commonly receivables, inventory, and long-lived assets), capitalizing expenses, or deflating contra accounts (allowance for doubtful accounts, depreciation, amortization, etc.), the financials will show a higher than truthful equity and profit. HealthSouth exaggerated assets balances to cover insufficient profits over a period of years. A transaction that debits an asset and credits an equity or revenue account "magically" creates profits.

In the case of the WorldCom financial statement fraud, leases of telephone lines were clearly an expense. Yet WorldCom's CEO convinced accountants internally and financial auditors externally to treat them as assets. Thus by moving millions of dollars of expenses to the balance sheet, the income statement suddenly looked much better.

CORRUPTION SCHEMES

There are four corruption subcategories of fraud schemes, and two of them have three microcategories. The four categories under corruption are conflicts of interest, bribery, illegal gratuities, and economic extortion.

Conflicts of Interest

A conflict of interest occurs when an employee, manager, or executive has an undisclosed economic or personal interest in a transaction that adversely affects the company. Conflicts of interest include three microcategories: purchases schemes, sales schemes, and other schemes. The difference between conflict of interest and other corruption frauds is the fact that fraudsters exert their influence (e.g., approving invoices or bills) because of their personal interest rather than because of a bribe or kickback.

Bribery

Bribery can be defined as the offering, giving, receiving, or soliciting anything of value to influence an official act or business decision. Bribery has been around for centuries. It is probably most often associated with politics. The famous Francis Bacon of England was promoted to the highest position in the king's court, Lord Chancellor, in 1618. A British landowner brought charges of bribery against Lord Bacon, and the subsequent investigation found an abundance of evidence that he had been taking bribes often to manipulate the judgments of cases. Bacon had to resign his office.

In the United States, President Warren G. Harding's administration was damaged by the "Teapot Scandal." In it, Secretary of Interior Albert Falls took bribes to allow private drilling of government oil fields and several other similar bribery schemes. But bribery is also prevalent in the business world when contracts and arrangements are involved.

According to the ACFE 2004 Report to the Nation, corruption schemes make up 30.1% of all frauds.[3] Corruption includes economic distortion, illegal gratuities, conflicts of interest, and bribery. Bribery includes three microcategories: kickbacks, bid rigging, and other. Kickbacks are undisclosed payments made by vendors to employees of purchasing companies to enlist their influence in gaining business with the entity, or in allowing the vendor to overbill. Bid rigging occurs when an employee fraudulently assists a vendor in winning a contact involving the competitive bidding process.

One example of bribery occurred in the U.S. automobile industry in the 1990s. Several Honda America executives were convicted of accepting bribes from local auto dealers.

Illegal Gratuities

Illegal gratuities are similar to bribes, but with illegal gratuities there is not necessarily an intent to influence a business decision. For instance, a person of influence could be given an expensive gift, free vacation, and so on for her influence in a negotiation or business deal, but the gift is made *after* the deal is over. Because it is afterward, it is hard to prove. But accepting a gift is usually illegal in most political entities and is prohibited in large businesses, above some small minimal value.

Economic Extortion

Basically, economic extortion is the opposite of a bribery fraud. Instead of a vendor offering a bribe, the employee demands payment from a vendor in order to favor the vendor.

ASSET MISAPPROPRIATION SCHEMES

A clear definition of asset misappropriation is helpful in recognizing this type of fraud. We begin with several to clarify the meaning of asset misappropriation in this book.

Black's Law Dictionary defines *misappropriation* this way:

> *The act of misappropriating or turning to a wrongful purpose; wrong appropriation, a term that does not necessarily mean peculation, although it may mean that. The term may also embrace the taking and using of another's property for sole purpose of capitalizing unfairly on good will and reputation of property owner.* [4]

The definition in *Webster's Dictionary* is a little different, and more in line with the use of the term in this book:

> *to appropriate wrongly (as by theft of embezzlement).* [5]

Joe Wells defines misappropriation in this way:

> *[Misappropriation] includes more than theft or embezzlement. It involves the misuse of any company asset for personal gain.* [6]

By far, the most common frauds are asset misappropriations (92.7% of all frauds involve asset misappropriation). There are 2 subcategories (Cash and Inventory and Other Assets), 5 microcategories (see Exhibit 4.2), 5 categories under microcategory Fraudulent

Disbursements, and 18 different schemes under them. Altogether, a total of 32 different individual fraud schemes are contained in this major category.

Cash

Cash schemes involve the taking of cash from one's employer. Cash schemes dominate the asset misappropriations cases, according to the statistics from the ACFE. In its 2004 RTTN, of the 471 asset misappropriation frauds, 93% involved the misappropriation of cash.

Cash schemes, in the ACFE fraud tree, are divided into three groups: cash larceny schemes, fraudulent disbursements schemes, and skimming schemes.

Larceny   Joe Wells defines cash larceny as the intentional taking of an employer's cash (currency and checks) without the consent and against the will of the employer.[7] Cash larceny is the outright stealing of cash. Because the cash stolen by an employee in a cash larceny scheme has already been recorded in the accounting system, the absence of the cash ought to be more easily detectable than a skimming scheme, which is "off the books." In order for an employee to commit a cash larceny fraud, she must have been placed in a position in direct contact with cash somewhere along the company's cash path—cash coming in and cash going out. That also means the employee was considered trustworthy.

Cash larceny schemes fall into three groups: cash on hand, from the deposit, and other schemes. According to the ACFE 2004 RTTN, 23.9% of all cash misappropriations are cash larceny, and the average loss is $80,000.

Fraudulent Disbursements   *Fraudulent disbursement schemes* are those in which a distribution of funds is made from some company account in what appears to be a normal manner. The method for obtaining the funds may be the forging of a check, the submission of a false invoice, the doctoring of a time card, and so on. The key difference between fraudulent disbursement schemes and cash larceny schemes is in the former, the money is moved from the company in what appears to be a legitimate disbursement of funds.

Fraudulent disbursement schemes fall into five groups: billing schemes, payroll schemes, expense reimbursement schemes, check tampering schemes, and register disbursement schemes. According to the ACFE 2004 RTTN, 74.1% of all cash misappropriations are fraudulent disbursements. The average loss in a fraudulent disbursement scheme is $125,000. These frauds occur much more often than other types of cash misappropriation, and are more costly than the average fraud ($93,000).

Billing Schemes *Billing schemes* use the company's accounting system to steal funds by submitting bogus claims in one form or another. If a vendor is in the authorized vendor list, and if an invoice has been approved by the proper person, the system will take care of the rest— to generate and/or send a check for the perpetrator to intercept and cash. The same is true of payroll checks and employees. Billing schemes include shell company schemes (phony vendor), nonaccomplice vendor schemes, and personal purchases schemes.

According to the ACFE 2004 RTTN, 52.1% of fraudulent disbursements are billing schemes. The average cost of a billing scheme is $140,000.

A *shell company scheme* involves using a fictitious company, created for the sole purpose of committing a fraud, to generate checks from the company's resources that will be directed to the culprit, to her benefit. Usually the fictitious vendor is a fabricated name, and often the address is a post office box. Sometimes the culprit will use a derivation of a legitimate vendor's name to confuse those who might see the checks or the fictitious vendor's name. For example, if ABC Corporation was a legitimate vendor, the fraudster might use ABC Co. as the fictitious vendor's name.

A description of the shell vendor process follows. The fictitious vendor must be added to the authorized vendor list, an invoice must be approved, a check must be written to the shell vendor, and the check must be intercepted by the fraudster or an accomplice. (This could be as simple as mailing it to the fraudster's post office box.)

Often the perpetrator is in a control position with the authority to add a vendor. Also, often the perpetrator is in an authority position to approve the phony invoice. Or the perpetrator could be depending on "rubber stamping" or inattention to approval review. The perpetrator usually also sets up a bank account in the name of the fictitious vendor—which is fairly easy to do. A check is processed and mailed, probably to a post office box (POB). The perpetrator intercepts or receives the check, deposits it into the bank account, and writes checks out to whomever he desires.

The *pass-through scheme* is a version of the shell vendor scheme where the perpetrator sets up a company, but in this scheme, she actually buys products through the pass-through vendor. The perpetrator sells the goods to his or her employer, but at an inflated price. Paying excessive prices for goods is possible because the perpetrator is in a position to approve invoices or vendors for purchases. By marking up the prices to exorbitant levels, the perpetrator can siphon off funds from his or her employer to her pseudo vendor.

Unlike the previous two vendor schemes, the *nonaccomplice vendor scheme* involves a legitimate vendor. However, the vendor is not an accomplice but rather an innocent party being used by the perpetrator. The perpetrator could bill or overbill the company using the vendor's invoices, and either intercept the check for the invoice or send the check to the vendor and ask for a refund from the vendor and intercept that check. Another version of the scheme involves the perpetrator deliberately ordering merchandise not needed, returning the merchandise for credit to a legitimate vendor, and intercepting the refund check from the vendor.

A *personal purchases scheme* is simply purchasing personal items with the company's money. With the advent of purchase credit cards (e-procurement), it is much easier to perpetrate this kind of scheme. The General Accounting Office (GAO) did an audit of its e-procurement system and found thousands of dollars that had been misappropriated for everything from brothels to expensive country club memberships.

Payroll Schemes   *Payroll schemes* are similar to billing schemes except instead of paying a vendor, the company is paying an employee. These schemes can be perpetrated in several ways: ghost employee scheme, falsified hours and salary scheme, commission scheme, or false workers' compensation scheme.

According to the ACFE 2004 RTTN, 19.6% of fraudulent disbursements are payroll schemes. The average cost of a payroll scheme is $90,000.

In a *ghost employee scheme,* someone receives a paycheck but does not actually work for the victim company. The ghost can be fictitious or a real person in collusion with the perpetrator. For example, a controller for a university in Texas set up several ghosts in the payroll system, including her son and some of his friends. She would have them either bring her the checks or split the money between them. She stole several hundreds of thousands of dollars in the scheme over several months.

The ghost employee process is similar to the shell vendor process: The ghost must be added to the employee master file for payroll, a time card or salary must be approved, a check must be written to the ghost, and the check must be intercepted by the fraudster or an accomplice.

Fraudsters have sometimes used the *falsified hours and salary scheme* to pay employees enormous overtime or exaggerated pay rates. At least on one occasion, an hourly employee was receiving paychecks for $2,000 a week on a rate of less than $20 per hour. In the *commission* scheme, fraudsters use several methods: generate bogus sales, overstate sales, increase the commission rate, or use some other means to gain more commission than was legitimately earned. The *false workers' compensation* scheme involves a worker faking an injury and collecting payment from the victim's insurance carrier.

Expense Reimbursement Schemes *Expense reimbursement schemes* are simple schemes: Submit a falsified business expense and gain a fraudulent reimbursement check from the victim company. According to the ACFE 2004 RTTN, 22.1% of fraudulent disbursements are expense reimbursement schemes. The average cost of an expense reimbursement scheme is $92,000. Schemes that fall under expense reimbursement include *mischaracterized expense schemes, overstated expense schemes, fictitious expense schemes,* and *multiple reimbursement schemes.*

Check Tampering Schemes *Check tampering schemes* are unique among the fraudulent disbursement schemes because it is the one scheme in which the perpetrator physically prepares the fraudulent check. In other cases, the fraudster causes the company to generate a check to herself by submitting some form of false document to the victim company (e.g., invoice, time card).

According to the ACFE 2004 RTTN, 31.3% of fraudulent disbursements are check tampering schemes. The average cost of a check tampering scheme is $155,000. This average figure makes this fraud scheme the most costly scheme or group of schemes of all the schemes.

Check tampering schemes include *forged maker schemes, forged endorsement schemes, altered payee schemes, concealed check schemes,* and *authorized maker schemes.*

A *forged maker scheme* involves the signing of another person's name to a check with fraudulent intent and the fraudulent alteration of a genuine instrument. A forged maker scheme usually starts with a blank check. The concern with forged maker schemes and checks is actually twofold. First, there is the concern over physical access to paper checks. The second concern is the digital access to check writing.

A *forged endorsement scheme* involves a culprit intercepting a company check intended for some other legitimate party and converting that check by signing (*forging*) the other party's name on the endorsement of the check. A forged endorsement check scheme starts with a completed check versus a blank check. For example, in a ghost employee scheme, the fraudster may use a real person, such as a former employee, as the ghost, intercept the check, and simply *forge* that person's name to cash the check. In a nonaccomplice vendor scheme, the fraudster usually intercepts a legitimate refund check from a legitimate vendor and *forges* the employer's endorsement on the back.

The *altered payee scheme* also involves intercepting a check written to another party, but in this scheme the culprit alters the payee designation so the check can be converted to himself or an accomplice. Sometimes the fraudster reverses the payee's name from the check, replacing his name with the original legitimate name, when the check is returned in the bank statement.

The *concealed check scheme* is a bold attempt to take advantage of "rubber stamping" or inattention to controls. The perpetrator prepares a fraudulent check and submits it along with legitimate checks to an authorized signer, whom the perpetrator hopes will sign it without a proper review. The perpetrator will likely wait until the check signer is busy or distracted before submitting the fraudulent check.

An *authorized maker scheme* involves a perpetrator who has check-signing authority and makes out fraudulent checks to herself for her own benefit. This kind of scheme is more difficult to detect because the person has *check-signing authority.* Obviously, this scheme succeeds only if controls are absent, circumvented, or too weak to be effective. In a small branch of a large chain of stores in

Mississippi, the only accountant of the employer was an authorized maker. For three years, she wrote herself checks that went undetected. Someone at the employer's bank found a check signed by "Mary," paid to "Mary," endorsed by "Mary," and deposited into "Mary's" personal account a little suspicious. She called the newly hired internal auditor of the branch and reported her suspicions. Eventually, over $250,000 worth of checks paid to Mary were uncovered. Remember, this business was a relatively small one.

Register Disbursement Schemes   *Register disbursement schemes* involve the removal of money from a register, where the removal is recorded on the register's system (tape, computer file, etc.). These frauds are among the least costly and least frequent of all frauds. According to the ACFE 2004 RTTN, 4.3% of fraudulent disbursements are register disbursement schemes. The average cost of a register disbursement scheme is $18,000. Register disbursement schemes involve two kinds of schemes: *false voids* and *false refunds*. Certain businesses have a higher risk for this fraud: restaurants, bars, street vendors, and any other cash business.

Skimming   *Skimming* is sometimes called front-end fraud, as funds are stolen *before* a booking entry is made. Thus it may be very difficult to detect a skimming scheme or to even notice that the money was stolen. Skimming is a common practice in cash businesses such as bars, restaurants, vending machines, home modernization contracting, gas stations, and retail stores. A good example might be the reported way Bugsy Seigel conducted business when he established casinos in Las Vegas. Supposedly Bugsy would take all of the cash from the day or week, "skim" off some for the Chicago mob to keep them happy and away from Vegas, skim some for himself (tax-free money!), and report what was left over as income. If the owner of a business, such as Bugsy, skims money from the incoming cash, then reports the balance to the books, it is *very* hard to catch such a fraud. In this example, who really cares if money is being skimmed? Maybe one or more government agencies, but they probably would have no way of knowing it was going on. The Crazy Eddie's fraud was exactly this kind of fraud. The family that owned the business skimmed millions of dollars from the electronics retail business, including almost all of its profits.

Skimming schemes fall into three groups: sales schemes (*unrecorded sales, understated sales*), receivables schemes (*write-off schemes, lapping schemes, unconcealed schemes*), and *refund schemes*. According to the ACFE 2004 RTTN, 28.2% of all cash misappropriations are skimming. The average loss in a skimming scheme is $85,000.

Receivables: Lapping Scheme   *Lapping* is a form of robbing one customer's payment to pay another's, because the latter's payment was stolen by the perpetrator. For example, a fraudster takes customer A's payment, steals it, and pays it back the next day with customer B's payment. Then in the next round, the fraudster steals from C and pays B's account with money from D, leaving C's and D's accounts overstated and unpaid on the books. The problem is that there often is a balloon effect from lapping. It is so easy to steal that the perpetrator takes a little more every time, and the balance grows larger and larger until the balloon bursts: There is not enough cash flow to sustain the scam any longer.

Several problems with the lapping scheme make it almost certain that the fraudster will get caught. First, eventually the customers' accounts get behind enough to be too problematic to hide. At that point, the fraudster may have to steal or alter customer statements to conceal the fraud adequately. Second, after several cycles of stealing, the fraudster also may have difficulty in knowing exactly which customers have sent in payments that have not been posted and how much the payments were. Sometimes a fraudster keeps separate set of books, usually near her desk. Last, the fraudster cannot take much vacation or sick leave, as the fraud will unravel fairly quickly if someone else begins to handle receivables payments and customers' accounts. These facts present some ways to detect or look for lapping schemes (e.g., employees who do not take vacation). They also offer some preventive measures (e.g., force vacation to be taken, force rotation of duties).

Inventory and Other Assets

Schemes involving inventory and other assets are not nearly as common as cash frauds, but the two are almost identical in average losses: cash averaging $98,000 and noncash averaging $100,000. In the ACFE 2004 RTTN, 22% of the asset misappropriation frauds involved noncash assets.

An employee can misappropriate inventory and other assets (excluding cash) in basically two ways. The asset can be misused (e.g., borrowed), or it can be stolen.

Misuse *Misuse* usually involves equipment, especially large and/or expensive equipment, such as backhoes, vehicles, and computers. Some surveys have estimated that over 50% of employees' use employer's computers and company time for personal business (e.g., establishing and maintaining eBay accounts to sell merchandise online). But this problem can be systemic if the employee culture considers the use of employer's assets as part of their benefits.

For example, one forensic accountant was hired to examine books for fraud based on multiple tips that the manager of a utility department for a municipality was abusing his position by employing a pass-through vendor scheme. In the process of interviewing people on site, he overheard one employee say to another late one Friday, "Did Joe get through with the backhoe?" The reply was yes. The first employee then said he was headed home and would be taking it. The forensic accountant approached the second employee and began to question him as to whether he understood what had just happened. The employee replied, "Oh, we do that all the time. Besides, Bill needs the backhoe for a job he is doing tomorrow." To his consternation, the forensic accountant was not able to convince the second employee that *anything* improper was happening. But clearly, the "borrowing" of the employer's equipment (especially to use in a side job for creating personal income) was a brazen, and in this case common, misuse of employer's assets. However, this example illustrates the fact that if misuse becomes a part of the culture, it may be hard to convince employees that this kind of fraud is really wrong. More important, rules against this type of misuse may be almost impossible to enforce. This example also proves that the existence of a policy, its communication, and its enforcement are critical steps in the deterrence of this type of fraud.

Larceny *Larceny* of inventory is the simple theft of inventory from the employer's possession. In some cases, an employee may just steal inventory and make no attempt to conceal the theft in the accounting records. Or an employee may create false documentation to justify the theft, as if inventory had been sold, shipped, or moved internally.

For example, an employee of a campus bookstore found the bay in the back always had the door up to improve ventilation in an area that was stuffy and too warm. The employee simply carried books out that door, down the street to an off-campus bookstore, and sold them for pennies on the dollar. He made no attempt to conceal the crime, which was his undoing. After weeks and months of stealing books, the internal accountant complained to the manager that profits were low and something was wrong. The manager believed that someone outside had managed to infiltrate their security and was walking away with expensive books, so he hired a fraud auditor. The fraud auditor examined the excellent security measures *inside* the store, then discovered the open door in the back of the storeroom. He immediately used the fraud theory approach and suggested to the manager that an employee might be taking books out the back door (*inventory—larceny* fraud). The manager was almost insulted, claiming he had only honest employees and there had to be another explanation. The fraud auditor followed up on his belief, found the off-campus store a block away, and eventually uncovered sufficient evidence to prosecute the fraudster.

SUMMARY

Successful fraud auditors and forensic accountants know the fraud schemes very well. They know how they are perpetrated and the characteristics of the various schemes, which enables them to perform their investigation or fraud prevention programs effectively.

This discussion of fraud schemes is a major part of the critical knowledge it takes for fraud auditors and forensic accountants to be able to do an effective job. Another major part is the understanding of the red flags associated with these fraud schemes. That is the context of the next chapter. Then in Chapter 6, we discuss how to apply the schemes (Chapter 4) and the red flags (Chapter 5) in fraud audits using computer-assisted audit techniques (CAATs).

ENDNOTES

1. ACFE, *2004 Report to the Nation* (Austin, TX: ACFE, 2004), pp. 6–36.
2. KPMG *Fraud Survey* (New York: KPMG, 2003), pp. 3–7.
3. ACFE, *2004 Report to the Nation* (Austin, TX: ACFE, 2004), pp. 10,12.
4. Garner, Bryan. *Black's Law Dictionary*, 8e, New York: West-Thomson, 2004, p. 708.
5. *Webster's Dictionary Online*, http://www.m-w.com/dictionary/misappropriation, last accessed April 25, 2006.
6. Wells, Joe. *Occupational Fraud and Abuse* (Austin, TX: ACFE, 1997), p. 61.
7. Ibid., p. 130.

CHAPTER 5

Red Flags and Fraud Detection

INTRODUCTION

The cornerstone of effective fraud prevention and detection is presented in the key subjects of Chapters 1, 2, and 4. The taxonomies introduced in Chapter 1 help to explain fraud with the fraud triangle and fraud taxonomy. They are of value in developing actual tests or conducting a fraud investigation. The fundamentals in Chapter 2 provide information of the fraud investigation process itself. The fraud schemes presented in Chapter 4 are critical to detecting and preventing fraud. A fraud auditor or forensic accountant *must* understand the *specific* frauds that are perpetrated and *how* each fraud scheme usually is committed. But these things come together in studying, analyzing, and using the red flags from fraud schemes.

For example, the fraud theory approach starts with identifying the most likely fraud scheme and how it might have been perpetrated. But in order to prove or disprove the resulting theory, the fraud investigator will look for signs of the fraud. This process usually is based on the *red flags* of *that* fraud.

A careful analytical review of the fraud tree (schemes) and the fraud triangle will bring to mind applicable flags. For example, in the fraud scheme of lapping, a person uses an elaborate method of taking some customer payments while applying payments from other customers in an overlapping fashion to those accounts stolen from earlier. It is easy to see that this type of fraudster cannot afford to take an extended vacation or else the scheme will be uncovered. Another example is the ghost employee scheme. Because the perpetrator has to intercept the check once it is printed, he cannot afford to *not* be there on payday. Thus a red flag is the absence of extended vacation taken by an employee. In addition, red flags come to mind when analyzing motivators, based on the fraud triangle discussed in Chapter 2. One motivator is excessive debt. Thus if a credit report shows that an employee has a high debt and a low credit score, that information is a red flag. In other words, the motivation leg of the fraud triangle is present for that employee.

Therefore, red flags are a critical success factor to detecting fraud. Red flags lead naturally to the design of effective detection methods and processes. And these detection methods lead naturally to the design of good controls. Often a good detective procedure can serve as a good control as well. This chapter analyzes red flags by the fraud schemes presented in Chapter 4 and, based on the red flags for a particular fraud scheme or group of schemes, presents some potentially effective detection methods.

PROFESSIONAL STANDARDS

Recent major fraud-related technical literature focuses on red flags to some degree. Most of the accounting professional organizations have followed the passage of the Sarbanes-Oxley Act (SOX) with the adoption of technical standards to accommodate SOX, or the spirit of SOX, and they generally include red flags as a key to the guidance. Three example professional groups and their standards are: the American Institute of Certified Public Accountants (AICPA), the Information Systems Audit and Control Association (ISACA), and the Institute of Internal Auditors (IIA). These were chosen because of their key role in auditing for fraud.

The AICPA's Statement on Auditing Standard (SAS) No. 99, *Consideration of Fraud in a Financial Statement Audit*, which codifies much of the SOX tenets and certainly the spirit of SOX, incorporates a list of red flags. Much of the work in identifying those red flags is associated with the work of the Association of Certified Fraud Examiners (ACFE) and founder Joe Wells in particular. Wells and the ACFE contributed to the development of the red flags contained in the appendix of SAS No. 99.

ISACA provides a similar list in its technical literature. The "Irregularities and Illegal Acts" guide (Standard 030.020.010) for "Procedures for Information Systems Auditing" became effective

November 1, 2003. Section 4.1 provides a list of "Audit Considerations" that include red flags, among other issues, especially in the "Application of CAATs [computer-assisted audit techniques]" segment.

The IIA literature is replete with examples of red flags. The IIA's technical and professional standards also address fraud. The IIA's International Standards for the Professional Practice of Internal Auditing states in section 1210.A2:

> *The internal auditor should have sufficient knowledge to identify the* indicators of fraud *but is not expected to have the expertise of a person whose primary responsibility is detecting and investigating fraud. [Emphasis added.]*

From the technical standards of these three organizations, it is clear that auditors are expected to be able to identify key indicators of fraud in the process of carrying out their duties and responsibilities. Because fraud audits are very different from financial audits, it is necessary for auditors to be trained in aspects of fraud identification and detection.[1] It is also important for auditors to use training, articles, seminars, education, and other means to develop an effective mind-set related to fraud. The data/transaction classification model that follows is intended to facilitate the auditor's ability to fulfill these responsibilities. Therefore, the process should start with some basic training or information about fraud schemes.

COMMON RED FLAGS

Generally speaking, some red flags are common to all frauds, or common to a set of frauds—a major category of frauds using the fraud triangle.

Asset Misappropriation

Those frauds categorized as asset misappropriation typically are perpetrated by employees, against the organization, for the benefit of the employee. According to Lux and Fitiani, general red flags include:

- Changes in behavior
- Inability to look people in the eye
- Increased irritability
- Irregular work history
- Character problems
- Consistent anger
- Tendency to blame others
- Change in lifestyle[2]

For persons with a higher personal code of ethics, the behavioral changes are more likely to occur (e.g., irritability, inability to look others in the eye); that is, their conscience will begin to bother them.

The last red flag, change in lifestyle, is perhaps the most common on this list. Of the fraudsters who get caught, many tend to take more and more assets over time. That is, if a fraudster gets away with a $15,000 fraud this year, he tends to steal more, perhaps twice that much, the next. If he gets away with $30,000 next year, he may double it again the next. This influx of tax-free money usually is spent, and spent in such a way that those around the fraudster can notice an increase in his lifestyle. One fraud was revealed by the purchase of cars, boats, an expensive second home, and rounds of beer every week for the bowling team—all on a salary of $30,000 a year! A next-door neighbor, who also worked for the same company, was suspicious, because she did not understand how he could afford such a drastic change. The fraudster claimed that a relative left him a lot of money. Not until months later, when a sharp internal auditor uncovered the fraud, did the neighbor realize that his change in lifestyle was because he had stolen over $1 million over a period of five years from their employer. Such a change in lifestyle is observable and is a red flag of frauds in general.

Other red flags would include employees who:

- Are disgruntled with employer or supervisor
- Never take a vacation (probable in lapping and ghost employee schemes)
- Have financial strains or debt problems
- Exhibit traits of psychotic problems
- Constantly complain about how the boss or company treats them

- Exhibit behavioral characteristics associated with egocentrics or control freaks
- Reject transfers, promotions, or other job offers

Financial Statement Frauds

Another major class of frauds is financial statement fraud. These frauds generally are perpetrated by senior management, for the organization (at least in part or indirectly), for the benefit of the organization and the fraudster.

For these frauds, the common red flags would be different from those associated with fraudsters who commit asset misappropriation frauds. Generally, these red flags would include:

- Accounting anomalies
- Rapid growth
- Unusual profits
- Internal control weaknesses
- Aggressiveness of executive management

But of these, the most telling common red flag of this category is the style or character of key executive managers. Usually a senior manager has a hard-to-observe weakness in personal ethics, but also exhibits an observable overly aggressive nature. For example, the executive could continually produce and approve overly optimistic financial goals. She could be domineering with employees, attempting to keep people under her thumb. She also probably would try to steer internal and external auditors around or away from those areas where the fraud would most likely be discovered. Being secretive or keeping certain financial information close to the vest is also a sign of this type of executive.

COMMON DETECTION METHODS

Based on the common red flags, some common detection methods should come to mind. These methods are independent of the particular fraud scheme.

General Methods

- Internal audit function actively engaged in proactive antifraud activities
- Financial auditors applying SAS No. 99
- SOX 404 results can lead to identification of weaknesses in internal controls that can cause a higher risk for fraud in that area or business process
- Horizontal and vertical analysis of financial reports, especially when comparisons are made between business units and their data
- Ratio analysis, especially trends over several years, and by business unit compared to other units and the entity as a whole
- Surprise audits and/or cash counts
- Anonymous, easy-to-use, tips and complaints system to which employees, vendors, and customers have access
- Improved internal controls, especially those embedded in business processes, and especially designed to detect fraud or red flags
- Data mine for applicable red flags using a CAAT software tool

Financial Statement Frauds

- An audit committee that meets SOX requirements and is actively engaged in an antifraud program, especially in holding executives accountable
- External auditors running background checks on executives
- External auditors maintaining a professional skepticism on *every* client

Asset Misappropriation

- Sending the bank statements to a person in the entity separate from accounts payable and any check-writing personnel, and having that person review the statement and cancelled checks, then forward them to the person responsible for the bank reconciliation
- Rotating duties or mandating vacation for key employees

- Examining all types of transactions that have a review/approval level, extracting all transactions just below that level, and classifying them by employee, vendor, and customer
- Reconciling inventory and confirming receivables regularly

SPECIFIC RED FLAGS AND DETECTION METHODS

Other red flags are peculiar to a specific fraud. This section illustrates some of the known red flags for each of the major fraud schemes. These red flags facilitate the development of some potentially effective detective methods for that specific fraud. This section is intended to make auditors familiar with red flags and possible detection methods in order to accentuate their fraud mindset.

Financial Statement Schemes

This category is broken down into six specific frauds. These six schemes are addressed in SAS No. 99 as well. For a detailed and lengthy list of red flags associated with financial statement fraud, see the appendix to SAS No. 99.

Red flags that apply to all types of financial statement schemes include (most are taken from SAS No. 99):

- Threats to financial stability or profitability by economic, industrial, or internal operational conditions
- Excessive pressure on management to meet aggressive financial requirements
- Evidence that executives or board members have a personal financial dependence on the performance of the entity
- Highly complex transactions or relationships to third parties
- Ineffective monitoring of executives
- Complex or unstable organizational structure
- Deficient internal controls, especially reportable conditions
- Unreasonable increase in gross margin, especially when compared to the industry average

- Recurring negative cash flows from operations, especially when coupled with increasing profits and overall positive cash flow
- Unusual profits, especially if well above the industry average
- Rapid growth, profits that are above the Standard & Poor's (S&P) average
- Significant transactions with related parties, especially when the other party is not audited or audited by a different audit firm
- Significant, unusual, or highly complex transactions at the end of the fiscal year
- Significant volume of sales to entities whose substance and owners are not known
- Unusual growth in revenues by minority of business units

Detection methods include:

- Horizontal and vertical analysis of financial reports
- Ratio analysis, especially trends over several years
- Beneisch's five earnings manipulation ratios
- Examination of generally accepted accounting principles (GAAP) tax rate versus cash tax rate
- Irrational price/earnings ratios: benchmark is 20 to 25, S&P average is about 36
- Financial auditors applying SAS No. 99

Timing Differences (Improper Treatment of Sales) This fraud centers around booking sales that are either premature or will be reversed in a few weeks or months. Thus red flags for this scheme center around the ways such improper transactions would be perpetrated. If the sale is a legitimate one, but posted prematurely, then a potential red flag would be a sale transaction that is posted too early (i.e., violation of GAAP). Channel stuffing red flags include excessive returns of merchandise, accompanied with sales credits.

Fictitious Revenues Fictitious revenues are created by simply recording sales that never occurred. Red flags associated with these types of transactions or their results include:

- Unusual increase in assets (the other side of the entry to create fictitious revenues)
- Customers with missing data (especially physical address and phone numbers)
- Unexplained changes in certain relationships or ratio trends (e.g., revenues grow but accounts receivable does not)

Concealed Liabilities (Improper Recording of Liabilities) Profits can be inflated unethically by moving liabilities off one entity's books to another. Liabilities can also be concealed by not recording legitimate liabilities. Red flags associated with those types of transactions include:

- Excessive transfers from one entity to a related entity (e.g., a sister subsidiary)
- Unusual or unexplained transfers from one entity to a related entity
- The employ of different audit firms for different subsidiaries or related business entities
- Vendor invoices and other liability transactions that are not recorded in the books

Inadequate Disclosures Improper disclosures can be the tactic of a fraudster to hide a fraud. Red flags include:

- Disclosure notes that are so obfuscated that it is difficult to determine the true nature of the event or transaction
- Discovery of undisclosed legal contingencies, or any other significant event
- Discovery of undisclosed fraud

Improper Asset Valuation Profits can be inflated by increasing asset values. That increase can be the result of adding value to the original costs or by decreasing the contra accounts that go with a depreciable asset. Red flags include:

- Unusual or unexplained increases in book value of assets (inventory, receivables, long-lived assets)
- Unusual trends in ratios or relationships of assets to other parts of the financial report (e.g., consistent increases in number-of-days in receivables ratio, changes in the ratio of receivables to revenues)
- Violation of GAAP in recording expenses as assets

CORRUPTION SCHEMES

There are four corruption subcategories of fraud schemes, six micro-categories, and a total of eight different individual schemes. Corruption schemes invariably involve two parties, even if one is unwilling.

Conflicts of Interest

A conflict-of-interest fraud involves an employee with a relationship with a third party by which the employee and/or the third party gain a financial advantage. The fraudster exerts influence for the benefit of the third party because of this personal interest in the third party. Entities should have a policy (ethics or fraud) that specifically forbids this kind of activity. Red flags include:

- A large volume of transactions with a particular vendor
- The discovery of a relationship between an employee and a third party that was previously unknown
- Weak segregation of duties in assigning contracts and approving invoices

Detection methods include:

- Classifying transactions by vendor and examining unusual, unexplained higher-than-expected volumes
- Random investigation of all vendors, including owners, major shareholders, and any relationship with employees

- Reviewing contracts and approval of invoices periodically, even if only a sample during each audit
- Verifying the authenticity of vendors as part of internal audits, even if it is only a sample

bureacratic

Bribery

Bribery frauds involve payments to influence an employee to send business to the vendor making the payments. The frauds in this group include kickbacks, bid rigging, and others. Red flags include:

- A change in lifestyle of an employee
- Discovery of a relationship between an employee and a vendor
- Weak segregation of duties in approving vendors and invoices

Detection methods include:

- Rotating duties of approving contracts and/or vendors, and bid responsibilities
- Segregating duties of approving vendors and awarding contracts or approving invoices

Economic Extortion

Basically, economic extortion is the opposite of a bribery fraud. Instead of a vendor offering a bribe, the employee demands payment from a vendor in order to favor the vendor. The red flags and detection methods are the same as for bribery.

ASSET MISAPPROPRIATION SCHEMES

Asset misappropriation schemes are the most common type of fraud. They involve the theft or misuse of assets, normally cash. Altogether, a total of 32 different individual fraud schemes are contained in this major category. The schemes or groups of schemes to be discussed were selected because of the probability of their occurrence (i.e., they occur more frequently than others) or higher costs (the schemes include the top 14 individual schemes).

Cash Larceny

Cash larceny is simply the theft of cash from the employer, occurring *after* it was recorded in the books of records. It includes cash and checks. Red flags include:

- Unusual or unexplained drops in the level of deposits in the bank
- Unusual or unexplained differences between the accounts or reports of activities and bank statement information
- Change in lifestyle of an employee

Detection methods include:

- Investigating shortages in cash drawers, deposits, etc.
- Investigating missing or altered sales records
- Having two people independently verify deposits on bank statements to postings in the general ledger
- Maintaining and reviewing daily cash availability amounts
- Having deposits delivered to the bank under dual control
- Secretly determining the deposit prior to its transmittal to the bank and then independently confirming with the bank the amount of the deposit
- Making sure deposits in transit are the first to clear on next statement (flag associated with lapping deposits)
- Conducting surprise cash counts
- Reviewing cash and check ratio of daily bank deposits (for those who steal only cash)
- Reviewing timeliness of deposits from remote locations to central treasurer function
- Observing cash receipting at all points of entry

Billing Schemes

Shell Company   In a shell company scheme, the fraudster establishes a fictitious company as the means to divert checks from the employer to the fraudster. Usually the fictitious vendor is a fabricated name, and often the address is a post office box. Sometimes the culprit will use a derivation of a legitimate vendor's name to confuse those who might see the checks or the fictitious vendor's name. Red flags include:

- Use of post office box (POB) for the only address of a vendor, or in place of a physical address
- Lack of sufficient contact data: missing phone number, and so on
- Use of Excel-generated invoices by a vendor
- Sequential invoice numbers from a vendor
- Address that matches an employee's address
- A vendor who only bills for services
- Use of round numbers for amounts on an invoice
- Use of unintelligible descriptions on invoices
- Odd items being purchased (e.g., gravel for an attorney)
- Lack of detail on invoice
- Irregular folds on invoices from same vendor (e.g., looks like it was delivered in a shirt pocket!)
- No Employer Identification Number (EIN) or improper one (i.e., does not fit the format of a proper EIN)
- No sales tax identification number or improper one
- Unusual or unexpected increase in cost of goods sold
- Irrational ratios
- Vendor who consistently gets paid more quickly than other vendors
- Applicable tips and complaints, especially from employees who can observe the fraud or evidence of the fraud
- Notations for "extra" or "special" charges

Detection methods include:

- Sorting payments by vendor, amount, and invoice number
- Expense exceeds budget, especially if it is exactly double (i.e., possibly producing two checks, one for the legitimate vendor, and one for the fraudster)

- Examining charges in largest expense account, as fraudsters often charge billing schemes to the largest account in an attempt to hide the crime
- Horizontal analysis
- Verifying service-only vendors' invoices
- Using a CAAT software tool to cross reference employees' addresses with vendors' addresses
- Testing for turnaround time from receipt of invoice to payment
- Verifying that vendors are legitimate. While this test may appear daunting, it can become manageable. Simply verify only the vendors added since last audit, and only ones peculiar to this business unit. Look them up in the phone book or in the online white pages. Use Google to search for the firm. Check with the local chamber of commerce. Contact others in the same industry.
- Asking the State Department for copy of the company's filing Look for post office box and no physical address, or address is same as one of the employees. Look for one person serving as all of the officers.
- Reviewing cancelled checks
- Not paying a suspicious invoice/vendor and seeing who follows up on payment
- Taking special precaution with those who can add a vendor to the authorized list: Segregate that duty if possible from invoice approval
- Data mining for as many of the red flags as possible
- Verifying the legitimacy of any vendor who uses Excel-generated invoices
- Printing the vendor list alphabetically and searching for two vendors with nearly identical names and data

Pass-Through Vendor A pass-through vendor scheme is similar to the shell vendor scheme. In the pass-through vendor scheme, the vendor actually does deliver product to the employer, but the price paid to the vendor is exorbitant. The fraudster sets up the pseudo vendor for the purposes of bilking the employer into paying much more for services or products than would be paid honestly in order to take the excess for himself.

Red flags include many of the same ones as for a shell vendor scheme, plus:

- Tips from employees that the entity is paying too much for certain goods or services
- Evidence that high prices are being paid for certain products or services
- Declining profits, increasing cost of goods sold
- Unfavorable variances on performance reports
- Poor internal controls, especially lack of segregation between adding vendors and approving contracts or invoices. (If the same person can do both, that is a red flag.)
- Amounts of invoices are just below an approval level, especially an excessive number of invoices below that amount by vendor or by employee who approved the transaction

Detection methods include some of the same ones as for the shell vendor scheme, such as turnaround time from receipt of invoice to payment of invoice, and the following:

- Examining all invoices just below the approval level, sorted by vendor or employee who approved the invoice
- Comparing market prices for prices on invoices, using a CAAT and some research
- Reviewing invoices for what is being bought and the prices

Nonaccomplice Vendor   In this scheme, the vendor is an innocent participant. In some manner, the fraudster entices a legitimate vendor to send a check, usually for a refund, to the employer. The fraudster intercepts that check and forges an endorsement to cash it for her own benefit. Red flags include:

- Use of invoice numbers outside the range of normal sequence
- Unusual or unexplained levels of purchases from a vendor
- Unusual or unexplained purchases of particular goods

Detection methods include:

- Sorting invoices by vendor and look for unusual invoice numbers
- Classifying vendor by invoice amounts and look for unusual amounts
- Verifying invoices (sample) and all invoices that led to vendor refunds
- Requesting that the bank notify the proper person if someone endorses a check where the company is the payee, and the company uses the stamp "For Deposit Only" for official endorsements

Personal Purchases In personal purchases frauds, the fraudster simply has the company pay for personal items. In the case of a General Accounting Office (GAO) audit of e-procurement purchases, auditors could not properly examine records because of a lack of sufficient detail in their records. The auditors contacted the credit card companies and obtained a copy of their data from the financial institution's database. They then sorted the data looking at the merchandise codes and pulled those that were incompatible with normal use. Those codes included merchants such as brothels, country clubs, and Victoria's Secret. Thousands of dollars of unauthorized expenses were detected in this manner. It is noteworthy that unauthorized expenses can be made for normal merchants (e.g., airlines, hotels, car rentals in this case), and they probably would not be detected using this specific audit procedure.

Red flags include:

- Unusual or unexplained activity on corporate credit cards
- Purchases of unusual items
- Consistently overbudget employee
- Pattern of purchases just below review

Detection methods include:

- Spot-checking expenditures on credit cards, looking for unusual vendors or items bought
- Surprise audits of an employee who is authorized to use credit cards or sign checks
- Examining unfavorable balances on performance reports
- Vendor payment trend analysis

- Extracting all purchases with no purchase order, summarized by both vendor and employee
- Extracting all purchases just below the review/approval limit, summarized by both vendor and employee

Payroll Schemes

Payroll schemes involve conning the company into paying wages that were not earned. The manner of such frauds varies, but they all lead to an unauthorized increase in a paycheck or an unauthorized paycheck period. Specific schemes include the ghost employee scheme, falsified hours and salary scheme, commission scheme, and false workers' compensation scheme.

Ghost Employee A ghost employee is perpetrated by a fraudster by adding a person, fictitious or real, to the payroll files. Then the fraudster manages to get pay approved for the ghost and intercepts the check or has it mailed to an accomplice or her own POB.

For example, a property management company had decided to expand into a neighboring state. The managers of the family-owned business decided to assign the management of the newly opened remote facility to their best employee, a woman who had worked for them for several years, had a great personality, and was fiercely loyal. She was sent to the new property as the only full-time employee of the business and was given a part-time "handyman." When the handyman quit, she decided to leave him on the payroll, continue to send in approved time, intercept the paycheck when it came back, forge his signature, and thus increase her personal income. In this case, the ghost was a real person—a former employee.

Other ghost employee frauds use fictitious people. The facts behind how these frauds are perpetrated lead to the red flags, which lead to effective ways to detect the fraud.

Red flags include:

- Unexplained or unusual increases in wages expense
- Paychecks for employees who:
  - Never take a vacation
  - Never take sick leave
  - Have no taxes withheld

- Have no deductions
- Have no social security number (SSN) or an invalid one
- Have a POB and no physical address
- Have an address duplicated by another employee, or it is the address of a relative or friend
- Have no phone number, or duplicate phone number, or the phone number is a work phone of the employer rather than a residence
- Have a duplicate direct deposit number
- Have a date of paycheck *after* termination of the employee

Detection methods include:

- Where feasible, reconciling employees in the payroll database with employees in the human resource (HR) database; the ghost should be missing in HR. CAATs can make this possible for 100% of the employees.
- Getting a copy of the SSN file and, at least once a year, reconciling that file with your employees' SSNs
- Periodically and unannounced, distributing checks manually, requiring ID to pick up check
- Investigating any payroll checks with dual endorsements (sign of an employee accomplice working with a real person who is serving as the ghost)
- Rotating duties of handling printed paychecks, or requiring vacation timed with issuance of payroll
- Data mining payroll data looking for these red flags:
  - POBs versus a physical address
  - A physical address that matches that of another employee (i.e., a "duplicate")
  - A direct deposit account number that matches that of another employee
  - Missing phone number, or a phone number that matches either another employee or a work phone
  - Dates of paychecks compared to termination dates (employees being paid after terminated, and used as a ghost by existing employee)
  - Employees who never take vacation or sick leave (if neither is taken, this is highly suspicious). (A fraud using a ghost employee,

for example, would result in that fictitious employee having neither, unless the fraudster creates fictitious leave.)

- Employees who have no deductions from paychecks
- Employees with no SSN, invalid SSN, or duplicate SSN

Commission Scheme   Commission schemes involve the fraudulent manipulation of commissions paid, either the rate or sales. Red flags include:

- Unexplained or unusual increases in commissions expense
- Changes in commissions rates over time
- Higher rate of returns or credits for one salesperson

Detection methods include:

- Randomly spot checking all of the transactions involved in sales commissions for a pay period or a salesperson
- Investigating higher rates of returns or credits for a salesperson
- Creating and reviewing a linear correlation between sales and commissions paid, by employee
- Tracking uncollected sales by employee
- Creating exception reports for employees whose compensation has increased over last year by some unusual percentage
- Having a designated and independent official verify all changes in commission rates

Falsified Wages   Red flags include:

- Unexplained or unusual amounts of overtime
- Unusual changes in pay rates
- Unusual or unexplained number of hours paid

Detection methods include:

- Data mining all transactions over a certain number of overtime hours (e.g., more than 20 hours per week)
- Creating exception reports for employees whose compensation has increased over last year by some unusual percentage

- Randomly verifying the pay rates in a pay period or for an employee over pay periods
- Having a designated and independent official verify all changes in pay rates
- Maintaining careful custody of time cards—after approval, process them immediately

Check-Tampering Schemes   The five check-tampering schemes make up the most costly of frauds. As such, they deserve extra attention in understanding them and in developing detection and prevention methods and controls. Check tampering essentially involves using the entity's checks in one manner or another to extract cash from the victim organization.

With the advent of Check 21 rules, many of the red flags (especially those associated with endorsements) became more difficult to observe, as checks are truncated by the banking system. Therefore, it is important to select the entity's bank carefully. Choose a bank that scans both the front and back of the check, and provides customers with access to both images (front and back) over the Internet.

Red flags include:

- Excessive number of voided checks
- Missing checks
- Nonpayroll checks where employee is the payee
- Alterations to payee or amount on cancelled checks
- Altered or dual endorsements on cancelled checks
- Questionable payees or payee addresses (e.g., POB)
- Duplicate or out-of-sequence check numbers

Detection methods include:

- Periodically rotating personnel who handle and code checks
- Using a positive pay system at the entity's bank
- Having the bank statement sent unopened to someone in management completely separate from accounts payable—in the case of smaller companies, perhaps the owner/manager. Review the statement and cancelled checks, even if it is online, before passing the statement on to the person who will do the bank reconciliation.

Skimming Skimming frauds happen *before* a booking entry is made. Because it is an off-the-books fraud, this type of fraud is the most difficult to detect. One methodology to detect skimming is to perform an "invigilation." Invigilation is the creation of a pristine, fraud-free environment for the purpose of benchmarking the total receipts that should be normal. This pristine effect can be created by a high-profile investigation, where everyone knows that fraud auditors are coming to look for fraud. Add cameras for surveillance and anything else that will increase the level of attention to the fraud audit. The intent is to create such a high level of perception of detection that the fraudsters shut down their skimming temporarily so the fraud auditor can determine the level of normal sales. That benchmark then can be compared to actual sales to determine if, and approximately how much, skimming is taking place. The individual skimming schemes are sales schemes (unrecorded sales, understated sales), receivables schemes (write-off schemes, lapping schemes, unconcealed schemes), and refund schemes.

Red flags include:

- Lower than expected revenues
- Actual profits that are less than projections
- Gross margins significantly less than projections

Detection methods include:

- Surveillance of employees at point of sale (e.g., cameras above registers and meal tables)
- Discovery of "markers" near registers (fraudsters use markers to keep up with the amounts skimmed; for example, a penny for $100, an nickel for $500)
- Investigating gaps in prenumbered receipts
- Checking registers for excessive no-sale transactions, voids, or refunds
- Posting a sign at the register or in plain view of customers: "If you did not receive a receipt, please contact the manager and your meal will be free."
- Using a trained secret shopper to look for signs of fraud
- Using an "invigilation" for an approximation of missing monies, or to determine if skimming is occurring
- Measuring variances in revenues by employee and by shift

- Doing a pro-forma income statement, using cost of goods sold and standard markups to ascertain the level of sales that should exist, then comparing it to actual for an approximation of missing monies
- Performing surprise audits or cash counts just after closing out a shift

Skimming: Receivables: Lapping Scheme   Lapping is skimming accounts receivable (AR) payments before they are posted. Lapping is more difficult to conceal than skimming cash in a cash business since the customer expects to be credited with a payment on account. Red flags include:

- Customer complaints about payments being posted long after checks were mailed
- Growing delinquency in accounts receivable or specific customers, incremental increases over time in number-of-days in receivables
- Employees who put in a lot of time after hours—sometimes necessary to keep a separate set of books on the lapping system

Detection methods include:

- Customer service phone calls: follow-up on customer complaints of delays in posting checks independent of the AR personnel
- Using a trend analysis of number-of-days in receivables, by business unit or AR clerk—follow up on those above the standard or organizational average
- Independent confirmation of AR balances and aging in particular
- Conducting surprise audits and/or cash counts
- Classifying write-offs and credit memos by employee, and investigating any irregularities (i.e., transactions that are not randomly distributed)
- Conducting random, unannounced customer satisfaction surveys—specifically asking questions about length of time from check mailed to posted on account
- Watching for employees who put in a lot of time after hours
- Conducting a surprise "desk raid," looking for a second set of books (lapping system) kept in the desk

- Spot checking daily deposits to AR, verifying that names on checks match postings
- Comparing dates of AR postings to dates of checks or date payment was mailed

FRAUD DETECTION MODEL

Auditors often come across transactions, accounting records, or accounting data that are not quite right, that constitute an exception of some kind. Primarily, they are exceptions to policies, procedures or internal controls. Many times, if not most of the time, these events and transactions are minor glitches in the recording of the accounting event, due to a number of possible reasons including human error. But sometimes they are actually evidence of a fraud.

A problem in recognizing these signs of fraud is their apparent benign nature, especially when considering a single transaction, document, or event. For example, an internal auditor is doing a file review of a vendor picks up an invoice and find a POB as the address. Many vendors want the check and remittance to be returned to a POB. But it is also true that a POB is a red flag for a billing scheme. So should it be ignored? By itself, does it mean anything? Probably not. But it should not be ignored. Thus some model of accumulating and classifying anomalies (exceptions) would be beneficial to auditors and antifraud concerns.

The model that follows is based on the concept similar to that of materiality and financial audits. When a financial auditor finds a misstatement that is not material to the account or class of accounts, she does not ignore the misstatement. Rather she puts that misstatement into a file to be accumulated with other misstatements. The purpose of the accumulation is to determine if the misstatements are material in the aggregate. The same process and goal should apply to fraud audits and anomalies (red flags in particular).

If a number of auditors are involved in an audit, it is conceivable that each of them observed one or two red flags but dismissed them. Their reasons would be quite valid on an individual basis. But a number of anomalies larger than any one person's were dismissed. The question that begs to be answered, therefore, is whether these anomalies, these red flags, are significant *in the aggregate*. There is no way to know without some formal process in the audit to accumulate anomalies.

A Model for Aggregating and Classifying Anomalies

Auditors need a structured approach to detecting fraud as they conduct their audits. Basically, they need a method to formally track the occurrences of possible red flags. One simple way to do so is to assess the probability and level of risk for a specific anomaly or exception. This model (see Exhibit 5.1) will use one measure that combines both aspects of the risk assessment.[3] The measures could be: (1) not likely to be fraud, low risk; (2) somewhat likely to be fraud, medium risk; (3) highly likely to be associated with a fraud, high risk. By *anomaly* or *exception,* we mean something in the data or transaction that is not correct. It could be missing data, a violation of policies or internal controls, or the presence of a fraud red flag.

For those anomalies identified, if the transaction (document, event, data) does not violate policies or controls, and does not specifically identify a fraud, then it should be classified as a level 1 anomaly. An example would be a POB for a vendor's physical address. The use of a POB is fairly common in billing schemes. If the use of a POB is not a violation of the entity's vendor policies, and if the auditor is reasonably sure it is not fraud-related (e.g., shell company), then it should be treated as a level 1 anomaly. These data or transactions are still suspicious because they contain a known red flag, but the degree or level of risk is low (low probability and low risk).

If the data or transactions do violate policies or controls, it should be assigned a level 2 anomaly (medium probability and medium risk). For example, if payroll policies are such that an employee should not receive but one check per pay period, then if an employee has two checks for the same pay period in the data, that is a violation of the payroll policies and thus is more risky than the level 1 type anomalies. The fraud auditor should examine these types of anomalies carefully to

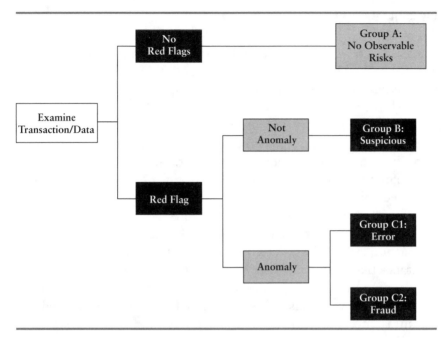

EXHIBIT 5.1   Data/Transaction Classification Model for Fraud

determine if it is an error or fraud. If it is an error, the level 2 remains. If it is not determined in a reasonable time to be an error, then it should be assigned a level 3 anomaly (high probability and high risk).

The fraud auditor should accumulate these levels by vendor, employee, and other factors to see if some aspect of the data as a whole level a high number of anomalies, too many occurrences of the higher levels, or the accumulation of an unacceptable total level of risk. Is, the numbers of 1s and 2s are too high to be ignored. Is it the accumulation of too much risk? For example, if one vendor has 10 different level 1 anomalies, and no other vendor has 3 anomalies of any level, then something could be amiss with that vendor. At best, something is wrong with the way that vendor's transactions are being handled in the computer system. Without a structured approach such as this classification and accumulation model, the 10 anomalies might be ignored in each case, and thus the vendor would be ignored overall.

Classifications of Transactions—Risk Analysis

The next step would be to group transactions with risk by the level of risk for each. The first group (Group A) in the analysis of data and transactions are those that have no apparent red flags or anomalies (see Exhibit 5.1). These transactions are indicative of normal transactions that have integrity. But just because a transaction has no red flag does not mean it is absolutely free of fraud. For example, the transactions in some of the major financial frauds (Enron, WorldCom, HealthSouth) were perpetrated by the chief executives, and they appeared relatively normal (no red flags). Other substantive procedures, especially related to generally accepted accounting principles or controls, may be necessary to provide adequate assurance that the transaction is indeed risk-free. Thus, external auditors need to provide assurance that transactions are not being falsified by an executive officer directing employees, and in such a way that the transactions exhibit no observable red flags. These additional, or different, procedures are always necessary for financial statement frauds, but probably not necessary for asset misappropriation—because the latter are perpetrated by employees and the former by executives.

The second group (Group B) is one where red flags exist, but they are not a result of violation of policy or controls. For instance, if a company does not have a policy about using a POB as the address for a vendor, then a POB as the physical address data for a vendor would not be a violation of policy. Because controls are a function of policy, it would also not be a violation of a control. But it would be a red flag because vendor schemes of the past have used no physical address but a POB instead. These types of red flags are not indicators of fraud per se but are suspicious because they are consistent with data patterns of certain fraud schemes of the past. Thus auditors would increase the nature, scope, and timing of audit procedures at that point to acquire a sufficient level of assurance on that transaction; that is, to ensure it is *not* fraud. Suspicious transactions can possibly be classified as anomalies where both red flags and policy/control violations exist. In this case, the transaction is treated as an anomaly (Group C).

For instance, most companies that sell on account have policies about qualifying customers to buy on account, including setting a credit limit for each customer. That set of policies usually includes one that disallows a sale on account if that sale puts a customer over its credit limit. Controls should be developed by applying corporate policies to business processes and implementing controls to ensure that corporate policies are adhered to or violations are detected. Therefore, if a transaction is in the database that puts a customer over its credit limit, that transaction violates company policy and/or internal controls. This violation is an "anomaly" because it is an exception to the corporate policies and controls. Anomalies (Group C) only have two plausible explanations: (1) an error has occurred (Group C1), or (2) it is a fraudulent transaction (Group C2).

These two subcategories carry the highest risk of the classifications and some action is required as a result of the anomaly. If it is an error, some internal control needs to be changed or implemented to prevent it from happening again. This catch-and-fix process is helpful in complying with SOX section 404, the evaluation of internal controls by management, and the subsequent opinion of the financial auditors on that assessment. But if it is fraud, an even more intense and specialized group of processes needs to be set in motion. It is recommended that an official fraud investigation be conducted. That investigation would seek to prove or disprove the apparent fraud. The entity's representative would have a goal of identifying the fraudster, if it is fraud, and gathering forensic evidence to prosecute the perpetrator. It is almost always advisable at this point to involve two key professionals: a lawyer and a forensic accountant to be that representative and fraud expert.

Exhibit 5.2 uses the three previously mentioned types of schemes and red flags to illustrate how the data/transaction classification model would work.

Model Implications to the Audit Procedures

This classification model is designed to serve as a first layer of examination. It is not an absolute fraud detection system, but rather a way to assess some cumulative level of risk on the assurance of data and transactions that are being examined by auditors, by providing them with a means to identify potentially fraudulent transactions or documents. The same model would be very useful in proactive antifraud

Fraud Scheme	Data Transaction Issue	Status
Vendor Scheme	PO box as physical address	Red flag (B)
	Two checks to same vendor for same bill/invoice	Anomaly (C)
Lapping Scheme	No vacation leave taken	Red flag (B)
	Customers calling in complaints about statements/balance	Red flag (B)
	Customer challenging a check that has cleared their bank but not posted to accounts receivable as payment on company's books	Anomaly (C)
Payroll Scheme	Duplicate check issued to same employee, same time period	Anomaly (C)
	Duplicate SSN on two different employees in payroll database	Anomaly (C)
	No vacation leave taken	Red flag/ Anomaly (B/C)

EXHIBIT 5.2   Examples of Data/Transaction Classification

techniques, such as data mining and other data analysis tools that provide many benefits in the prevention and detection of fraud. With these tools, the fraud auditor would use the red flags to develop the tests, metrics, or benchmarks for the software tool.

The model filters through transactions and assigns them some level of risk beginning with low for Group A, moderate for Group B, and high for Group C. However, it should be stated clearly that fraud could exist in any of the three major groups, including Group A where no observable red flag exists.

It also must be noted that even if a transaction had a red flag in a financial fraud, which is probably being perpetrated by a chief executive who is directing others to deliberately falsify the records, then none of the model classifications matter—except to the external financial auditors. Therefore, the financial auditors *must* exercise due diligence in its examination of the records for possible red flags. SAS No. 99 aims at ensuring that due diligence.

SUMMARY

In order to have a high probability of detecting fraud, a fraud auditor or forensic accountant needs to understand as many red flags of fraud as possible. Fraud auditors, and especially internal auditors, need to understand the "general" red flags that are indicative of a fraud but not necessarily associated with a specific fraud scheme. These red flags include changes in lifestyle, changes in behavior, and tips or complaints from other employees. But an identification of those red flags associated with specific fraud schemes is even more important. They are crucial to detecting fraud in the lives of auditors in their everyday activities, whether they are internal or financial auditors. A study of the top fraud schemes, and the red flags of each, is a key success factor in detecting fraud. In fact, a thorough understanding and analysis of known red flags lead to potentially effective detective methods.

In the next chapter, these red flags and detective models will be used to develop potentially effective CAAT procedures and tests to look proactively for fraud, red flags, and evidence of fraud.

ENDNOTES

1. Joseph Wells, "Sherlock Holmes, CPA, Part I," *Journal of Accountancy* (August 2003), pp. 86–90.
2. Allen G. Lux and Sandra Fitiani, "Fighting Internal Crime Before It Happens," *Information Systems Control Journal* Vol. III (2002), pp. 50–51.
3. Obviously, most larger organizations will find this approach too simple. However, it should be intuitive how to expand the risk assessment to all of the possible combinations of probabilities (low, medium, high) and levels of risk (low, medium, high).

CHAPTER 6

Fraud and CAATs

INTRODUCTION

There are many circumstances in which a fraud audit is simply not possible without the aid of computer-assisted audit techniques (CAATs). For instance, one forensic accounting firm was asked to review an organization's transactions over a period of 10 years. The annual budget was $500 million a year, and thus the volume of paper documents was staggering. The only way the forensic accountants could have reasonably audited these transactions is with the aid of CAATs, which they did successfully.

CAATs are really quite simple tools in concept and provide a simple ability: an efficiently automated audit of data. It is critical to note up front that *any computer system performs only what it is programmed to do and should mimic the noncomputerized business process being automated.* Various kinds of CAATs exist, and they have matured to the point where solutions are cost effective. In fact, sometimes software already in use in much of the business world can be used as a CAAT (e.g., Excel, Access). Regardless of the tool used, it must be strategically adapted to the situation, the audit objectives, and the audit procedures.

CAATs are targeted toward likely risks in transactions and data. In fraud audits, this targeting means incorporating common fraud schemes and their red flags into the CAATs' application. With the right approach, CAATs can be seamlessly integrated into and add value to the audit strategy, plan, and procedures. They can also bring benefits in terms of either efficiency or effectiveness (specifically, being able to do more with the same amount of resources).

BENEFITS OF CAATS

Although the term CAATs gives the connotation of the use of computers in auditing, in fact, CAATs refer more specifically to software capable of auditing data. CAATs include software designed to a wide variety of things associated with various kinds of audits. In regard to fraud, one is most interested in the ability of CAATs to audit the data and transactions, specifically data integrity. Data integrity can be affected by poor program logic, improper data entry, fraud, and other manipulations. The power of CAATs lies in the ability to audit data efficiently on a large scale, and their ability to audit 100% of the data with relative efficiency. Without CAATs, auditing large volumes of transactions or data (information systems, systems of financial reporting, and any other system) would be a daunting task. Without CAATs, auditing 100% of the data or transactions likewise would be daunting.

The true leverage available in CAATs is analyzing large quantities of data in a customized fashion. Data, after all, are the critical ingredient of all accounting and business systems; data are the input and output of all systems. The databases residing in organizations today are invaluable to those entities and sometimes worth more than the entities themselves. How much are the Department of Defense's databases worth? How valuable are the databases at Wal-Mart and Amazon.com?

How can CAATs provide value in auditing data? They add value by allowing auditors to integrate customized audit procedures into CAATs, performing the audit more efficiently by analyzing data quicker than humans, and more thoroughly by evaluating more data, in more depth than humans. This process means the first year, auditors spend time developing appropriate tests and audit procedures. Most CAATs allow you to automate those procedures. In ACL, that is done using the "BATCH" command that works like a batch file or macro. Then the following years, the auditor can run all of those tests with a single command, and have the results documented by the software; in ACL, that is done in the "LOG." The auditor may also develop new tests or audit procedures that can be added to the previous set of procedures. At this point, the audit using the CAAT "batch" takes on some serious efficiency.

Also, to utilize CAATs to their potential, auditors have to build a connection among the business processes, audit procedures, and software. Said differently, CAATs are as useful as the extent to which their implementation accurately audits the appropriate transactions and the data, although they certainly have intrinsic benefits.

Therefore, there are six major benefits to using a CAAT in a fraud audit (and other types of audits, of course).

1. The tool can be used to audit 100% of the data, not just a random sample. By doing so, the trained auditor can look for a plethora of red flags. Only a couple of the fraud schemes, such as skimming, are off-the-books schemes. That means about 95% of all schemes are on the books. And if a fraud is on the books, then some evidence of that fraud does exist somewhere in the data. If it does exist in the data, with the right tools and techniques, a trained auditor has some possibility of discovering or uncovering that evidence and thus has some potential to detect the fraud.

2. Current CAAT software products use commands and procedures that are familiar to auditors. Thus the learning curve is relatively short. With a little training from an expert, most auditors can quickly pick up on using a CAAT effectively and efficiently in auditing for fraud. As providers of training in this area, the authors have seen this result on many occasions among internal and external auditors.

3. Today's advanced CAATs have built-in tools to document the work and results of audit procedures as the auditor uses them (e.g., ACL IDEA, PanAudit, and Monarch). In other words, CAATs make it easier for the auditor to create appropriate audit work papers of the tests and results.

4. CAATs typically can import data of many formats. That compatibility is significant, as organizations often have varying forms of data and these commonly need to be integrated to effectively audit. Almost all computer systems can export data from accounting and finance databases as a text file (ASCII), and CAATs can read text files. CAAT software also can import vendor specific files. Depending on certain constraints, it is possible to import the data into Microsoft Excel and Access, software that generally is available in the entity.

5. CAATs typically are read-only; they utilize a copy of data and cannot actually edit the data, thus preserving the integrity of the data. That feature is a very important one for fraud audits. Not only is the integrity of the data maintained, but is this security feature is compatible with custody of evidence as well. Using CAAT software eliminates a lot of mistakes that can happen in using Excel or Access as a CAAT.

6. Today's advanced CAATs also allow auditors to automate the running of the tests. That is, an inventory of audit procedures or tests can be built to identify exceptions or anomalies. If proven to be effective, these tests or procedures can be saved in the software and called on to be run in a batch sequence, where all of the tests are run back-to-back and documented in a log of some kind. So in the years subsequent to the initial year of implementation, the audits will go faster, without sacrificing the ability to fine-tune or add to the procedures. Over time, the fraud auditor can easily adapt previous procedures that were automated into a batch to accommodate changes in the environment. Such a feature means that with a little time, and a little training, the audit procedures are not only automated but programmable. It also means the auditor is "scanning" for fraud evidence or red flags proactively during each audit.

FRAUD AND CAAT ISSUES

One of the primary issues in a fraud audit (and other types of audits) is the potential efficiency advantage of using CAATs over traditional audit techniques—specifically substantive testing of a sample of the audit trail. With a CAAT, an auditor can evaluate 100% of the data in 100% of the transactions, assuming the data provided are all of the data. With the public, governmental, and business community pressures to look for fraud, it is much easier to do so if an auditor can review 100% of the transactional data efficiently.

A second issue is the volume of data and transactions. For example, a 60-gigabyte hard drive can hold the equivalent of over 27 million pages. If they were stacked up, that stack would be 18 times the height of the Washington Monument. How is it possible to examine that volume of paper documents? A review of that set of transactions is humanly possible, or economically feasible, only with a CAAT.

There also is the issue of proactive audits versus reactive audits. According to the most recent Association of Certified Fraud Examiners (ACFE) Report to the Nation (2004), over 60% of all frauds are detected either by a tip or accident. That leaves a lot of room for proactive methods. One excellent proactive method is to build an inventory of effective audit procedures (tests) in a CAAT that searches for the existence of specified red flags, such as anomalies (exceptions) or certain characteristics of data. Over time, the audit program could be doing an extensive search of 100% of the data for known red flags. That approach is clearly proactive. And in many, if not most, cases, that is feasible.

In addition, financial auditors must consider the Statement on Auditing Standard (SAS) No. 94, *The Effect of IT on the Auditor's Consideration of Internal Control in a Financial Statement Audit.* This technical literature piece was written in response to the explosive growth of information technology (IT). The use of IT significantly changes the methods that firms employ to gather and report financial information. SAS No. 94 provides guidance to financial auditors concerning the proper assessment of internal controls in IT systems. The standard states that CAATs are needed to test the automated controls in those systems. According to the standard, *"It is not practical or possible to restrict detection risk to an acceptable level by performing only substantive tests."* Therefore, SAS No. 94 suggests that financial auditors rely more on analytical procedures, CAATs, and techniques other than substantive tests. The standard provides specific examples and even examples of when it is *not* appropriate to use CAATs. But, where applicable, the tests of controls required under this SAS are possible with CAATs.

NEED FOR COMPUTER TOOLS

It should be obvious that one of the best, if not the most effective, tools or techniques to mitigate risks and threats is computer technology. Technologies often are used to protect and defend computer and financial assets from damage of any kind, including fraud. Certain types of CAATs are software tools and techniques that work with computer systems in general; that is, they are not proprietary to any one vendor or system. These software types of CAATs are often referred to as generalized audit software (GAS).

Generalized audit software, such as ACL, IDEA, PanAudit Plus, Monarch, and others, has proven to be of immense value in detecting irregularities, fraud, and computer crimes in information systems and information technology. Using GAS and computer-assisted audit techniques and tools (CAATTs) is a powerful way to counter the use of computers or attacks on computers by malicious individuals. The use of GAS can bring both effectiveness and efficiency to the protection of computers and information. *One of the major benefits of GAS regarding fraud is the fact that auditors are able to examine all of the records, not just a sample.* To use CAATTs or GAS to detect computer-related fraud, the auditor should follow seven steps:

Set the audit objectives.

Meet with the owner of the data and a programmer.

Formally request the data.

Create or build the input file definition of the GAS.

Verify data integrity for the data imported.

Gain an understanding of the data.

Analyze the data.

In step 5, it is necessary to develop a technique to bring some level of assurance that the data given the auditor are in fact the exact data on the operational computer.

The GAS will have many commands and audit procedures that can be applied to steps 4 through 7. From a fraud perspective, these tests are chosen to assist the fraud auditor in detecting fraud, collecting evidence to prove or disprove a fraud, and so on. Some of the types of tests run to meet these objectives include:

- *Reasonableness tests.* Are the data reasonable under the circumstances?
- *Completeness tests.* Are all the data there that should be?
- *Gaps.* Are there any gaps in check numbers, invoice numbers, and so on? Are there gaps where none should be, or vice versa?

- *Duplicates.* Similar to gaps. Are there duplicate transactions or data where there should be none, or vice versa?
- *Sort.* Sorting is a quick way to spot anomalies (exceptions).
- *Classify.* Classifying is a quick way to spot abnormal levels of activity in a vendor, customer, employee.
- *Stratify.* Stratifying is a quick way to examine the distribution of data, especially to see if it is a "normal" distribution by layers.
- *Period-to-period (trends).* Many frauds can be detected by spotting the incremental increases or decreases in certain accounts, vendors, customers, or ratios. Trends can be especially useful in comparing a specific business unit to other business units or the entity as a whole.
- *Regression analysis.* Regression analysis serves a similar purpose as trends, and also can be especially useful in comparing a specific business unit to other business units.
- *Statistical analysis.* Statistical analysis is always a good way to fulfill step 6, and it too can be especially useful in comparing a specific business unit to other business units.
- *Transaction matching.* This is used to spot evidence of a fraud by an employee.
- *Filters.* Filters are used to locate anomalies (exceptions).
- *Benford's law.* Benford's law is an arithmetic law of leading digits. Digits do not randomly occur as the leading digit or digits. This law is used to spot anomalies (exceptions) in the leading digits of amounts.

SAMPLE TOOLS/CAATS

There are many tools available in the market from which to choose (see Exhibit 6.1). Only a few are mentioned here, and they are mentioned to illustrate the kind and the practicality of tools available.[1]

The first general category would be spreadsheet-enabled tools. An electronic spreadsheet is a tool in and of itself. But there are also spreadsheet "plug-ins" that bring more power and audit-friendly commands to the aid of the auditor. One example is Information Active products: Active Audit and Active Data. The end result of installing these products is the auditor has many of the specific techniques listed in the section below as a menu in Microsoft's Excel. However, there are data limitations to using a spreadsheet; Excel's limits are 65,536 rows by 256 columns. It is likely that even a small business will have annual data in *some* files that are simply too large for Excel to handle. Excel also is limited in data integrity *during the audit*. That is, values in cells can be inadvertently changed or deleted, causing serious problems with audit procedures performed. The values can be locked in Excel to prevent this mistake from occurring, but locking and unlocking might require a lot of back-and-forth work.

An example of using Excel as a CAAT is worth illustrating. One fraud case involved a known shell company scheme, reported by a tipster who became aware of the fraud and reported it to the risk manager, but the organization did not know which vendor was involved.[2] The firm had over 10,000 vendors. So the fraud auditor loaded all of the vendor demographic data into Excel and added a column for "Red Flags." He then used the "AutoFilter" option in Excel to filter the data for red flags (e.g., post office boxes as physical address, no phone number, improper or missing Employer Identification Number [EIN]). He simply added "1" to the Red Flags column for each occurrence from the "tests" using AutoFilter. He then used AutoFilter to determine which vendors had the most red flags. At that point, he had only six vendors with the most red flags. He pulled a sample of three invoices for each of the six vendors and was able to quickly recognize which vendor was the phony one (because it was an Excel-generated invoice with no contact data and was for services, not products). This entire process of eliminating over 10,000 vendors took about half a day, and could take less time than that. And it was done with a conventional copy of Excel.

The second category is database software, such as Microsoft's Access. Auditors can do more with the capabilities of Access than Excel. Access also can handle a lot more data than Excel, but it too is limited in the amount of data it can handle. Namely, Access files are limited to 2 gigabytes and tables are limited to 255 columns. Still, Access is an upgrade from spreadsheet tools and allows better filtering through the use of querying (filtering data in multiple ways from multiple data sources). Using Structured Query Language (SQL) or Access's query feature, a trained auditor with SQL/Access skills can look for red flags and anomalies. Using Access successfully does take more skill and ability to than Excel, but the potential advantages are greater.

EXHIBIT 6.1   Sample Fraud CAATs

Type	Vendor	URL
Spreadsheet		
Active Data	Information Active	www.informationactive.com
Active Audit	Information Active	www.informationactive.com
Excel->AutoFilter	Excel	www.microsoft.com
Database		
Access	Microsoft	www.microsoft.com
Statistical Software		
SAS	SAS Institute Inc.	www.sas.com
SPSS	SPSS Inc.	www.spss.com
Data Mining Software		
ACL	ACL Services Ltd.	www.acl.com
IDEA	Audimation Services Inc.	www.audimation.com
PanAudit	Computer Associates (CA)	www.ca.com
Monarch	Datawatch	www.datawatch.com

The third category is statistical software. Software normally used to do statistical analysis for research can also be used effectively to run audit tests for anomalies and red flags. Examples would include software such as SAS or SPSS. Because they are mainframe compatible, they may be more readily compatible with operational computer files. They can also handle vast volumes of data and not be limited by the same constraints as Access and Excel regarding size of data files. There is a trade-off, however: They are much more costly and complicated to use than the previous two types of CAATs. In fact, it will take a specially trained person to use statistical software successfully as a CAAT (e.g., a programmer and IT auditor).

The last category is data mining software (DMS). The history of DMS goes back to the late 1960s, and its evolution has been affected by the audit profession and its needs. The term *data mining software,* as used in this book, is the comprehensive CAAT and audit software tool that includes commonly used audit tests or procedures as commands in the menu and is generally either platform independent or imports a wide variety of files (essentially making it platform independent). This kind of software is relatively easy for auditors to learn, as the procedures will be intuitive to them with a little training.

Almost anything a fraud auditor would need to do to data to examine them for fraud can be done by one of the commands in DMS. The range of commands is extensive. Some of the premier tools in this category are ACL, IDEA, Panaudit, and Monarch. Because of the authors' experience with ACL, it will be used to demonstrate the capabilities of DMS for fraud audits.

CAAT METHODOLOGY

The key elements to CAAT methodology are basically four steps.

(1) The auditor needs to choose the appropriate CAAT, and obviously needs to have an adequate level of competence with that tool.

(2) The auditor must get all of the appropriate data. Usually the fraud auditor will have to go through the information systems (IS) department or personnel in order to get the data files. A word of caution concerning fraud and this process: If someone in IS is involved with a fraud, they can deliberately falsify the data downloaded from the operational system and given to the fraud auditor.

(3) The auditor must verify that she has the right data and that their integrity is intact. For example, it is possible for the IS person to make a mistake in downloading the data or misunderstand precisely what data need to be downloaded. Since it is critical to have the right data, this step is usually the most important of the steps involved. On a social note, IS people tend to be busy and unresponsive to auditors, especially fraud auditors. It is extremely helpful to become "friends" with the IS personnel, to treat them with courtesy, and so on.

(4) Then the auditor must import that data into ACL (or another CAAT), which usually is a simple process for the trained person. For example, most systems can export data files as text (also known as ASCII) files. ACL can then read that data in as a text file and create the ACL files using a wizard with little effort on the auditor's part. Many systems can export smaller files as Excel spreadsheets. ACL can read a variety of different

file types, including Excel, Comma Separated Value (CSV), Access, and the increasingly popular (for its format compatibility) eXtensible Markup Language (XML). Hint for importing Excel files into ACL: If auditors use the first row of a spreadsheet to label the column headings and then enter data contiguously beginning on the second row, ACL can read that Excel file easily using its wizard, even establishing the column headings and data types.

In regard to creating the ACL files, it might be beneficial to consider an ACL server approach. That is, have a super user create the ACL files on a server to which all auditors have access. By definition, a super user has the expertise in both computer technologies and ACL to create the files without a lot of assistance. Then the rest of the auditors, who are probably not super users, need only enough training to be able to use the files in ACL. That minimizes the level of expertise necessary in the internal audit function, external audit team, or fraud audit team in order to audit the data files adequately. It is much more doable to train all the users on ACL commands and audit procedures, then only rely on one or two super users to set up the more intricate work of creating the ACL files. Super users would also be useful for in-house training of auditors and for advanced ACL features, such as BATCH.

Once the tool is chosen (ACL in this chapter) and the data are imported, the auditor is ready to begin the fraud audit program. As previously discussed, any audit is based on the associated risks. With regard to fraud, the common risks in transactions and data are associated with red flags.

Red Flags

The fraud audit is critically dependent on the identification of red flags (see Chapter 5 for a detailed discussion of fraud schemes and their associated red flags). If the audit is reactive—that is, the auditor is hired to find a fraud—then these red flags would either be self-evident or would be developed in the fraud theory approach process (see Chapter 2). If the fraud audit is proactive or part of a regular internal or financial audit, then the red flags are not self-evident. In the latter case, an auditor would need to rely on established red flags in the antifraud professional literature, combined with possible red flags associated with the particular policies, procedures (especially computerized ones), and internal controls of the specific entity. Some reputable sources include Joe Wells's book *Occupational Fraud and Abuse*; the fraud flags listed in SAS No. 99, *Consideration of Fraud in a Financial Statement Audit*; and the red flags listed in the ISACA IS Audit Procedure *Irregularities and Illegal Acts* (#030.020.010) (see Exhibit 6.2). Fraud author and researcher Howard Schilit provides tools through his Center for Financial Research & Analysis, including the newly released "Industry Risk Assessment Profile Library," which is based on red flags of certain industries.[3]

Once the suggested red flags have been reviewed in the current context, the design of GAS/CAATs tests and procedures is rather easy to determine. For example, if the risk of a shell company fraud is high and the audit is a proactive one, then the auditor would use as many red flags as possible regarding a shell company scheme. From the antifraud literature, those red flags include: post office boxes (POB) for physical address, missing contact data, names similar to legitimate vendors, invalid or no EIN, and so forth. Then by thinking through the policies, procedures, and internal controls of accounts payable, other flags might come to the auditor's attention. For instance, if the entity has a policy that all vendors are required to provide an EIN from the Internal Revenue Service (IRS), then all vendors should have a valid value in that field. In the case of the latter, the test could be just to look for missing EINs or EINs that do not fit the format of a proper EIN (i.e., ##-#######). The results (one without an EIN or with an improperly formatted EIN) would be anomalies/exceptions. As the terms are used in this book, anomalies or exceptions have two possible explanations: error or fraud. The identified anomalies probably would need to be combined with other tests to determine if further investigation of that vendor is necessary.

Without the identification of applicable red flags, the fraud audit will end up looking for a needle in a haystack. As noted, CAATs are not really designed for this approach, nor should they be, as this shotgun approach ignores situational circumstances and known probabilities. Therefore, the adequate identification of a sufficient and relevant list of red flags is critical to the success of the fraud audit.

☐ Identify high-value credit notes, balances, and invoices.
☐ Report on gaps in the sequencing of invoices generated.
☐ Identify duplicate invoices, credits, or receipts.
☐ Determine credits, receipts, and invoices not in proper sequence or range.
☐ Report gaps in the sequence of generated invoices.
☐ Identify adjustments to discounts.
☐ Summarize large invoices without purchase orders, by vendor.
☐ Compare voucher or invoice amounts to purchase orders or contact amounts.
☐ Determine duplicate item or serial numbers.
☐ Determine percentage change in sales, price, and/or cost levels by product/vendor.
☐ Match inventory receipts with vendor ledger and report variances.
☐ Show items depreciated to cost in order to highlight assets greater than cost.
☐ Calculate turnover by inventory class and/or item.
☐ Match inventory receipts with vendor ledger amounts and report variances.
☐ Identify unusual delivery addresses.
☐ Identify items with high return or allowance rates.
☐ Extract all payroll checks where amount exceeds set amount (by category of employee).
☐ Identify persons on payroll with no time off for vacations or sick leave.
☐ Identify stale purchase orders, or purchase orders with only partial orders received.
☐ Identify purchases by ordering clerk for each vendor.
☐ Compare inventory levels and turnover rates.
☐ Check for split contract (same vendor, same day).
☐ Identify duplicate vendor numbers on master vendor file.
☐ Match vendor and employee names, addresses, and phone numbers.
☐ Test credit card balances against credit limits.
☐ Determine duplicate return transactions.
☐ Identify voided transactions followed by no sale.
☐ Identify items sold for less than the selling price.
☐ Calculate the number and amount of voids by sales clerk.
☐ Determine inventory day sales by store.
☐ Compare selling prices across stores.
☐ Compare products on work orders and sales orders for net demand analysis.
☐ Compare master planning orders to capacity to improve schedules.
☐ Identify items (labor, materials) charged to project that are already completed.
☐ Compute ratios such as cost of goods/revenue.
☐ Generate vendor cash activity summary to support rebate negotiations.
☐ Calculate market value of collateral for outstanding loans.
☐ Duplicate claims for the same time period.
☐ Identify duplicate invoices.
☐ Identify duplicate invoice addresses.
☐ Identify outstanding checks.
☐ Identify uncleared pending/clearing items in accounts.
☐ Determine cash over/short by sales clerk.
☐ Determine cash balances (overdrafts).
☐ Verify computer access controls are appropriate.
☐ Verify computer processing exceptions are followed up and missing tranactions are processed.
☐ Verify computer rerun analysis.
☐ Verify computer fault analysis.
☐ Verify computer usage analysis capacity planning, analysis, and management.

EXHIBIT 6.2   ISACA 030.020.010: Application of CAATS by Area

Structured Approach

Identifying individual red flags is generally just the beginning of gathering evidence of a fraud, especially in a proactive fraud audit. Chapter 5 discussed the need to have a structured approach to accumulating red flags. That is true whether the auditor uses a CAAT or not, but is probably easier when using a CAAT. The purpose or goal is to accumulate red flags in much the same manner as financial auditors accumulate misstatements. Misstatements may not be material in individual accounts, but it is possible they are material in the aggregate. That concept or theory is even more important in fraud audits because it is tempting to overlook an anomaly or red flag or to not even notice that one is present in the transaction, data, or document the auditor is handling. A fraud auditor should also consider accumulating red flags by some meaningful entity: vendor, customer, or employee. For example, if red flags were accumulated by employee and then examined across all employees, differences between the employees might reveal the fact that a fraud is being perpetrated.

CAAT and Fraud Audit Plan

To begin this process of classification and accumulation, the fraud auditor should gain an understanding of the data. Some of the CAAT's commands are intended to provide results for this purpose (e.g., PROFILE, STATS in ACL). Those commands are identified as GENERAL in Exhibit 6.3. The GENERAL commands fall under step 6, gaining an understanding of the data.

The STATS can be used to provide a quick overview of the data in a file before the detailed analysis begins (step 7). However, it might also reveal evidence of a fraud. For example, one fraud was discovered by using STATS. In ACL, STATS shows the average, standard deviation, absolute value, five highest values, and five lowest values for any numeric field. An auditor in this case ran STATS on the *Inventory Receipts* file and got the results shown in Exhibit 6.4.

EXHIBIT 6.3 Sample ACL Commands

Type	Command	Description
General	*PROFILE*	Maximum, minimum, total, absolute values (numeric field)
	SORT	Arrange a file in some sequence: e.g., check number, largest to smallest amount (invoices, etc.)
	STATS	Average, Std Dev, absolute, 5 highest and lowest values
	STRATIFY	By layers (e.g., sales invoice amounts)
Specific	*AGE*	Difference in dates: date invoices received to date paid
	BENFORD'S LAW	Natural occurrence of leading digits
	CLASSIFY	Classify (group) transaction data by vendor, customer, sales person, etc.
	DUPLICATES	Duplications: check numbers, invoice numbers, etc.
	FILTER/QUERY	Limited only by creativity, to search for anything
	GAPS	Gaps in a sequence: check numbers, invoice numbers, etc.
	JOIN	Two or more tables: e.g., vendors and employees to see if a vendor has an employee's address
	SORT	To look for anomalies in a data list: sequence exists where none should, or absence of sequence where it should be
Conventional	*AGE*	Aged accounts receivable trial balance
	CONFIRMATION	Standard confirmation of accounts receivable letters (or customized to fraud)
	SAMPLE	To take a statistical sample for substantive testing
Post	*BATCH*	Batch together multiple ACL tests to run automatically and consecutively, documenting the results in the LOG
	LOG	Automatically store the commands and results of ACL tests, which are easily exported to word processors, etc.

EXHIBIT 6.4 ACL STATS Example

	Number	Total	Average
Positive:	1,821	85,587	47
Zeroes:	0	0	0
Negative:	180	−470	−3
Totals:	2,001	85,117	43
Abs Value		86,057	
Range:		106	
Std Dev:		12.07	

Highest:	98 98 96 95 92
Lowest:	−8 −6 −3 −3 −3

How easy is it to spot the anomaly (exception)? How is it negative inventory? The auditor then proceeded to examine the cause behind the negative numbers and discovered that the inventory warehouse manager was entering negative receipts of inventory to cover up missing inventory. By making sure the numbers in the system matched the physical inventory, the manager was able to obtain a performance bonus. Therefore, in the process of gaining an understanding of the data, the fraud auditor came across evidence of impropriety.

In step 7, the fraud auditor would begin to look for *specific* anomalies or red flags, developed as discussed earlier. The ACL commands associated with these specific audit procedures are labeled as SPECIFIC in Exhibit 6.3.

For example, credit card companies use AGE to spot fraud perpetrated by their own employees. AGE actually can measure the difference between dates of fields. The fraud auditor developed an audit procedure based on these assumptions: If a credit card holder has not used her credit card for several months (e.g., 12), and if an employee of the company notices that the card is basically inactive, and if the employee were so inclined, she could charge expenditures to that card in the hopes that it would go unnoticed by the holder or the employer. Using AGE, the auditor identified all credit cards for which charges had been made recently but, prior to that time, there was at least 12 months of inactivity on the card. Then the auditor used CONFIRMATIONS to send a letter to these card holders to confirm whether they had authorized the charges. A significant number of the letters were returned because of bad addresses (the card holder had moved). Also, a number of the card holders replied that they had *not* authorized the charges. Together, those numbers represented over 50% of the total credit card holders tested.

Another example is worth noting regarding the use of Benford's law. Benford's law is a mathematical rule about the frequency of the various numbers as the leading digit or digits in a large number of random amounts. The law basically says that the leading digits do not occur randomly. Although one might think that the digits 1 through 9 would appear equally as the leading digit of a number (about 11% each), they do not. Proven mathematically to be true, the digit "1" appears about 30% of the time as the leading digit in a random and large set of numbers. The digit "2" appears about 18% of the time, and the percentage decreases down to 4% for the number "9."

A couple of illustrations are worth noting. First, if the company has a level of approval, and someone is abusing that level of approval to commit fraud, then the fraudster may have distorted the nature occurrence of leading digits for that data. A bank vice president (VP) died suddenly of a heart attack. In cleaning out his desk drawers, the company discovered numerous loans, the original papers, in his desk. A closer inspection found that the majority of the loans were made out to the same person, an acquaintance of the VP's. Those loans had very few payments made against them. The VP had managed to intercept late notices and hide the fictitious loans from the bank, and from its auditors—a Big Four accounting firm. The bank had a limit of what a loan officer could approve without bringing the loan proposal to the bank's loan committee. That approval level was $50,000. Each of the loans was for the same amount: $49,999.99.

This particular fraud may have been noticeable if a Benford's law test had been done on the loans file. Exhibit 6.5 presents a possible result (i.e., the result is based on the case, but the data were made up) of this test for this actual case. ACL could also have detected this fraud if the FILTER command was used to search for transactions.just below the approval level of $50,000.

The second case involves the well-publicized Equity Funding Fraud. When the chief executive officer (CEO) decided to commit fraud by creating bogus insurance policies and fraudulent accounts receivable based on the phony policies, he knew he needed a way to keep up with those policies. So the CEO simply used a "99" prefix to the phony policies in the policy number. Then, any time he saw a policy with the 99 prefix, he knew it was one of the phony ones. Because all of the policies were in the computer system, the computer helped the CEO perpetrate the fraud by identifying the real insurance policies from the phony ones. When the fraud became public, two-thirds of the $3 billion of accounts receivable was phony. A Benford's law test anytime during the seven years the fraud was being perpetrated would have been revealing. The "9" digit would have been off the scale (67% occurrence versus an expected 4%).

All of the other commands in this section are highly capable of detecting certain frauds. They can detect exceptions and anomalies, such as an authorized maker who is pulling checks from the bottom of the stack to write checks to herself. They can detect gaps and duplicates where none are expected, or not find them where they are expected. For example, if a test is run by vendor for sequencing of invoice numbers, and the auditor finds one vendor's list of invoice numbers are sequential, that appears to mean that we are its only customer. Why would we be the only customer? Perhaps because it is a shell vendor or pass-through vendor scheme.

The auditor may also want to use some of the traditional audit procedures, such as an aged accounts receivable trial balance using the AGE command. The other traditional commands are identified as CONVENTIONAL in Exhibit 6.3.

Finally, after the audit tests and procedures are complete, the auditor can do some special postaudit commands. These are identified as POST in Exhibit 6.3. For example, the fraud auditor probably would want to document his findings. The ACL command LOG can greatly assist this process. The auditor probably will also want to "save" most, if not all, of the tests and procedures that proved to be effective. This "macro" archive of ACL tests can be amended using the command BATCH. Thus the next time around, the auditor will be able to significantly reduce the time spent in creating the ACL tests and procedures. The auditor can also fine-tune the procedures next time very quickly, and thus the ACL batched procedures basically become programmable, with relative ease. The super user referred to earlier might perform this task.

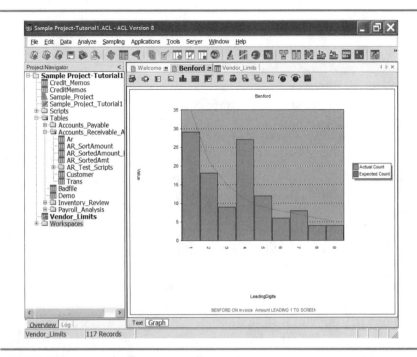

EXHIBIT 6.5 ACL Benford's Law Example

SUMMARY

There are significant benefits to employing CAATs, for both efficiency and effectiveness. Auditors can gain an advantage in performing their duties by becoming proficient in a CAAT tool, even if it is only one person from the audit group.

Fraud audits are particularly good subjects for the use of CAATs. For example, CAATS are adept at looking for exceptions or anomalies, which is what red flags of fraud often are. They also can examine 100% of the data, which is otherwise probably infeasible. The commands and procedures are compatible with the audit language and procedures, making the learning curve relatively short and certainly doable.

This chapter illustrated the range of tools available today and the general way these tools can serve fraud audits. These tools range from existing ones, such as Excel, to complicated statistical packages, such as SAS, to comprehensive data mining CAAT packages, such as ACL.

The chapter also illustrated the data mining tools by demonstrating some of the commands and how they could be applied to fraud audits, and fraud detection in particular. Specifically, the value of CAAT was shown in its ability to search 100% of the data and transactions for certain exceptions, anomalies, and fraud red flags.

In order to ensure successful usage of CAATs, the entity should employ the "champion" tactic. That is, select a super user—someone with the right set of skills and knowledge—to be the leader of the cause: making sure the CAAT is implemented and used. That person champions the cause by answering questions, training others, running interference with IT personnel in getting data, and even possibly setting up a server with data files that can be used to do the fraud audit.

With the focus on detecting fraud in today's business environment and the proliferation of computers, fraud auditors and forensic accountants must become competent in CAATs. That is not to say that every fraud auditor should be competent, but it certainly means that every auditor entity (fraud, internal, or financial auditors) should have at least one person who is sufficiently competent in CAATs/GAS, and the proper techniques that go with them, to be employ them as often as necessary. And today, their use is becoming more and more necessary.

ENDNOTES

1. A fairly exhaustive list is contained in an article by Nancy Bagranoff and Laurie Henry, "Choosing and Using Sarbanes-Oxley Software," *Information Systems Control Journal* Vol. II (2005), pp. 49–51.
2. A special thanks to Dr. Thomas Buckhoff for sharing this experience with the authors.
3. Available from Schiltt's research center web site: http://www.cfraonline.com.

CHAPTER 7

Fraud Prevention and Control

INTRODUCTION

In developing a fraud control system, it is very difficult to know what to protect and how to protect it if one does not first perform a risk assessment to see where the risk lies in the entity. That would include the assets with the most risk, the fraud schemes most likely to occur, and the residual risk considering what controls are in place to mitigate the risks present. Fraud prevention and risk assessment (see Chapter 8) both deserve a thorough discussion, so they are separated in this book. Because controls must be considered in the risk assessment, this book addresses prevention first. These two topics are highly interconnected.

The goal of any antifraud program is to prevent fraud, not just detect it. The old axiom of "An ounce of prevention is worth a pound of cure" is an understatement with regard to fraud. The passage of the Sarbanes-Oxley Act of 2002 (SOX) puts into law tenets to *prevent* fraud. Although detecting fraud is important, it obviously would be better if fraud could be mitigated or minimized—prevented to the degree possible. Detection is inevitably tied to prevention, and the two together provide the system of fraud control. This chapter presents the components of a successful fraud control system.

PERCEPTION OF DETECTION

Based on years of law enforcement and criminal justice experience, experts say the best deterrent to crime, including fraud, is the perception of detection. Because white-collar criminals who commit fraud tend to have some personal code of ethics, this technique is even more effective in preventing fraud than it is for "street" crimes. The fear of jail, humiliation, or loss of family ties is enough of a deterrent for many potential fraudsters to cause them to stop, think, and decide it is not worth the total cost. The best thing any entity can do to minimize fraud is to find an effective way to increase the perception of detection. Some ways to increase the perception of detection include:

- Surveillance
- Anonymous tips
- Surprise audits
- Prosecution
- Enforcement of ethics and fraud policies
- Catch me if you can!

Surveillance

In those places where assets are at high risk, such as mailrooms where mail that contains checks and/or cash is opened, surveillance cameras or other surveillance can be a good perception of detection method. If surveillance is going to be employed as a counter measure against fraud, it is best to announce it to the world that it is in place. A word of caution: One must make sure to monitor the surveillance in such a way that people will know someone is actually following up on suspicious activities. Unethical employees will test the effectiveness of surveillance to see if it is really monitored and used by someone to actually follow up on suspicious activities.

Anonymous Tips

This detection method was discussed in Chapter 5. Tips have been shown to be the best method to date in detecting frauds. However, they are also a prevention measure. The reason is simple. If employees know there is an anonymous tips system and that anyone who sees something suspicious can turn them in, then it begins to serve as a perception-of-detection preventive measure.

Surprise Audits

Internal audit really does serve some purpose and have some value in fraud detection. In fact, internal audit is the highest-ranked proactive method of detection. But surprise audits by either the internal audit function or hired fraud auditors are even more effective. Not only will these audits serve a similar purpose in detecting frauds, but the fact that the surprise audit is unannounced creates a perception of detection. Fraudsters do not know when the fraud auditor is going to show up, so they cannot prepare to fool the auditor. In fact, in at least one fraud that the authors know of, the announcement of a surprise audit that was fictitious (the internal auditor was attempting to play a joke) caused the manager of the business unit to confess to a fraud.

Prosecution

Enormous benefits can be gained by prosecuting fraudsters to the maximum extent of the law. It is true that there is some downside risk in a public trial, and even some risk that the prosecuting agency may fail to do its job effectively. But the upside is not merely obtaining justice for the single incident and justice for the fraudster. Prosecuting someone sends a strong message about perception of detection: If one commits a fraud and gets caught, this company is going to seek prosecution and perhaps imprisonment. Most experts agree that prosecution is *key* to maintaining an effective level of perception of detection.

Think of the signal that was sent in this case. A bank vice president (VP) stole about $5 million from his bank in fraudulent loans. When caught, the bank decided it was in its best interest to not prosecute. The VP was fired and never paid a penny back to the bank. So what would a rational VP of this bank think about working for the employer? Would she be deterred or would she decide that the fraudster VP had found a better retirement plan?

There are numerous stories of people who commit a fraud, do not get punished, and move on to commit another one at the next employer. This scenario is likely if a company chooses to not prosecute but rather just fire the employee. It seems we could learn from Mr. Spock in the *Star Trek II* movie where he deliberately entered the nuclear reactor room to fix it, at the expense of his own life. While

Spock was dying inside the room, Admiral Kirk asked him why he did it. Spock replied a famous philosophical quote: "The good of the many outweigh the good of the one or the few." The business world should take that philosophy to heart in dealing with fraudsters.

Enforcement of Ethics and Fraud Policies

The same philosophy is true for compliance with fraud policy, ethics policy, and corporate policy in handling frauds. A company should have determined beforehand what it would do if a fraud occurred; in particular, what penalties would be meted out for what kinds of frauds and levels of fraud. Then the company would need to make sure to follow through with its stated penalties for fraud. Failure to follow its own guidelines for punishment of frauds is worse than having no fraud policy at all.

Catch Me If You Can!

Oddly enough, perhaps the greatest perception of a detection measure is to catch a fraudster, prosecute him, and highly publicize what has been done. A recently busted fraudster can significantly increase the perception of detection, as it serves as a living example and reminder that this entity is serious, capable of detecting frauds, and willing to prosecute. Additionally, rewarding employees who contribute to detecting fraud contributes to an antifraud culture.

CLASSIC APPROACHES

A review of the classic approaches to the reduction of employee theft, fraud, and embezzlement is helpful in developing an effective fraud prevention and control program. Here are the classics:

- *Directive approach.* The directive approach is confrontational and authoritative. It says: "Don't steal. If you do, and we catch you, you'll be fired." When an entity does little or nothing to prevent fraud, it is probably taking this approach. If a fraud did occur and was detected, management would probably fire the employee—and probably would not prosecute the fraudster. Management probably also would be shocked that someone would perpetrate a fraud against the company.

■ *Preventive approach.* In the preventive approach, potential fraudsters are screened out using various means. Management could employ background checks to verify employment, check for a criminal record, examine credit reports, and/or check references. Psychological testing for honesty and integrity is another front-door screening mechanism. The purpose of these two screening policies is simply not to hire a potential fraudster up front. Under this approach, management could also use polygraph tests for existing employees to identify fraudsters.

Internal controls can be used in the preventive approach. Namely, segregation of duties can mitigate the risk of fraud at least to the point where management must override controls or persons must collude to commit fraud, which are always possibilities. Separation of duties requires constant oversight.

■ *Detective approach.* In the detective approach, management sets up accounting controls and an internal audit function to monitor potential frauds. The internal audit function periodically verifies the legitimacy of transactions and confirms the existence of assets. Between the periodic audits, management depends on the accounting controls to detect any fraud that might occur.

■ *Observation approach.* The observation approach relies on physical observation of assets and employees. Management monitors employee conduct for suspicious behaviors or activities. The level of stocks of valuable and portable goods is also monitored in person or by other means, such as cameras. The goods include valuable and portable inventory, cash, and other such assets. This approach also inspects outgoing parcels for accuracy and completeness.

■ *Investigative approach.* Based on investigative results, the investigative approach follows up on discrepancies. For example, the company would follow up on allegations of theft. For unfavorable, or certain favorable, variances in inventory, goods, materials, supplies, and product costs, the company would follow up to determine the nature and extent of the loss and who the likely culprits might be.

■ *Insurance approach.* This approach depends on adequate insurance coverage to cover losses that might occur due to a fraud. Although this approach clearly does not reduce employee theft, it does soften the financial blow when fraudulent losses occur.

But employee theft may occur even if a company adopts all of these classic approaches. Two types of frauds can always occur: collusion between two persons and management override of controls. Additionally, the nature of these frauds mean they can continue on a large scale undetected. That fact seems to be the experience of many firms today, as evidence by the results of the Association of Certified Fraud Examiners (ACFE) 1996, 2002, and 2004 Report to the Nation (RTTN), where each survey showed fraud costs were 6% of total revenues.[1] What other options are available to minimize the rate of fraud and the amount of loss from frauds? The best bet is to focus on the company's ethical climate and culture.

PREVENTION ENVIRONMENT

A key to successful fraud prevention is to look at the culture and try to change it, if necessary. Some activities and attitudes can help in achieving this goal. The important prevention elements that are discussed next are generally applied to an entity, and not necessarily directed toward a specific fraud.

Policies and Procedures

The prevention environment begins with the policies and procedures of the entity, more specifically the policies. It is from the policies that internal controls are developed. It is from the policies that actions and transactions are determined to be unethical and it is from those policies that it is determined how fraudsters or violations of the corporate culture will be treated. Therefore, the foundation for an antifraud culture and environment for any company serious about preventing fraud is a fraud policy and carefully crafted accounting policies.

SOX essentially requires publicly traded companies to have an ethics policy. Companies without a written ethics policy must state so in their 10-K forms and explain why they do not have one. A fraud policy is probably even more valuable in fraud prevention, as it becomes the source document for developing fraud prevention measures and an antifraud culture or climate.

To have an effective fraud policy, a company must:

- Design an antifraud program/policy.
- Define *frauds*.
- Describe incident reporting procedures.
- Describe investigation policies and procedures.
- Describe actions taken in fraud audit.
- Describe resolutions to frauds.
- Describe the analysis of evidence.
- Describe publication and communication of policy.
- Describe implementation of controls for antifraud.
- Describe testing of antifraud controls.
- Describe training.
- Describe proactive fraud audit measures.

But the creation of a written ethics or fraud policy is insufficient by itself. Effective systems include a means of communicating that policy adequately to all involved. An example would be to include ethics and fraud in employee orientation programs. Crucial to the success of the policy is a monitoring and compliance system. In research conducted on frauds and cooperatives, it was found when all three—policy, monitoring, and compliance—are present, fraud instances were significantly less than any other situation. Only about one-tenth of the entities with an ethics policy had any compliance mechanism in place.[2]

Ethics policies can also be based on values or principles. Instead of a detailed list of policies and procedures, a handful of values are selected as symbolic of the entity. With this approach, employees must buy into the values, which must be engrained in the culture and reinforced by actions.

Importantly, entities must consider the human element of the organization's culture. Although a myriad of factors influence culture, some are more important than others. The people present are one large component of culture. Building an antifraud culture that fits the people, the business operations, and the organization as a whole will ensure that fraud is mitigated to the degree possible.

Tone at the Top

Although it is a worn-out phrase, sometimes ignored, often misused, it is still a key to preventing fraud. If one reviews the major scandals of recent years, in almost every case, an executive was involved. That executive typically mistrusted people and kept as much of the financial affairs as possible secreted away from auditors. Thus there was clearly no antifraud tone at the top in Enron, WorldCom, Tyco, and others.

If key managers, and the board of directors where it exists, continually talk about fraud, communicate fraud policies, and encourage everyone to be involved in preventing and detecting fraud, then the entity eventually will develop an antifraud culture. Without the emphasis and support of key management, it is almost impossible to have such a culture.

Good Corporate Governance

Prior to the passage of SOX, research had shown that weak corporate governance was associated with all of the major financial frauds. For instance, the COSO Landmark Study (1998) studied 200 of the 300 fraud cases handled by the Securities and Exchange Commission (SEC) from 1987 to 1997.[3] The researchers found a distinctive pattern of weak boards for those entities investigated. The weakness included:

- Board members who were not independent
- Board dominated by insiders
- Board members with significant equity holdings
- Board members with little board experience
- Boards and audit committees that did not meet
- Audit committee members who knew little about finances or auditing
- No audit committee
- Audit committee did not meet
- Top executives involved in the frauds

Seventy-two percent of the cases named the chief executive officer (CEO), and 43% named the chief financial officer (CFO). In addition, according to *Wheel, Deal and Steal,* the vast majority of the boards are chaired by a former or current CEO.[4]

SOX addresses these issues by requiring more independence and expertise as well as a number of other activities that relate to good corporate governance. For instance, audit committees are responsible for implementing an anonymous tips and complaints system and a whistleblower system. SOX also requires the audit committee to hire external audit firms and set its fee for the financial audit. SOX recommends a high level of interaction between the audit committee with both internal and financial auditors. In summary, good corporate governance includes active, independent boards and audit committees. Since the purpose of SOX is to mitigate risk, those who created the legislation believed good corporate governance would do just that.

Overoptimistic Goals

Another common element of the major frauds was the overoptimistic goals set for corporate performance. Almost every goal and strategy of the company revolved around increasing profits to an abnormal level for that industry and/or that company. If the company's leaders, especially the board, can avoid setting unrealistic financial goals, there will be less pressure on the executives to cut corners to reach those financial goals. Balancing those goals with any negative impact they might have is a delicate task.

As discussed, one of the legs of the fraud triangle is *pressure (motivation),* and unrealistic financial goals automatically create this leg. As executives, board members can override controls, which is a second leg of the fraud triangle—*opportunity.* That situation means only the executive's ethics (*rationalization*—the third and final leg) will prevent that executive from committing a financial fraud.

PREVENTION MEASURES

Outside of the general (environmental, cultural, and corporate) prevention measures, many specific prevention measures can be employed to minimize fraud. The key employees—those who have control or access over valuable and portable assets such as cash or checks—need to be the object of prevention measures and fraud countermeasures. A company should consider the appropriate prevention measures that would hold these employees accountable for handling valued assets.

Surveillance

Surveillance increases the perception of detection. Although it is a detection measure, it does serve as a prevention measure if it is highly publicized and then monitored correctly. Cameras in key places where valuable portable assets are accessible could be an effective prevention measure.

Invigilation

A variation of surveillance is invigilation. In invigilation, the fraud auditor creates a pristine environment that should be fraud-free. That is, it is a high profile, well-staffed fraud audit. Because employees will be very careful to not commit fraudulent activities during such a time, the invigilation serves as a benchmark of what the entity *should* be earning in revenues. By analyzing the revenues during the invigilation against other time periods, a fraud auditor can determine if frauds are occurring regularly outside the invigilation.

Regular Audits

The fact that auditors are coming around on a regular basis can serve as a prevention measure. Again, this measure would increase the perception of detection, and that is why it would serve as a prevention measure. By its nature, regular audits are detection measures. However, if the auditors use some effective audit tools and techniques to look for fraud aggressively, those audits will also serve as prevention measures. A key to these effective audits is to review and analyze anomalies.

In at least a couple of the major financial frauds of recent years, the internal audit function was crippled and not allowed to do anything serious with financial information, but kept busy with other kinds of audits. The CEOs for those companies were taking no chances that some rogue internal auditor might stumble across their scams. That happened where one internal auditor came in late at night and secretly examined financial records to which she was not allowed access during the day by the senior executives. Eventually she uncovered the financial fraud and exposed the fraudster CEO.

A case illustrates just how important a prevention device regular audits can be. A small university newspaper office had one accountant who did all of the accounting. A retired accounting professor was conducting regular audits of the newspaper accounts. In April of a certain year, the retired professor notified the university president that this year would be his last audit. He suggested that the president find a replacement or put an internal audit function into place. Up until this time, the university did not have an internal audit function. In mid-October, a university VP got a call from the newspaper printing vendor. The vendor representative said the company was not going to print the next issue of the university newspaper because it had not been paid in some time. The VP checked into the records and found the accounting clerk had stolen thousands of dollars. Oddly enough, she began to steal in May of that year. Clearly the regular audit had served as a perception-of-detection measure for her, but once removed, she was able to rationalize the fraud.

Surprise Audits

Although regular audits serve as a prevention measure, surprise audits serve even better. Not knowing when the auditors are coming can psychologically wear on a person.

Periodic Fraud Audits

They may not be feasible, but periodic fraud audits would surely increase the perception of detection. Bringing in experts to conduct fraud audits generally only leads to good things. Even if they do not find fraud, they probably will find ways to improve the entity's antifraud measures.

Background Checks

One potentially effective prevention measure is to use background checks for key employees. Although a background check can reveal potential problems, it is not a 100% effective means of identifying potential fraudsters. A background check could reveal a criminal record and/or high debt. Either of them would be justification to not hire the person. The high debt is evidence that the *pressure* (economic or financial pressure in this cases) leg of the fraud triangle is already present. The criminal record shows the history of committing crimes before. However, according to the ACFE 2004 RTTN, only 12% of those fraudsters caught had a prior conviction for a fraud-related offense.

Internal Controls

The fraud triangle includes *opportunity*, which, as discussed in Chapter 1, is basically a synonym for internal controls. Of the three legs, a fraud auditor or professional has little ability to affect *pressure* or *rationalization*. Those aspects happen predominantly in one's mind. They are difficult to observe directly for the same reason. Therefore, internal control is the best place to focus as an auditor if one wishes to employ prevention measures.

Historically, the most common flaw in internal controls is no segregation of duties where there should be. Other internal controls include:

- Proper authorization procedures
- Adequate documentation, records, and audit trail
- Physical control over assets and records
- Independent checks on performance
- Monitoring of controls

If SOX is truly a compilation of best practices, then section 404 of SOX is the best solution in an attempt to minimize fraud. Section 404 requires annual evaluations of the internal controls by management, within 90 days of the audit date, and an opinion from the financial auditors on that evaluation. The fact that this evaluation is annual brings focus and improvements to internal controls. The fact that financial auditors opine on it adds to the effectiveness of the process. And improved internal controls have the potential to prevent fraud in the first place.

ACCOUNTING CYCLES

One way to address prevention measures is to examine the accounting business processes in their natural cycles. Considering some of the common characteristics of frauds in these areas is way to develop effective prevention measures therein. Here we present examples of what can be done. Related concepts are addressed further in Chapter 9.

Generalizations

First, it should be noted how accounting transactions and cycles are specific to any given organization. The specificity can be due to the industry, strategy, size, culture, organizational structure, capital structure, and various other factors. The important fact to glean from this is that to prevent or detect fraud, one must understand the underlying processes and the situational environment. No frauds occur within a box.

Organizational size is one of the most important factors to consider in fraud control. Size greatly impacts segregation of duties, a critical area to fraud prevention and detection. Size is also a factor when it comes to the type and amount of fraud committed (as noted in Chapter 4). Size is a factor when it comes to the control method; large organizations are innately more complex, and therefore more difficult to control in most aspects, but have more control resources to expend. The opposite is true for smaller organizations. This generalization does not always hold true. For example, segregation of duties is hard to implement in small organizations as a preventive control but is easier to detect as the organizational structure is generally much thinner and more tightly connected. Again, the critical point here is to understand the organizational context and the fraud environment factors at hand.

Although each organization's accounting transactions and cycles differ, on some level they are the same. Only a handful of basic accounting cycles exist. Though fraudulent transactions therein take on many forms, their substance is the same. (See Chapter 9 for AIS and more on cycles.)

Sales Cycle

One common scheme in the sales cycle is *lapping*. For a person to carry on a lapping scheme for an extended period of time, she cannot afford to take more than a day or so at a time off work. Two possible prevention measures for lapping are: (1) forced rotation of duties and (2) forced taking of vacation. Segregation of duties can help prevent frauds such as *larceny* and *write-off schemes*. From a detection standpoint, careful observation is the best monitoring technique. Employees who "hold their cards close to their chest" or are reluctant to undergo inspections, audits, and the like can be guilty of lapping. In many cases, a simple independent authorization step needs to be added to the business process.

Purchases Cycle

In the purchases cycle, the highest percentage of frauds revolve around fraudulent disbursements. One common fraud is a *shell company*. To prevent this fraud, an independent party needs to add vendors to the authorized list. Again, many fraud schemes could be stymied by segregation of duties, often a simple independent authorization step. This measure should help prevent *check tampering, false voids*, and *false refunds*, for example. Transactions with related parties, both in prevention and detection controls, should be carefully scrutinized, as this situation is another common area for fraud in disbursements. From a detection standpoint, the use of computer-assisted accounting technology (CAATs; see Chapter 6) can automate common signs of fraudulent payments.

Payroll Cycle

In the payroll cycle, there are some common schemes to consider. For example, *ghost employees* are a common fraud scheme in payroll. An independent party could be used to add employees to the authorized payroll file. Another prevention method is to cross-check payroll against human resource (HR) records, if possible. A ghost employee will be in the payroll but not the HR file. If done properly, this cross-check would detect the first occurrence and thus serve as a prevention measure. Forced rotation of duties and vacations in the payroll manager area is probably a good prevention measure as well (ghost employees).

Notably, many organizations have outsourced at least some of the payroll function in order to cut costs. This decision can be a dangerous area for fraud control. One of the largest payroll outsourcers in the United States has been found to have repetitive instances of fraud. Any organization outsourcing this function should require a *SAS 70 Type II* report (which requires independent evaluation of the *design and operating effectiveness* of internal controls) as a fraud prevention measure. That report should be scrutinized by business process and systems owners. SAS 70 audits also aid in the evaluation of processes, controls, and financial data in the 404 and financial audits, which often reveal potential improvements to be made in the control system.

Another critical point is the attention to people in and associated with the organization. HR, of course, is highly focused on getting the right people and, after all, *people commit fraud*. A thorough hiring process can be an effective fraud prevention technique.

As noted, detection techniques would ideally include CAATs for any disbursement since these frauds are usually easily visible and detectable in the data. When CAATs are not possible, monitoring becomes essential. In the end, the key is to ensure any exceptions (anomalies, problems, etc.) found in monitoring are pursued, resolved, and documented for retention. Strong, self-learning antifraud programs will study exceptions over time and cyclically implement them into the fraud prevention and detection control system.

SUMMARY

It is obviously more desirable to prevent fraud than to detect it after it occurs. There are a limited number of prevention methods (e.g., perception of detection) an entity can employ, but they are essential to a fraud-free environment. There are environmental issues that can enhance those preventive methods. A careful analysis of the business processes in the accounting cycle provide valuable input into preventive measures. Together, the counter measures and concepts herein should enable auditors to assist management in developing an effective anti-fraud program that can minimize frauds.

ENDNOTES

1. ACFE, "Report to the Nation," Austin, TX: 1996, 2002, and 2004.
2. Singleton, T., Messina, F., and Turpen, R. "Waving the Red Flag," *Rural Cooperatives*, Volume 70, Number 4 (July-August 2003), pp. 13–14.
3. COSO, Landmark Study on Fraud in Financial Reporting, 1998.
4. Daniel Quinn Mills, *Wheel, Deal, and Steal: Deceptive Accounting, Deceitful CEOs, and Ineffective Reforms* (Upper Saddle River, NJ: Financial Times Prentice Hall, 2003).

CHAPTER 8

Fraud Risk Assessment

INTRODUCTION

Since Enron and other frauds, there has been a significant focus on fraud, internal controls, and risk assessment—all of which are interrelated. The passage of Sarbanes-Oxley Act in 2002 (SOX) brought both more attention to these issues and put many tenets related to them into federal law. The Securities and Exchange Commission (SEC), and its accounting arm the Public Companies Accounting Oversight Board (PCAOB), have been focused on these issues. The Committee on Sponsoring Organizations (COSO) has also made significant efforts in the area of risk assessment, producing its COSO model for enterprise risk assessment.

The heart of an effective internal controls system and the effectiveness of an antifraud program are both contingent on an effective risk assessment. The fraud risk assessment is dependent on the fraud concepts (flags, cycles and accounting information system) covered in Chapters 4 through 7 and Chapter 10. This chapter discusses the risk assessment concepts and tools to aid in that process.

Technical Literature and Risk Assessment

Much of the technical literature for auditors suggests or outright dictates that audits start with a risk assessment. *On one level, section 404 of SOX is simply a risk assessment for financial reporting.* Additionally, the PCAOB's Auditing Standard No. 2 (AS2), *An Audit of Internal Control over Financial Reporting Performed in Conjunction with an Audit of Financial Statements,* dictates the SEC guidelines for satisfying section 404 of SOX and includes information on conducting a risk assessment. AS2 includes a recommendation that auditors use some internal control model to perform the required management evaluation of internal controls. Broadly speaking, PCAOB standards are infused with language, content, and suggestions regarding risk assessment.

The American Institute of Certified Public Accountants (AICPA) adopted Statement on Auditing Standards (SAS) No. 99, *Consideration of Fraud in a Financial Statement Audit*, which provides guidance for financial auditors, including brainstorming during the planning phase, and forced recognition of certain fraud techniques, such as revenue inflation. More broadly, the AICPA standard requires consideration of a host of organization-specific factors, such as industry, strategy, and so forth. Auditors are required to adjust the nature, timing, and extent of audit procedures if the circumstances warrant it, based on a risk assessment during the brainstorming step.

The Institute of Internal Auditors (IIA) promotes the idea all of the internal audit function audits and activities should begin with a risk assessment (e.g., sections 2010 and 2600 of *Standards of Professional Practice in Internal Audit* (SPPIA). The Information Systems Audit and Control Association (ISACA) also has the same requirement in its technical literature. Statement on Information Systems Auditing Standards (SISAS) 5, *Use of Risk Assessment in Audit Planning*, outlines certain requirements related to fraud for information technology audits. Many other ISACA standards address risk assessment as well, most notably SISAS 8, *Audit Considerations for Irregularities*.

Factors to Consider

The probability of fraud, theft, or embezzlement in any work environment is a product of the personality of the executive and employees, the working conditions, the effectiveness of internal controls, and the level of honesty therein (the organizational culture or environment). Different perspectives should be included and/or examined in the risk assessment process.

Corporate Environment Factors   Employee fraud, theft, and embezzlement are more prevalent in some organizations than in others. Conventional wisdom among members of the audit and security communities suggests that the organizations most vulnerable are those with the weakest management, accounting, and security controls. Organizations that are most vulnerable to employee occupational fraud and abuse can also be

EXHIBIT 8.1   Corporate Fraud Environment: Potential for Fraud
Source: Jack Bologna, *Forensic Accounting Review* (1985).

	High Fraud Potential	Low Fraud Potential
Management Style	Autocratic Profit focused	Participative Customer focused

Management Orientation	Low trust
	X theory
	Power driven
	Management by crisis
	Issues and personal
	  differences are skirted
	  or repressed
		High trust
		Y theory
		Achievement driven
		Management by objective
		Issues and personal
		  differences are confronted
		  and addressed openly

Management Structure and Controls	Bureaucratic Regimented Inflexible Imposed controls Many-tiered, vertical	Collegial Systematic Open to change Self-controlled Flat structure, horizontal

CEO Characteristics	Swinger
	Braggart
	Self-interested
	Driver
	Insensitive to people
	Feared
	Insecure
	Gambler
	Impulsive
	Tight-fisted
	
	Number- and things-
	  oriented
	Profit seeker
	Vain
	Bombastic
	Highly emotional
	
	Partial
	Pretends to be more than
	  he/she is
		Professional
		Decisive
		
		Fast-paced
		Friendly
		Respected by peers
		Secure
		Risk taker
		Thoughtful
		Generous with personal time
		  and money
		Products and market
		  oriented
		Builder
		Self-confident
		Helper
		Composed, calm, deliberate,
		  even disposition
		Fair
		Knows who, what, and
		  where he/she is

Authority	Centralized, reserved by
	  top management
	Rigid rules strongly
	  enforced
		Decentralized, delegated to
		  all levels
		Reasonable rules fairly
		  enforced

Planning	Centralized Short range	Decentralized Long range

EXHIBIT 8.1   *(continued)*

	High Fraud Potential	Low Fraud Potential
Performance	Measured quantitatively and on a short-term basis	Measured both qualitatively and quantitatively, and on a long-term basis
	Critical feedback	Positive feedback
	Negative feedback	Supportive feedback
Reporting	Routine reports only	Exception reporting
	Everything documented—a rule for everything	Adequate documentation, but not burdensome—some discretion allowed
	Formal, written, stiff, pompous, ambiguous internal communications	Informal, oral, clear, friendly, open, candid internal communications
Primary Management Concerns	Preservation of capital	Human, then capital and technological asset utilization
	Profit maximization	Profit optimization
Reward System	Punitive	Reinforcing
	Penurious	Generous
	Politically administered	Fairly administered
	Mainly monetary	Recognition, promotion, added responsibility, choice assignments, plus money
Business Ethics	Ambivalent: rides the tides	Clearly defined and regularly followed
Values and Beliefs	Economic, political	Social, spiritual
	Self-centered	Group-centered
Internal Relationships	Highly competitive, hostile	Friendly, competitive, supportive
External Relationships/ Competitors	Hostile	Professional
Peer Relationships	Hostile, aggressive, contentious	Cooperative, friendly
Success Basis/Formula	Works harder	Works smarter
Human Resource Problems	High turnover	Not enough promotional opportunities for all the talent
	Burnout Grievances Absenteeism	
Financial Concerns	Cash flow shortage	Opportunities for new investments
Company Loyalty	Low	High
Growth Pattern	Sporadic	Consistent, steady

distinguished from those that are less vulnerable by the environmental and cultural contrasts shown in Exhibit 8.1.

Internal Factors   Internal factors that enhance the probability of fraud, theft, and embezzlement include:

Inadequate Rewards	• Pay • Fringe benefits • Recognition • Job security • Job responsibilities
Inadequate Management Controls	• Failure to articulate and communicate minimum standards of performance and personal conduct • Ambiguity in job roles, duties, responsibilities, and areas of accountability
Lack of or Inadequate Reinforcement and Performance Feedback Mechanisms	• Failure to counsel and take administrative action when performance levels or personal behavior falls below acceptable standards
Inadequate Support	• Lack of adequate resources to meet mandated standards
Inadequate Operational Reviews	• Lack of timely or periodic audits, inspections, and follow-through to ensure compliance with company goals, priorities, policies, procedures, and governmental regulations
Lax Enforcement of Disciplinary Rules	• Ambiguous corporate social values and ethical norms
Fostering Hostility	• Promoting or permitting destructive interpersonal or interdepartmental competitiveness

Other Motivational Issues	• Inadequate orientation and training on legal, ethical, and security issues
	• Inadequate company policies with respect to sanctions for legal, ethical, and security breaches
	• Failure to monitor and enforce policies on honesty, loyalty, and fairness
	• General job-related stress or anxiety

RISK ASSESSMENT PROCESS AND DOCUMENTATION

Leader(s)

The risk assessment process should include an appropriate person or group, and ideally include a team. For organizational management, the appropriate person normally would be someone from the internal audit function, if one exists. If not, the next best alternative is an appropriate consultant. The value of having a person experienced and proven to be effective in assessing risk involved with any risk assessment function cannot be overstated.

Team

The team should be chosen carefully. Although it should start with the internal expert and/or consultant, it must include a broad cross-section of the entity. That cross-section should involve different levels of the entity, especially levels of management. The team should represent all of the major business units, business processes, key positions, and perspectives necessary to provide a quality risk assessment. People who think creatively, reason logically, understand the business and industry well, and can effectively play devil's advocate should be sought, regardless of their position.

Documenting risk assessments is critical, most particularly because the documentation can be reviewed afterward when the risk as assessed has or has not been realized. Documentation can then serve as a learning tool for more effective assessments and preventive measures. Documentation also establishes accountability for persons involved in the process. Several tools can be used to conduct the risk assessment, which would serve a dual purpose of documenting it as well. Exhibit 8.2 provides some checklists to serve as examples of how to organize a risk assessment.

Brainstorming

The risk assessment process is not altogether different from other business decision-making issues. One common management technique for group decision making is to use brainstorming. In fact, SAS No. 99 requires financial auditors to use brainstorming at the beginning of the audit, during the planning phase. Brainstorming is a key success factor in conducting an effective risk assessment. The brainstorming team should be a cross-sectional representation of the entity being assessed as just described.

Frequency

Risk assessment should be conducted regularly, probably every 12 to 24 months. With the requirements of SOX section 404, every year would be congruent with internal control evaluation necessary to comply with section 404. Performing this evaluation on a timely basis is not easy and usually does not happen.

One thing is sure: Timely section 404 evaluations can improve 404 report results and can better strengthen the internal control system. The timeliness and overall quality of management's evaluations speaks to its culture, which affects any audit. Timely evaluations from a section 404 audit perspective allow management time to remediate controls, because in the 404 report, the external auditor expresses an opinion on control *design* and *operating effectiveness*. Basically, management can provide some time to remediate controls that can potentially be done so appropriately in order for the financial auditors to be able to accept them as reasonable in design and operating effectively.

The more often and timely management performs its evaluation, the stronger the internal control will become. Management's evaluation and audit results should stimulate appropriate reactions o strengthen controls where there is room for improvement. Financial and 404 audit reports are, for public companies, in the public domain, and the investing public market will judge companies on said results.

RISK MANAGEMENT CHECKLISTS AND DOCUMENTATION

The checklist shown in Exhibit 8.2 is designed to assist accountants in assessing and managing the risk of fraud in their organizations and those of their clients. Generally, all "No" answers require investigation and follow-up, the results of which should be documented. Where there is such additional documentation, the purpose of the "Ref" column is to cross-reference the checklist to the appropriate working paper (or to the notes on the reverse).

This checklist is intended for general use only. Using the checklist does not guarantee fraud prevention or detection, and the checklist is not intended as a substitute for audit or similar procedures. If fraud prevention is an especially vital concern or if fraud is suspected, a specialist's advice should be sought.[1]

Fraud Schemes Checklist

Another approach to risk assessment is to use an appropriate taxonomy of fraud schemes and do an audit-focused risk assessment. For example, the Association of Certified Fraud Examiners (ACFE) fraud

	Yes	No	N/A	Ref

1. Does the organization have an adequate level of fraud awareness and are appropriate policies in place to minimize fraud risk? Specifically:

  a. Generic risk factors

    ☐ *Has each employee been assigned a maximum "opportunity level" to commit fraud; for each employee, has management asked itself: "What is the maximum amount of which this employee could defraud the organization, and does this represent an acceptable risk?"*   ( ) ( ) ( ) _____

    ☐ *Has a "catastrophic" opportunity level been set; that is, has management asked, "Have we ensured that no single employee—or group of employees in collusion—can commit a fraud that would place the organization in imminent risk of survival?"*   ( ) ( ) ( ) _____

    ☐ *Is it the organization's policy to immediately dismiss any employee who is found to have committed a fraud?*   ( ) ( ) ( ) _____

    ☐ *Is it the organization's policy to report all frauds to the authorities and press charges?*   ( ) ( ) ( ) _____

    ☐ *For any and all frauds that the company has experienced in the past, have the reasons that led to the fraud been evaluated and corrective action taken?*   ( ) ( ) ( ) _____

  b. Managing individual risk Factors (i.e., to promote moral behavior and minimize the motivation to commit fraud)

    ☐ *Does the organization have a corporate mission statement that includes as an objective good corporate citizenship (i.e., maintaining good standing in the community)?*   ( ) ( ) ( ) _____

    ☐ *Does the organization have a written code of ethics and business conduct?*   ( ) ( ) ( ) _____

    ☐ *Does the organization conduct ethical and security training for new employees with periodic updates for existing employees?*   ( ) ( ) ( ) _____

    ☐ *Does management set the right example? Does it follow the corporate mission statement, code of ethics and business conduct, and other organization policies, and do the employees clearly see it doing so?*   ( ) ( ) ( ) _____

EXHIBIT 8.2   Risk Management Checklist

	Yes	No	N/A	Ref

☐ *Does the corporate culture avoid characteristics that promote unethical behavior (e.g., high or even hostile competitiveness within the organization, pushing employees to burnout, rigid and/or petty policies, or overcentralization of authority)?*   ( ) ( ) ( ) _____

☐ *When hiring, does the organization, to the extent possible, seek out individuals of high moral character and weed out those of low moral character?*   ( ) ( ) ( ) _____

☐ *For especially sensitive positions, are screening and/or testing procedures used (e.g., psychological testing, drug testing, lie detector tests where legal)?*   ( ) ( ) ( ) _____

☐ *Does the organization provide and/or encourage counseling for employees with personal problems (e.g., alcohol and drug abuse)?*   ( ) ( ) ( ) _____

☐ *Does the organization have fair employee relations and compensation policies (e.g., salaries, fringe benefits, performance appraisal, promotions, severance pay)? Do these policies compare favorably with competitors' and promote an environment that minimizes disenchantment and similar motivations to commit fraud?*   ( ) ( ) ( ) _____

☐ *Are fair mechanisms in place for dealing with employee grievances?*   ( ) ( ) ( ) _____

☐ *As a feedback mechanism on its policies with respect to employee relations, does the organization conduct exit interviews of departing employees?*   ( ) ( ) ( ) _____

c. **Management awareness**

☐ *Overall, does management exhibit an awareness of fraud and its possible manifestations: signs of employee problems such as drug addiction and low-paid employees who suddenly appear with trappings of wealth?*   ( ) ( ) ( ) _____

EXHIBIT 8.2   *(continued)*

	Yes	No	N/A	Ref

2. Does the organization have an adequate system of internal controls? Specifically:

a. Fraud integral to internal controls
   ☐ *Has the need for fraud prevention been explicitly considered in the design and maintenance of the system of internal controls?* ( ) ( ) ( ) _____

b. Control over physical and logical access
   ☐ *Does the organization have a policy and practice of locking doors, desks, and cabinets after hours and when unattended, especially for areas with valuable assets, including files and personnel and payroll records, checks and other accounting documents, customer and vendor lists, corporate strategies, marketing plans, and research?* ( ) ( ) ( ) _____
   ☐ *Does the organization have a policy and practice of using IDs and passwords for general computer access?* ( ) ( ) ( ) _____
   ☐ *For sensitive files and applications, does the computer system require additional access controls? Does the access control of each user ID limit him/her access? Are there additional layer(s) of access control for remote access (i.e., smart cards, temporary PINs, biometrics, etc.)?* ( ) ( ) ( ) _____
   ☐ *Does the organization have a stated and enforced policy that access is restricted to those requiring it to perform their job functions, including a strict policy against employees allowing access to unauthorized personnel by lending keys, sharing passwords, and so on?* ( ) ( ) ( ) _____
   ☐ *For especially sensitive areas, are there additional computerized security and/or electronic surveillance systems?* ( ) ( ) ( ) _____
   ☐ *To an impartial observer, does the workplace appear to have adequate access controls?* ( ) ( ) ( ) _____

c. Job descriptions
   ☐ *Does the organization have written and specific job descriptions?* ( ) ( ) ( ) _____
   ☐ *Do employees and managers adhere to them?* ( ) ( ) ( ) _____

EXHIBIT 8.2 *(continued)*

	Yes	No	N/A	Ref

☐ Does the company have an organization chart that reflects and is consistent with the employee job descriptions? ( ) ( ) ( ) _____

☐ Are incompatible duties segregated (i.e., handling of valuable assets, especially cash and related records)? ( ) ( ) ( ) _____

☐ Is the purchasing function properly segregated (e.g., to ensure that one individual cannot requisition goods or services, approve and make the related payment, and access accounts payable records)? ( ) ( ) ( ) _____

☐ Are especially sensitive duties duplicated (i.e., the double-signing of checks over a specified amount)? ( ) ( ) ( ) _____

☐ Do job descriptions specify that annual vacations must be taken? ( ) ( ) ( ) _____

☐ Overall, has the process of formulating job descriptions been an integrated one, giving adequate consideration to the importance of fraud prevention? ( ) ( ) ( ) _____

d. **Regular accounting reconciliations and analyses**

☐ Bank reconciliations, for all accounts? ( ) ( ) ( ) _____

☐ Accounts receivable reconciliations (month to month, general ledger to subledger)? ( ) ( ) ( ) _____

☐ Accounts payable reconciliations (month to month, general ledger to subledger)? ( ) ( ) ( ) _____

☐ Variance analysis of general ledger accounts (budget to actual, current year versus prior year)? ( ) ( ) ( ) _____

☐ Vertical analysis of profit and loss accounts (i.e., as a percentage of sales, against historical and/or budget standards)? ( ) ( ) ( ) _____

☐ Detailed sales and major expense analysis (i.e., by product line or geographic territory)? ( ) ( ) ( ) _____

e. **Supervision**

☐ Do supervisors and managers have adequate fraud awareness? Are they alert to the possibility of fraud whenever an unusual or exceptional situation occurs, such as when supplier or customer complains about its account? ( ) ( ) ( ) _____

EXHIBIT 8.2   (continued)

	Yes	No	N/A	Ref

□ *Do supervisors and managers diligently review the work of their subordinates (e.g., accounting reconciliations), and, where appropriate, even have the employee re-perform the work?* ( ) ( ) ( ) _____

□ *For smaller businesses or where division of duties is not possible, is close supervision in place so as to compensate for the lack of separation?* ( ) ( ) ( ) _____

□ *Is supervisory or management override (a manager or supervisor taking charge of, altering or otherwise interfering in the work of a subordinate) prohibited, and are others in the hierarchy alert to this situation as a fraud "red flag"?* ( ) ( ) ( ) _____

f. Audit

□ *Is there an internal audit function?* ( ) ( ) ( ) _____

□ *Does the internal audit function perform regular checks to ensure that fraud prevention mechanisms are in place and operating as intended?* ( ) ( ) ( ) _____

□ *Are external audits performed on a regular basis (quarterly for larger businesses)?* ( ) ( ) ( ) _____

□ *Does management fully cooperate with external auditors with respect to its work in general and fraud matters in particular (i.e, through the audit committee)?* ( ) ( ) ( ) _____

3. Has the organization addressed the following fraud prevention issues?

□ *Promoting an ethical environment?* ( ) ( ) ( ) _____
□ *Risk financing?* ( ) ( ) ( ) _____

EXHIBIT 8.2 *(continued)*

tree could be used to determine at least the initial list of fraud schemes. The columns of this form of risk assessment include (see Exhibit 8.3):

- The fraud scheme
- An assessment of inherent risk for that fraud in the particular entity or business process
- The factor internal controls has in mitigating that risk
- The "residual risk" left over after the mitigation of existing internal controls related to this fraud scheme in this entity or business process
- Business process, where the scheme is likely to occur, if it does occur
- Red flags, which could be used to detect this scheme

Fraud Schemes	Inherent Risk	Controls Assessment	Residual Risk	Business Processes	Red Flags
General Antifraud					
Fraudulent Statements					
Financial:					
Overstate Revenues					
Timing Differences					
Fictitious Revenues					
Concealed Liabilities					
Improper Disclosures					
Improper Asset Valuation					
Asset/Revenue Understated					

EXHIBIT 8.3   Fraud Schemes Risk Checklist

Different Entities to Assess   If an organization is large enough, a single risk assessment may not be as useful as separate risk assessments. In this case, it is recommended that a different assessment and team be used for each major business unit, each significant business process that crosses business units, the corporate unit (executives, etc.), and any other entity or element that the leaders and team identify. It is possible the company is so large that different layers may be necessary: for instance, business units rolled up to subsidiaries, rolled up to corporate, where higher risks are rolled up with specifics as to the unit associated with the specific risk. A potentially more effective, though more challenging, way to assess risk at a high level in large organizations is by business processes, as these can more accurately reflect the fraud risks present.

Fraud Schemes   There are a variety of ways to determine the fraud schemes to list in the first column of Exhibit 8.3 (Inherent Risk). However, one should start with some established taxonomy (see Chapter 1) and add or delete from that list as needed. Then, using other taxonomies, or good judgment about specific schemes that are risks to this particular entity, one should make any necessary additions or deletions. Herein is the value of using brainstorming—teams using shared criteria to make sure that important schemes are not missed and that irrelevant schemes are not considered (at least for specific entities certain fraud schemes may be irrelevant). Once the list is compiled, the team and leaders should evaluate each line item using the remaining columns.

Measures and Relationships   Measuring risks in a quantitative sense is usually quite difficult. Some base must be used as a corollary to the potential losses of a *possible* fraud. What is a relevant, reliable, and representative indication of the risk needing measurement? Such a determination should be made and agreed on by the *team* according to shared criteria. The critical and difficult job of measuring risks is again a testament to the importance of selecting a diversified, organization-encompassing team able to make logical decisions during the risk assessment process.

Inherent Risk   The team should determine what the inherent risk is for this fraud scheme for this entity or business process. The assessment could be a percentage (1 to 100%) or simply low, medium, or high. A number of factors can be considered here, some of which are industry, strategy, market volatility, and organizational structure.

Controls Assessment   Using the auditors and other key people on the team, one should determine what controls are in place to mitigate the specific fraud scheme. The assessment would, of course, match the method of assessing inherent risk (percentage or tier). One must be sure to consider that people in key positions can best evaluate weaknesses in internal controls and risks; but those same persons are potentially the ones to commit fraud in the given area.

Residual Risk   A simple mathematical function of subtracting the level of control mitigation from the inherent risk will leave the residual risk. Again, it would take the form of whatever was chosen for inherent risk. Residual risk will inevitably require one of two responses: no action, as the remaining risk is accepted, or action to remediate through additional prevention or detection procedures. The response taken should be documented.

Business Processes   This column is a notation column to identify which business processes are involved with this scheme. It may be that only those rated a "high" residual risk (or greater than some percentage) would be noted. The business process owner should be documented as the responsible party for the area and, if applicable, for responding to unacceptable residual risk.

Red Flags   This column is also a notation column. Here the team, probably the auditors, would identify the red flags that could be associated with this scheme.

Red flags are available from a variety of literature sources. They include:

- ISACA's standard 030.020.010 (a.k.a. SISAS 8), *Audit Considerations for Irregularities*
- AICPA SAS No. 99, *Consideration of Fraud in a Financial Statement Audit*[2]

- PCAOB Standard No. 2
- *Occupational Fraud and Abuse*[3]
- Corporate policies, procedures, and internal controls

SPECIAL CASES

Banking Industry[4]

Cash is the inventory banks carry, so it should be no surprise that banks suffer extensively from embezzlement at the teller level. But most teller embezzlements create relatively small total losses as compared, for example, to the damage a bank's own money traders or its commercial lenders could cause. In this era of computerized banking, one might also think that electronic funds transfer clerks, who handle hundreds of millions of dollars a day, must be stealing like mad. The authors have seen little proof of that. There have been reports from banks in Los Angeles, Chicago, New York, London, and Zurich of attempts to fraudulently wire transfer bank funds, involving $10 million in one case, $20 million in another, and $60 million in still another. None of these attempts was successful.

But for the sake of experiential learning, one can compare the relative risks of bank funds transfer clerks committing acts of embezzlement vis-à-vis bank tellers, lenders, traders, purchasing department personnel, bookkeeper-accountants, operations supervisors, and so on, using the matrix form in Exhibit 8.4. When the exercise is complete, one can compare the assessment. How close are the responses? What factors does the bank's internal auditor rate more highly and why?

Risk Financing

An embezzlement risk assessment indicates whether the risk of fraud, theft, and embezzlement could be reduced with better controls, better personnel practices, better management, or all of these. But fraud, theft, and embezzlement cannot be reduced to zero. Depending on the nature of the risk, its frequency and severity, there are some options for management. Management can elect to finance the risk in

Functional Roles	Probability of Occurrence[a]	Severity of Financial Loss[a]	Severity of Image Loss[a]	Weighted Average
Tellers				
Lenders				
Purchasers				
Funds Transferors				
Bookkeepers/ Accountants				
Operations Supervisors				
Operations Clericals				
Data Input Clerks				
Computer Operators				
Programmer Analysts				
Systems Programmers				
Senior Management				

[a] Risk Level = 3 HIGH; Risk Level = 2 MEDIUM; Risk Level = 1 LOW

EXHIBIT 8.4   Embezzlement Risk Assessment in the Banking Industry

part or in whole, with insurance. If the risk is of catastrophic proportions, most management would opt to transfer all or a large part of it to an insurance carrier.

External Auditors and Risk

External auditors do not view the risk of fraud, theft, and embezzlement from the same perspective as management does. Their concern is a defensive one. External auditors see fraud from the perspective of professional liability; that is, if fraud is there and we miss it, will we be sued by the client, its shareholders, or even a third-party lender? External auditors are inclined to focus on transaction frauds, that is, expense voucher padding, and so on.

In addition, SAS No. 99 requires financial auditors to "identify the fraud risks that may result in a material misstatement", and "assess the identified risks after taking into account an evaluation of the entity's {anti-fraud} programs and controls."[5] Based on that assessment, the auditor should design the audit to provide reasonable assurance of detecting frauds, errors and irregularities that are material to the financial statements."

SUMMARY

Risk assessment is a critical starting point for audits in general. In this chapter, risk assessment is used as a tool for an entity's antifraud program, where the entity is trying to minimize its fraud risk. As such, this step does not occur during the fraud audit processes. Rather it is a tool to identify the risks and address the most important ones. It is recommended that any business, especially a publicly traded one, go through this exercise. Risk assessments, done properly, will almost always lead to more benefits than the costs of the process.

ENDNOTES

1. Abstracted from G. J. Bologna, Robert I. Lindquist, and Joseph T. Wells, *The Accountant's Handbook on Fraud and Commercial Crime* (New York: John Wiley & Sons, 1993).
2. AU316, pp. 30–34.
3. Joe Wells, *Occupational Fraud and Abuse* (Austin, TX: ACEF, 1997).
4. Jack Bologna, Computer Protection Systems, Inc., 1994.
5. AICPA, Statement on Auditing Standards (SAS) No. 99, "Consideration of Fraud in a Financial Statement Audit."

CHAPTER 9

Fraud and the Accounting Information System

INTRODUCTION

Except for certain limited "off the books" schemes, fraud transaction data are almost always contained in the accounting information system, even if the fraudster destroyed the paper trail. Therefore a proper understanding of the accounting cycles (business processes) and the accounting information system (nearly always a computerized system) is critical to the success in preventing and detecting fraud. The discussion of the accounting system here will further discuss the concepts of fraud control in accounting cycles discussed in Chapter 7.

Notably, accounting information systems can take on a manual or computerized form. Though few in number, completely manual accounting systems exist and no accounting system can be absolutely automated. Systems fall somewhere in between, automating in areas where efficiencies can be attained and using manual procedures where risks, preferences, or technological limitations make it necessary. Clearly the trend is toward automation, but computer technology cannot replace some human capabilities.

In the end, the same concepts discussed in this chapter apply to both manual or automated systems unless noted otherwise. While concepts may take different forms in one system or another, they are the same in substance. The discussion in this chapter addresses those accounting concepts that apply to any system and covers technology in accounting systems in detail.

ACCOUNTING CONCEPTS

Revenue Cycle (Sales and Receipts)

The revenue cycle includes all systems that record the sale of goods and services, grant credit to customers, and receive and record customer remittances (see Exhibit 9.1). The details of a product sold for a price, or of professional services rendered for a fee, are set out in a document called a sales invoice. Details of all sales invoices are listed in the sales journal.

When the customer pays, the company records the payment on a deposit slip ultimately listed in the cash receipts journal or receives notification of an electronic funds transfer (EFT) payment. Business organizations keep a list of those customers who owe money, produced by comparing the sales journal and the cash receipts journal, which is called accounts receivable. It is usually prepared monthly and shows, for each customer listed, the balance owed and the aging of the receivable—that is, if the customer has owed the money for 30, 60, 90, or more than 90 days. Customer ledgers are used depict a specific customer's sales and payment transactions and are often analyzed for critical customers or customers whose account is significantly aged (especially over 90 days past due).

Thus the system of sales, receipts, and receivables constitutes the revenue cycle of any company. The primary documents are the sales invoice (evidence of the sale to the customer) and the deposit slip

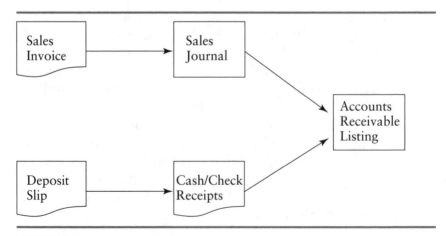

EXHIBIT 9.1 Revenue Cycle

(evidence of the customer's payment to the company). The best evidence of payment is a customer's canceled check. With the advent of Check 21, checks are truncated at some point of the banking system and not physically returned to the payer.

EXPENDITURES CYCLE (PURCHASES AND DISBURSEMENTS)

The expenditures cycle includes all systems that record the acquisition of goods and services for use in the business exchange for payment or promises to pay. Exhibit 9.2 charts this cycle.

In order to produce its product for sale, a company makes various types of expenditures. These may be for acquiring land, buildings, and equipment; purchasing materials and supplies; and paying company employees. Purchases are made from many different suppliers. A supplier's invoice is evidence of a transaction. This invoice is sent to the company and sets out the details of the transaction. The company lists certain details of the supplier's invoice in the purchase journal.

If the company has the funds available, the supplier usually is paid within 30 days. This payment is evidenced by the company's canceled check. All checks are recorded in the company's check disbursements journal when they are issued. This journal is simply a list

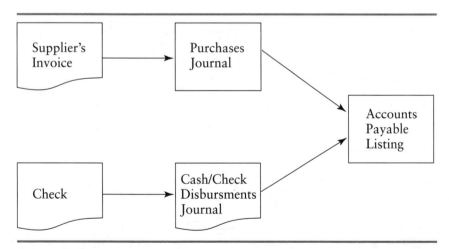

EXHIBIT 9.2   Expenditures Cycle

of the checks paid to the various suppliers and other creditors and individuals doing business with the company.

Most companies attempt to keep track of what they owe suppliers. This accounting is usually done monthly. The company prepares an accounts payable listing by comparing what is recorded in the purchases journal with what is recorded as paid in the check disbursements journal. This list may detail how long various suppliers have been owed (e.g., 30, 60, or 90 days). Accounts payable listings for specific customers are known as vendor ledgers.

The most common group of asset misappropriation frauds is fraudulent disbursements. Therefore, this cycle is ripe with possibilities of fraud detection in the average organization, if a fraud occurs. These frauds often involve collusion or override of controls, so monitoring and supervision are key to control.

BANK RECONCILIATION

The monies the company receives (as recorded in the cash receipts journal) and the monies the company pays out (as recorded in the check disbursements journal) are processed through the company's bank account. To ensure that the transactions recorded in these journals agree with those shown on the bank statement, a monthly bank reconciliation is prepared. Exhibit 9.3 charts this process.

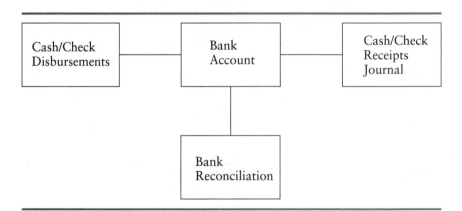

EXHIBIT 9.3 Bank Reconciliation

In regard to fraud, the bank reconciliation is perhaps the most important function management can oversee. That fact is true because *in the end, the money must go somewhere and it always leaves a trail*. The most common frauds are disbursement frauds, and the bank reconciliation can often reveal the fraud.

Too often, however, the bank reconciliation is not done or is done by the perpetrator. Management should consider at least segregating the bank reconciliation step from all other steps in the disbursement cycle. For instance, if a manager had the bank statement sent directly to her and at least reviewed the statement, even if she did not do the bank reconciliation step, there is a chance that manager could spot a disbursement fraud or even lapping and other frauds.

GENERAL LEDGER

Transactions listed in each of the four journals (sales, receipts, purchases, and disbursements) are totaled and entered into the general ledger. General ledger reports can be organized in a variety of ways: by journal totals, by primary accounts (assets, liabilities, and equity) and in total, by month or other cross-sections. More important than the form is the fact that adjusting journal entries are sometimes made directly to the general ledger account and not through the applicable journal.

Nearly all systems have a way to place a journal entry into the general ledger through the general journal. Mistakes and errors do occur in accounting. To correct them, an entry is made in the general journal. This journal is kept for the specific purpose of adjusting the general ledger to make necessary changes, including the correction of errors.

Such an entry bypasses several steps in the accounting process. Normally, sales occur that will be related to receipts; those receipts and the process of matching sales to receipts provide a paper trail. The sale gives credibility to the receipt and vice versa. The process and credibility of general journal entries is dependent on how controlled adjusting entries are.

Adjusting entries should set out a documented explanation for the correction and normally contain some evidence of management approval. A general journal entry has the effect of taking an amount from one account, say ABC, reducing the total in the ABC account, and transferring that amount to the other account, XYZ, thereby increasing the total in XYZ. In this manner the general ledger balances are corrected or distorted. Either way, once the adjusting entries are completed, the general ledger serves as the basis for preparing financial statements. Exhibits 9.4 and 9.5 illustrate the components and end product of the general ledger.

Due to the critical role the general ledger plays in producing financial statements and other reports, *entries to the general ledger present a significant fraud risk.* Financial statement frauds often employ journal entries to either create fictitious revenues or assets or to cover up the fraud. Normally, valid and invalid adjusting entries occur at the end of fiscal years or other time periods (months, quarters,

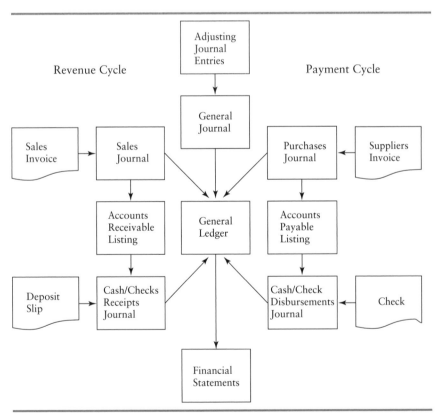

EXHIBIT 9.4   Documents in the Revenue Cycle

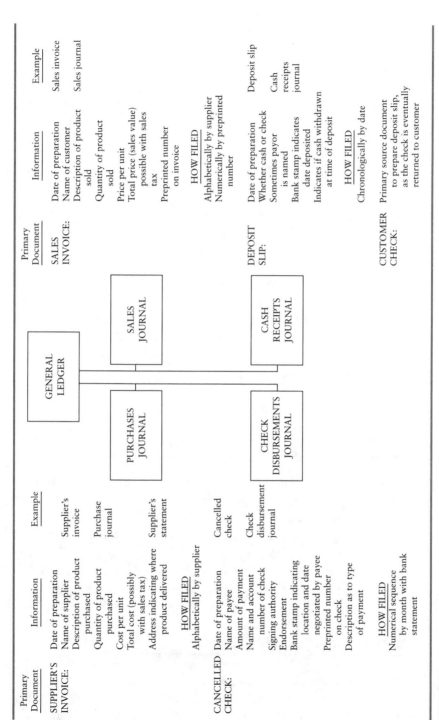

EXHIBIT 9.5 Documents in the Payment Cycle

Primary Document	Information	HOW FILED	Example
SUPPLIER'S INVOICE:	Date of preparation Name of supplier Description of product purchased Quantity of product purchased Cost per unit Total cost (possibly with sales tax) Address indicating where product delivered	Alphabetically by supplier	Supplier's invoice Purchase journal Supplier's statement
CANCELLED CHECK:	Date of preparation Name of payee Amount of payment Name and account number of check Signing authority Endorsement Bank stamp indicating location and date negotiated by payee Preprinted number on check Description as to type of payment	Numerical sequence by month with bank statement	Cancelled check Check disbursement journal

Primary Document	Information	HOW FILED	Example
SALES INVOICE:	Date of preparation Name of customer Description of product sold Quantity of product sold Price per unit Total price (sales value) possible with sales tax Preprinted number on invoice	Alphabetically by supplier Numerically by preprinted number	Sales invoice Sales journal
DEPOSIT SLIP:	Date of preparation Whether cash or check Sometimes payor is named Bank stamp indicates date deposited Indicates if cash withdrawn at time of deposit	Chronologically by date	Deposit slip Cash receipts journal
CUSTOMER CHECK:	Primary source document to prepare deposit slip, as the check is eventually returned to customer		

217

etc.). Frauds have been discovered many times when managers, especially executives, booked fictitious revenues in the last quarter of the year to increase the profits of the organization. From an internal perspective, controls over all adjusting general ledger entries should be strong and firmly in place. From a fraud audit perspective, inspection of journal entries can be an effective technique for detecting frauds.

CASH PATH

In regard to fraud, the asset misappropriation type of fraud (generally perpetrated by employees) is almost always associated with cash coming in or cash going out of the business. Theft of inventory or other assets is a small percentage of asset misappropriation frauds. Therefore, the positions that employees hold along the trail of cash coming in and going out are key positions and critical control points to prevent and detect fraud. The employees who hold these positions generally are believed to be trustworthy. Before putting a person in this tempting position, organizations should consider running a background check or other means of ensuring the integrity of that person on the cash path.

SEGREGATION OF DUTIES

An analysis of the cycles provides insights where segregation of duties should be employed. Specifically, within a cycle, the steps in that cycle should be segregated as much as possible. When not possible or feasible, the compensating control of formal supervision and monitoring is necessary to help mitigate the risk of fraud. The illustration of sending bank statements directly to management or internal audit is one type of formal supervision that could be used.

COMPUTERIZED ACCOUNTING SYSTEMS

Essentially, there are three major elements in a computerized accounting system: (1) key personnel, such as management, security, database management, and change control; (2) computer hardware—the physical equipment that includes processing and communications units (mainly various types of servers, network devices and personal computers) and "peripheral" devices from keyboards to laptops, mobile phones and BlackBerrys; and (3) computer software—the programs or instructions that enable the computer to perform a business function (including protecting and managing other computer systems and data) using the data input by personnel.

It is important to note that these elements are over and above those in conventional (noncomputerized) accounting systems, where the normal procedures are presumed to be in place. The major difference is fewer personnel are directly connected with the actual use of data in a computerized system. Otherwise, the only real difference is the computer processes the data and produces the report instead of people, who simply manage the data in an automated system.

Auditors have to understand the technology, the process, and the control to truly provide assurance over the state of security in the system. As many users have access to data through applications, the process for granting user access to software is quite important. However, many applications in today's market are intranet, extranet, or web applications, especially intranet applications. Often user access to the network automatically grants access to the software program, which again authenticates the user and authorizes the person to have certain privileges or permissions in the given application. When such is the case, access to the network *almost completely* reduces the possibility of users who were removed from the network gaining access. This is just one example of how the systems infrastructure can affect security over data; *each system is unique. Fraud auditors need to be sure to truly understand the process and controls in order to effectively conduct a fraud audit uising the accounting information system.*

KEY PERSONNEL

Specifying the typical information systems, or information technology (IT), department is difficult, but some generalizations can be made. While some decentralization usually exists, most organizations have a centralized IT department servicing the entire organization. The employees in that department are technology specialists of some kind, with regards to security, administrators, databases, software, or systems projects. The IT department develops, maintains, and supports systems and data for the rest of the organization, especially end (systems) users and business owners. This section briefly describes the jobs in the IT department.

Management

Both systems and business management over the accounting system are important in regard to fraud for two reasons:

1. The importance of culture cannot be understated and management creates that culture in the environment it manages.
2. Management ultimately controls what happens within its department; management can always override controls that do not reach above the given management's level of authority.

Security

The gatekeepers to networks, systems, applications, and, most important, data, are security personnel. Besides managing physical access, they manage user access (adding, editing, and removing), to systems (digital access). Controlled physical access, except in unique industries and government, is not normally as essential to security as controlled digital access.

Depending on the information system infrastructure (hardware, software, data, and communications devices), different areas of physical and digital access are high risk. Whatever the systems infrastructure, *keeping user access up to date is critical* and study after study has found neglecting to do so greatly increases the possibility of fraud. Periodic reviews of user access, especially when aimed at high-level and terminated users, are the best single control when done thoroughly; reviews should reconcile accounts with user responsibilities. To maintain access to data, an effective line of communication must exist, well-defined processes and procedures must be in place, and personnel responsible for reporting changes to user access must understand the importance of this area and act accordingly.

Security personnel also manage parameters, settings, and technology related to security. Parameters and settings refer to the options available to customize security in infrastructure components. For example, security management software has parameters/settings for the use of password requirements.

Experienced security personnel know solid password requirements—such as length (requiring six to eight characters), complexity (including a capital letter and a number or special character), expiration (enforces a change of password after a set number of days), and lockout (after a set number of failed attempts to access the system, the user will be locked out for a set time period), are a basic tenet of good security. Experienced security personnel also know that end users have to be aware of the importance of passwords and know how to protect them, especially by not leaving them in the drawer right beside the computer or, even worse, taped to the computer screen. It happens too much, too often!

Most IT departments have specialized security personnel who manage the integrity of networks, critical applications, and other high-risk areas specific to the organization. They deal with issues such as encryption of data, remote (VPN) access, application and data security, and surveillance and monitoring. These types of personnel perform the technical security work, for example, selecting a firewall, customizing it to the business process and needs, and monitoring it. They may also assist in developing, testing, or monitoring systems, as well as probing them for weaknesses. Security personnel are in a good position to relay any system weaknesses, although they are also in a good position to attempt to defraud systems.

Administrators

The term *administrator* is used quite loosely but generally means someone who oversees, or literally administers, some kind of system or data. For example, database administrators oversee a database or association of databases to ensure the data has integrity (is as it should be). Database administrators help maintain database structures, jobs (small, automated, and usually automatically run programs that edit or communicate data), data types, settings, relationships, access to, content in, and other aspects of databases.

Any kind of administrator has what is often called "power-user access." That generally means administrators can manipulate the system within their domain however they please. Administrators need this kind of access, although it must be balanced with monitoring; an excellent control here is the ability to automatically alert and log changes made by administrator users, which is usually fairly easy to track.

Change Control

The change control department provides quality assurance over the process of changing programs, databases, settings, and infrastructure components. It needs to be an independent group that ensures program developers and business users are on the same page and that both follow a controlled change process. Change control is critical because most changes are program changes, which can affect how applications or jobs (tasks) manipulate data. Other critical areas are changes to security settings, to databases, or to significant infrastructure. Change control should, at a minimum, ensure that:

- Change requests are approved and valid.
- Changes made resolve the request and cause no other problems.
- Testing is performed and documented.
- Changes are moved into production (the version currently in use) by the appropriate person.

End Users and Business Owners

The end user inputs all of the data to be processed by the computer. Data in an accounting context are usually classified as being processed in batch or in real time. With batches, data accumulate and assimilate into groups over a period of time when transactions take place; later, at some specified time or when users send a command, the batch is sent to be processed. Real-time processing, simply put, process data in real time, as it is entered into the program. End users, especially those with a lot of experience in a given area, know software rather well and could be a good source of understanding how it does and does not operate and the intended business purpose, when relevant.

The term *business owner* refers to the employee responsible for the system. The designation is usually made departmentally. For example, the vice president of finance at a bank would be responsible for a capital management and forecasting system. Business owners are helpful in understanding the business process ins and outs: how it was, how it is and how it should be. Generally, business owners are at a high enough level of management to override controls, and the culture they create is an important factor in a fraud audit.

Project Management

Managing IT projects is one of the most difficult jobs in systems. Project management is supposed to successfully implement a new or highly revised component of the organization's IT system to fulfill a business need. Projects are hardly ever built to intended specifications, much less in the projected time frame and on budget. This is one reason why project management is important to an organization and may become important in a fraud audit.

Project management best practices include documentation every step of the way, approvals by business owners and other appropriate persons at project milestones, thorough testing with a comparison of expected to actual results, and possibly a pilot to test the system change in the field before rolling out to the rest of the organization. The process must be adhered to, but people must perform the process well also. System analysts and designers, developers, and quality assurance specialists all play key roles in the process.

The systems analyst works with the various user departments to determine how their needs can best be met, what data must be entered, what processing must be carried out on the input data, what output must be produced, and with what frequency. Systems designers convert those needs into system specifications. The programmer carries on from the specifications, writing, debugging, and installing new system components based on specifications and the systems design. Developers are expected to document new programs in detail and to update the documentation when programs are changed. Quality assurance staff members examine and evaluate all of the project steps to date and thoroughly test the system to ensure it is working as intended.

Other Personnel

Computer operators mainly exist in mainframe environments, where they direct the execution of various mechanical tasks by means of a console terminal. When operators are in place, they usually deal with a significantly important application, operating system, and/or server. Operators schedule tasks for the system to complete and are responsible for the proper use of input and output devices. Operators monitor for any problems and perform backup activities. They should be required to document key, if not all, activities, if automated logging is not in place.

In addition to their central corporate computer, many organizations now have a network of "clients" (personal computers, terminals, desktops, etc.) linked to that computer. The client may be linked via a local, wide, or wireless area network via telephone lines, networking cables, or even satellite. Traditional terminals and mainframes are often in the same building or a building nearby and wired, if indirectly a bit, together. In opposition, the link could be remote (VPN) access, securely tunneling through the Internet over a cell phone or other wireless device, completely untethered.

Users using mobile clients, external networks, and remote access enter data directly into internal computers. Clearly, this decentralized system of processing increases the vulnerability of computer systems because more people have access to the computer under conditions less easily controlled. Passwords and other methods of restricting access have to be relied on heavily, to prevent people from tampering with programs and files.

The librarian stores and retrieves programs and data, usually at a location away from the computer site. Programs and data normally are stored on magnetic tape or disk and serve as a backup if the original software or transaction files are destroyed. The librarian also maintains, under normal circumstances, a log of borrowings from the library.

COMPUTER HARDWARE

Computer equipment may be online or offline. An online system permits the operator to access and manipulate information in the computer, changing the database immediately and receiving information from the computer immediately. In contrast, offline systems involve an intermediate step of some kind before processing takes place.

Generally, computer hardware includes: (1) equipment for preparing data for processing, (2) input devices, (3) a central processing unit (CPU), (4) output devices, and (5) communications devices. All of these devices provide some convenience at the cost of risks exposed by their presence; these risks do not change anything from a fraud audit perspective, but potentially provide new means to perpetrate a fraud.

Data Preparation Equipment

This equipment is used to convert the data into a machine-readable format. Depending on the method of inputting the information into the computer, numerous devices can be employed. In former days, these devices included magnetic tape, optical character readers, and paper-punch tape. Data are almost always entered directly via online computers, but offline systems and associated data conversions are still found in operation and prevent unique risks.

Input Devices

Input equipment includes such components as keyboards and video screens that show what is being entered, display instructions, and formats for inputting. Modern computer screens respond to touch. A wireless, optical "mouse" is not unusual. Scanners and cameras can bring imaging to every desktop and even cell phones. Tablet personal computers (PCs) take the convenience of a small laptop to a whole new level and can store a vast amount of data. Computer software is available that will respond to a range of voice commands as input. New technologies are developing constantly and potentially provide new vehicles for fraud.

Central Processing Unit

The CPU is the heart of the computer; it contains a series of operating programs and a translator that converts data into machine language (binary) on which the CPU itself operates. It stores programmed instructions and data; reads, writes, and moves data and instructions; interprets and performs programmed tasks; and synchronizes all of these activities. The CPU is really the technological processor, managing itself and processing according to mathematic functions; software is the business processor, processing data according to business functions.

Output Devices

Output equipment includes printers, video display screens, and plotters. The technology of output as well as input devices is constantly being improved, because these devices constitute the interface between human beings and computers. Note that output devices, to date, do not edit data and therefore are not particularly relevant to fraud audits.

Communications Devices

A host of communication devices exist in the typical organizational systems infrastructure. Routers connect networks, switches and hubs connect devices within a network, modems and communication protocols ensure interoperability, e-mail servers process countless messages per day. Cell phones, two-way radios, PDAs, and BlackBerrys, all with Internet capabilities, have flooded Corporate America, and there is no return. Again, with regard to fraud audits, the point is that there are more means available to commit fraud.

COMPUTER SOFTWARE

Software is the generic name for computer programs and their documentation. A program is a set of instructions that directs the computer to perform a task. Software is divided into two main classes: operating and application.

Operating systems (O/S) software consists of the programs that keep the computer running as automatically as possible. They coordinate computer functions between the application software and the computer hardware (e.g., printing a check from a payroll application). O/S can also control access to file directories ("paths") and directly to files, although limited security exists in most operating systems. Actually, most O/S are constantly sending out upgrades ("patches") to fix identified security weaknesses and outdated systems increase the chance of fraud.

Applications software consists of computer programs that apply the computer to the user's needs by carrying out an organizational task the user wants performed (e.g., processing a payroll). The normal four-step sequence of instructions in an application program is:

1. Read the information entered.
2. Process it (add, subtract).
3. Update existing files in the computer's memory with new information.
4. Output the new information by displaying, printing, or storing it (or all three).

Applications have increasingly taken on networked forms, meaning application software is often accessed and used over the Internet, extranet, and most popularly through the intranet. As intranet applications are internal to the organization, they provide more security than other "web-enabled" applications. Intranet software presents some unique risks, especially in "multilayered" applications, where different parts of the program reside on different computers and interact in a more process-oriented and hierarchical fashion. Again, what is important in the context of a fraud audit is to understand the new ways fraud can be perpetrated.

MEDIA STORAGE

The means used to store computer data are vulnerable to abuse and misuse. Most systems are connected via a network and centralized servers. These systems also often use databases. Between the two technologies, almost everyone in the organization can potentially access the data files. From a PC, a person can possibly steal, alter, or destroy data or data files. Stored data are extremely vulnerable to abuse. The subject of storing data is explained in more detail in Chapter 10.

NEW FORMS OF MEDIA

The trend in new forms of media has been toward portability—chief among them compact discs (CDs), digital video recorders (DVDs), flash drives (thumb drives, jump drives), personal digital assistants (PDAs), optical storage media, Internet and intranet storage, and even cell phones. These types of media present users with many advantages, particularly in the amount of information they can store and the convenience, speed, transportation, and cost with which that information may be accessed. But, of course, they represent new opportunities for fraud and new challenges for hackers. Fraud auditors and especially forensic auditors should be aware of, know how to search for, and understand how to handle the various forms of media storage.

Although e-mail does not quite fit the term *media,* it deserves special attention because of its similarities to media. E-mail stores data. Actually, e-mail stores a vast amount of data, sometimes critical to the organization and sometimes revealing a fraud. In several of the noted frauds in the late 1990s and early 2000s, e-mail communications supplied evidence of fraud. With the business world tightly connected and ever communicating, *e-mail will undoubtedly become a critical aspect of fraud auditing.*

Magnetic Media

Although hard drives, CDs, and DVDs predominate, magnetic tape is still in use. Information is stored on a magnetic tape in the same manner as on a floppy disk. The magnetic disk resembles a magnetically coated phonograph record and has a series of concentric paths that encode the information. The major advantage of disks is that computers can access information directly, anywhere on the disk, with great speed. The density of these disks determines the amount of information that can be stored on them. In contrast, a magnetic tape must be read sequentially to find the relevant data or instructions. Searching magnetic tape for fraud or anything else is tedious work and fraud auditors should consider that fact f this medium appears in a fraud audit.

Because they are small and light, floppy disks are easy to steal. When left lying about, they present a tempting target. Because their surfaces are easily damaged, and the magnetic dots can be obliterated by careless handling, floppy disks are quickly becoming antiquated technology.

Hard disks, however, are much less vulnerable, because they are protected by being housed within the computer's disk drive. Nevertheless, the data on both types of disks are susceptible to tampering. Critical hard disks are servers that serve important business functions and hard drives in personal computers of key employees, such as executive management. With hard drives, physical security plays more of a control than it does in other areas.

PAPER AND MICROFILM

Data can be stored in hard-copy form, such as on paper or microfilm. Hard copies can show the result of data manipulation or processing by the computer, but not necessarily the transactions that occurred in arriving at the output. Paper is a familiar and stable medium but is bulky to store; as a result, more companies are using smaller, cheaper digital media. Many organizations are even going to a "paperless office," where all documents are scanned onto network media storage devices and only critical, original paper documents are physically retained. Imagine a tax, law, or accounting firm *not* retaining the abysmal amounts of paper they use.

AUDIT TRAIL CONCEPT

In every transaction, there is a bigger process occurring than the transaction itself. The accounting cycles described earlier depict the typical processes overlying business transactions. Whether manual or automated systems are in place, a trail exists when transactions move through these processes.

Financial auditors often refer to the audit trail as the series of items that show a transaction from beginning to end, through the accounting information system. Single items of evidence are associated with other evidence and form the path the transaction has taken, such as a sales invoice, cash receipt, and bank deposit. Certain elements connect those documents and verify each other; certain actions are taken involving these documents, like approvals on paper or in electronic form. In financial audits, the amounts, approvals, and other transactional details found in the audit trail are of critical importance to the audit, as it is self-authenticating, and *one connection can reveal everything needing to be known about the process*. The same is true in fraud audits; following the audit trail concept can be vital to locating substantial evidence capable of ending the investigation.

Although computerized systems do not leave physical trails of evidence, the audit trail concept still applies. The data either went somewhere or it did not, was edited or was not, and is correct or it is not. The difficulty in proving either of those in an automated system is that the audit trail tends to be a bit more complex, vague, and can be less reliable. Computers are dependent on elements humans are not, and they are programmable. The ability to create, measure, monitor, and report important transactions of data is vital but can be manipulated or simply turned off.

Physical, digital, and abstract forms of evidence exist. Successful criminal investigations usually have physical ("hard") evidence. Other revealing types of evidence exist, such as computer records and behavioral manifestations. Like an audit trail, discovering one item of evidence can literally open up the investigation. In this regard, criminal investigations echo the validity of the audit trail concept.

The audit trail concept is dependent on one assumption: *some indication always exists of what has transacted*. Cash is predominantly the root of most audit trails. If cash is involved in a transaction, it went somewhere. If it was not transacted, it is still as it was. On one level, those are the only two options. On another level, there are the matters of what was supposed to transact and how and why what occurred really happened. Determining such matters requires an objective and investigative mind-set and a walk through the trail.

CHAPTER 10

Computer-Related Fraud

INTRODUCTION

A computer-related crime, in very broad terms, means both a crime that has been committed or abetted through the use of a computer and a crime in which a computer itself is the victim. The usual crimes committed by computer include embezzlement, theft of property and proprietary information, fraud, forgery, and counterfeiting. Crimes committed against computers include sabotage, vandalism, electronic unauthorized access (gaining illegal access by impersonating an authorized user), and exceeding one's own authority (insider hacker).

Before there were computers, there was no computer crime, but there was crime—both the white- and blue-collar varieties. There were also crimes of violence (crimes against people) and crimes against property. Computer-related crime, therefore, can be viewed as a phenomenon brought about by advances in information technologies. The computer did not usher in a new wave of crime; it merely changed the form of older crimes. Embezzlers can now steal by making electronic entries in books of account rather than by pen and ink or electromechanical entries.

Basically, computer-related crime is an occupational crime. That is, it is committed mainly by people with the requisite skills, knowledge, and access. Access can be gained more easily by organization insiders (employees) than by outsiders (intruders, hackers). Research on this subject finds that about 70 to 80% of computer-related malicious acts are perpetrated by insiders versus outsiders.[1] Therefore, insiders represent a greater potential computer crime threat than outsiders, despite mass media commentators, who often suggest the opposite.

One might therefore conclude that computer-related crime is a phenomenon that involves knowledgeable people with questionable dispositions. But that also is too simple to be true. The idea that criminals are born crime prone has not won much favor from behavioral scientists. They suggest that cultural and environmental conditioning is more significant factors in understanding crime. Therefore, it is important to view computer-related crime from a number of perspectives:

- The individual criminal and his motivations
- The external environmental factors that exacerbate motivations to commit computer crime
- The internal organizational cultures that minimize or maximize the probability of such crimes

Nature of Computer-Related Crime

Crimes like embezzlement and employee thefts of funds were not unheard of before computers came into being. Accountants attempted to discourage such crimes by requiring a separation of duties between people who handled cash or other assets and those who made entries in the books of account. Accessibility to assets and accountability for recording transactions concerning such assets were divided, on the theory that requiring two people to conspire to commit a theft of assets would reduce the probability of such a theft.

An added control measure accountants instituted is called the paper trail or audit trail. In essence, this control measure requires that all business transactions be entered into journals and be supported by paper documents (e.g., vendor invoices, purchase orders, receiving reports, cancelled checks, disbursement vouchers, sales receipts, or customer invoices) to establish accountability.

But despite these control measures, employee thefts, frauds, and embezzlements are still possible. Accounting systems are not designed to be absolutely foolproof or fraud proof. A determined defrauder could still find ways to circumvent or override controls even in the era of manual accounting. Computers have not changed that human disposition. Fraud, thefts, and embezzlements are still possible in the computer era.

Value of Stored Data

With the advent of computers, a new form of asset has been created: the data held in the computer. The data eventually may cause money to change hands as in electronic funds transfer (EFT) systems. Although the data are not a negotiable instrument (as is a bank check), they nonetheless have value. Further examples of these assets are bank-to-bank transfers, accounts receivable balances, inventory levels, funds and deposit balances, fixed assets listings, and accounts payable balances. Other more intangible assets include valued or confidential programs, scientific data files, programs a company can sell for a profit, confidential financial information, and computer time.

In today's world of endless computing, financial data are the most treasured asset in financial reporting. The financial statements that so heavily influence public markets and society in general are the end product of a long process of financial data creation, calculation, and processing many times over until organized into a set of financial statements. Section 404 of the Sarbanes-Oxley Act of 2002 requires auditors to understand and evaluate that process and control over data during the financial reporting process, legitimizing the importance of financial data from a more holistic viewpoint than traditionally has been the case.

HISTORY AND EVOLUTION OF COMPUTER-RELATED CRIMES

Electronic computers were first introduced for commercial use in the United States in 1954, when General Electric (GE) became the first U.S. business to employ a computer. Before then, the few computers that existed were used for governmental purposes (for tabulating the national census, for military applications, and for scientific research). The history of the computer crime begins in the mid-1950s.

Stanford Research International

Until 1958, no systematic tracking or tabulation of computer-related crime existed. That year, Stanford Research International (SRI) began tracking publicly reported incidents of computer abuse, some of which were criminal and others that involved the breach of civil laws, such as the copyright and patent acts. SRI grouped these incidents into four categories:

1. Vandalism (against computers)
2. Information or property theft
3. Financial fraud or theft
4. Unauthorized use or sale of (computer) services

The first year in which 10 or more of these incidents were reported was 1968. There were a total of 13 incidents that year. Reported incidents rose until 1977, but in 1978 they dropped dramatically. SRI discontinued tabulating such abuses after 1978 for several reasons. For one thing, the publicly reported incidents bore no relationship to all incidents. Many, perhaps most, incidents of computer abuse were not publicly reported.

Tabulating reported incidents by year could create the impression that computer abuse was growing or declining when, in fact, the reported incidents might not be fairly representative of all actual incidents of abuse. With more and more computers being used, one could expect an increase in the number of incidents of abuse. Figures of abuse would shed no light on the phenomenon itself or its causative factors. SRI elected to look at each case individually for whatever insights it could glean on causations and other variables, such as the mental dispositions of the computer abusers and the employment conditions that made abuse more likely—demographic characteristics of abusers.

Equity Funding Scandal

One of the earliest historic events regarding computer-related fraud was the Equity Funding scandal that was exposed in 1973. Managers at Equity Funding Corporation of America used a series of frauds beginning in 1964 to show false profits, thus increasing the company's stock price. The primary fraud was the use of phony insurance policies. Equity Funding used several tactics to perpetrate the fraud.

One was to use different external auditors in order to confound the audit process and prevent detection of the fraud. Another deceptive tactic was used during confirmation of receivables. When the external auditing firm tried to confirm receivables (policies) by phone, the Equity Funding switchboard operator simply patched them through to Equity Funding employees in the building. The most amazing fact of the case is that it went undetected for so long. Many people inside the company knew about the fraud, and yet the fraud was a better kept secret than some of our military secrets of the time.

The fraud was exposed when a disgruntled ex-employee blew the whistle. In March 1973, the Securities and Exchange Commission (SEC) suspended trading of Equity Funding stock. The subsequent audit by Touche Ross was definitely not traditional. First, the auditors were trying to prove something (insurance policies) *did not* exist. Second, it was a fraud audit, not a financial audit. The audit took two years to complete. Touche Ross found about $2 billion of phony insurance policies—two-thirds of the policies Equity Funding claimed to have in force.

Because it was so pervasive, the fraud clearly should have been caught by the external financial auditors or the SEC. All bogus policies were coded to department "99." The auditors did not review the computer processes themselves but treated the computer as a black box (i.e., audit around the information technology [IT]). The use of audit software by the external auditors could have detected the fraudulent policy file. The SEC could be accused of some neglect as well. An SEC staff member wrote memos 15 months prior to Equity Funding's collapse reporting rumors of irregularities. The SEC, however, dropped the investigation shortly after receiving the memos.

The popular press treated the fraud as a computer fraud, but it was also a management fraud using the old familiar fraudulent statement scheme (similar to Enron, Waste Management, and numerous others before and since). Equity Funding management probably could not have perpetrated the fraud without the use of computers. Indeed, it was a computer fraud because executives perpetrated the fraud using the computer. The public's perception of the part that the computer played in the fraud caused a new wave of interest in audit procedures where computers were a component of the accounting system.

The prevailing belief at this time was that traditional audits (those that audited around the computer) were sufficient to detect the existence of frauds. Others, primarily IT (electronic data processing [EDP]) auditors, had espoused the need for auditing through the computer. These people were now receiving attention from accountants, auditors, and management. Equity Funding did more for the rise of IT auditing (i.e., more IT auditor jobs) than any other single event up until the passage of SOX.

COMPUTER-RELATED FRAUD THEORIES AND PRINCIPLES

As stated, computer-related crime is either a crime against computers or using computers to perpetrate a conventional fraud or crime (e.g., fraudulent disbursement, fraudulent financial statements, etc.). Thus fraud principles, such as the fraud triangle and the fraud tree, apply to computer-related frauds as well. One theory of computer-related crime is a concept known as MOMM.

Computer-Related Fraud Theory: MOMM

MOMM is an acronym for *motivations*, *opportunities*, *means*, and *methods*. Notice the first two come from the fraud triangle (omitting only the rationalization leg). Means is closely related to opportunities and internal controls, with the addition of technology. Methods applies the systems model to computer-related fraud, but with clear inferences to the fraud tree for the schemes being committed using those methods. The computer-related theft can be depicted as an iterative process (see Exhibit 10.1).

Economic motives indicate that perpetrators have money as a main purpose. They have a need or desire to secure a financial gain from the crime. The object of the fraud does not have to be money, just something that can be converted into or exchanged for money.

Ideological motives are demonstrated when perpetrators feel impelled to seek revenge against someone or something they believe is oppressing or exploiting them. Terrorist bombings of computer

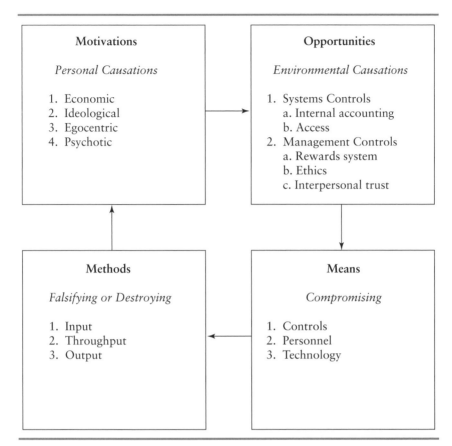

EXHIBIT 10.1   Computer Theft Iteration

centers exemplify that mindset. Sabotage against computers by disgruntled employees is another example. Such criminals may think that computer technology threatens their economic and political survival or well-being.

Egocentric motives are those associated with egos, power, and pride. Most frauds include this motive to some degree. Young enthusiasts who seek the thrill of the challenge to commit computer frauds or crimes exhibit egocentric motives.

Psychotic motives include a distorted sense of reality, delusions of grandeur or persecution, and exaggerated fears of computers. There have been few reported incidents of computer abuse where psychotic motives were attributed to perpetrators.

Environmental conditions that have provided motives for computer-related crime and abuse include both the internal environment of the firm that operates a computer and the external environment (the world or marketplace in general). Internal influences that can add to the motive for computer-related crime and abuse include:

- Work environment
- Reward system
- Level of interpersonal trust
- Level of ethics
- Level of stress (pressure for performance)
- Level of internal controls

Externally, motives for computer-related crime and abuse may be provided by the current mores and social values of society, competitive conditions in the industry, and economic conditions in the country or the world.

Categories in Computer-Related Fraud

Computer-related crimes can be grouped into three categories that parallel the three stages of data processing: input, output, and processing crimes. Input crimes involve the entry of false or fraudulent data into a computer; data have been altered, forged, or counterfeited—raised, lowered, destroyed, intentionally omitted, or fabricated. Input scams are probably the most common computer-related crimes yet perhaps the easiest kind to prevent with effective supervision and controls (i.e., separation of duties and proper audit trails). Output crimes, such as theft of computer-generated reports and data files (customer mailing lists, research and development results, long-range plans, employee lists, secret formulas, etc.) seem to be increasing in this era of intense competition. Throughput crimes usually require knowledge of technology, unless the system is uncontrolled, and access to the computers or application programs.

A similar categorization of fraud criminals exists: internal and external. Internal criminals are more far greater in number. In fact, the most common type of computer crime is probably theft of assets by employees. They have fraud opportunity from being inside the organization; with some pressure to steal (personal cash flow problems) and weak personal ethics, the fraud triangle is complete. If a weakness exists in the controls, the temptation can become too great for the employee to resist stealing from the organization.

Then there are those who break in from the outside. One type of these attackers comes to "steal, kill, and destroy"; in other words, they have malicious intent. Fraudsters from outside an entity would fall into this group. Others come to play—possibly bringing a system down and making it unavailable. But all cause damages and bring about costs. As such, the crimes they commit are computer crimes. One example is spamming. Several states have passed anti-spamming laws, making spam a computer crime.

Financial Computer-Related Crimes

To better understand computer-related financial crimes, it is helpful to know the more commonly committed crimes. Fraudulent disbursement of funds is a common financial fraud committed through computers. It usually requires a data entry clerk in accounts payable, payroll, or the benefits section, either acting alone or in collusion with an insider or outsider (depending on how tight the internal controls are). At higher management levels, the typical fraud involves overstating profits by the fabrication of such data as sales, which are increased arbitrarily (sales booked before the sales transaction is completed), and the understatement of expenses, which are arbitrarily reduced or disguised as deferrals to the next accounting period.

There are numerous variations on these two main themes—overstatement of sales and understatement of expenses. One of the more common ploys to overstate profits is to arbitrarily increase the ending inventory of manufactured goods or merchandise held for sale. That ploy results in understating the cost of goods sold and thereby increasing the net profit.

Executive compensation often provides the incentive to overstate those profits. If bonus awards depend on income or if they own a great deal of company stock, executives have an economic incentive to fudge the numbers. Manipulations of this type often require line executives and personnel in accounting and data processing capacities to conspire together. The pressure on executives for high performance grows each year. Because of the position on managers, they always have the opportunity to commit fraud, as they can override controls.

CHARACTERISTICS OF THE COMPUTER ENVIRONMENT

Computerized accounting systems are a natural progression from manual accounting systems. Still, they have special characteristics that make them more susceptible to crime. To understand the potential impact and extent of computer-related crime, it is necessary to understand these characteristics.

Connectivity

Computer communications may be defined as the ability to transfer messages between independent devices. In order to communicate, the computer devices must, of course, be connected in some way. *The increase in connectivity of information technologies has increased vulnerability to computer crimes*

Networks increase the vulnerability of computer systems. Information can be stolen by copying it through a workstation or by tapping into communication wiring. There can be unauthorized entry through public telephone lines or Internet access. Data can be downloaded easily and quickly to a nearly invisible flash drive.

The Internet exasperates risk as it opens the network up to anyone in the world with the knowledge and opportunity to commit computer fraud. All that needs to be true for a computer fraud to occur is for one of these computer experts to become motivated to attack an organization's computer. The Internet provides the opportunity to connect, almost any time, from almost anywhere, to millions of people around the world.

The idea of connecting computers has taken on new forms of note. Networks are now connected wirelessly, through a virtual private network (VPN)intranets and extranets, with numerous types of other networks and "clients" (devices to connect to a network). Distributed computing allows for more risk exposure than the traditional mainframe computer environment, as (parts of) applications and databases are integrated although separately stored on multiple servers in distant locations. Inevitably, a trade-off is always made in connectivity decisions: convenience or security.

Concentrated Data

Computer systems collect and combine data from all departments within an organization. These data are processed and typically centrally stored. Centralization for security purposes is advantageous, but the location of data *in one location* makes data vulnerable to risks. Simply by obtaining the appropriate password or physical access, a person can access any or all of a company's financial or other records. Nature, human error, or system failures can destroy records forever if a contingency plan is not in place or does not work.

The list of other characteristics follows.

- *Obscure audit trail.* The sheer volume of transactions, together with the online access and networks available on many systems, may result in confused or incomplete audit trails.
- *Misunderstood technology.* Understanding the substance of technology is difficult and requires knowledge of and an ability to see through the technical aspect of systems.
- *Built-in unsecurity.* Much of the hardware and software in use today was designed without much real security, and even secure technology constantly must be updated.
- *Instant access.* Access to hardware and software is abundant. Once a person is granted access, computers can only mitigate the risks of fraud.
- *Invisible records.* Permanent records are often stored in machine-readable form. Any abuse of these records, whether to data or actual programs, is less likely to be detected by nonspecialists.
- *Untraceable changes.* Manual records may reveal tampering or alterations, whereas computer records stored on a magnetic medium may be altered by writing over a record, obliterating the previous record without leaving any trail of the source of the change.

- *Vulnerable storage medium.* Assets are widely recorded in magnetic form. This storage medium is volatile and easily abused, making the stored information vulnerable.

Positions of Trust

By the very nature of their jobs, database administrators, programmers, and data entry clerks are in a position to manipulate records. A high degree of trust must be placed in them, and a corresponding degree of risk. For a fraud to occur, generally speaking, the person had to first be trusted.

Many computer analysts and programmers are not knowledgeable about accounting controls or the general principles of internal control. Thus most systems are designed without adequate controls, usually because they are standardized, not customized to the organization's structure and processes. In addition, many programs that have been operating for a long time have undergone extensive changes, with changes poorly documented, the "patched" programs little understood, and few personnel to support them. If systems are current, they are probably still maturing and have extensive program changes, data conversions, and other projects occurring. Either way, anyone with sufficient knowledge of the given computer area conceivably *could* manipulate or change programs and/or data to their benefit without a change being discovered.

INFORMATION SECURITY (INFOSEC)

One aspect of the *m*eans iteration of the computer-related fraud theory model (MOMM) is "compromising technology." In MOMM, all of the *m*ethods are computer-related as well. Therefore, the security of systems has become a dominant aspect of computer fraud and crime. Protecting the technologies, systems, and information is a critical success factor in the advanced technological environment of today.

A survey was conducted by Computer Security Institute and the FBI's San Francisco computer crime squad. The seventh annual survey polled 503 U.S. corporations, government agencies, financial and medical institutions, and universities. It reported that about 90% of respondents detected computer security breaches in the past year. Survey respondents said they lost at least $455 million as a result of computer crime, compared with $377 million the previous year. In both surveys, only about half chose to quantify their losses. Thirty-eight percent of the respondents said their Web sites have been broken into over the past year, and 21% said they were not sure. Eighteen percent reported some sort of theft of transaction information, such as credit card numbers or customer data, or financial fraud.[2]

Critical issues in information security are:

- Access controls
- Ethics
- Data integrity (accuracy, validity, and completeness of data)
- False entries
- Auditing fraudulent financial statements
- Logging
- Authentication
- Hacking
- Availability
- Counterfeiting
- Piracy
- Privacy
- Proprietary information theft
- Social engineering
- Terrorism
- Embezzlement
- Viruses

Risks and Threats

A critical organization policy is the security (or information security [InfoSec]) policy. Management needs to establish fundamental security objectives tied to business objectives and identify assets that need protection from identified risks. A good policy is contingent on a proper and thorough risk assessment.

One goal of the security policy is to emphasize to all stakeholders (employees in particular) that information and data are assets that have a value, and are not just computer files. A security policy will remind employees of the importance and value of information they handle and the risks or exposures that exist. That is, it will help to make a corporate culture that is security conscious. CERT (Computer Emergency Response Team) presents a good overview of why to have an InfoSec policy and how to develop it.[3]

Somewhat surprisingly, the greatest risk is from the organization's own employees. Disgruntled employees, recently terminated employees, embezzlers, former contractors or consultants, and others may be bent on revenge and be motivated to perpetrate a cyberterrorist-type attack. In fact, a recent study found that vengeful employees are now the biggest security worry for 90% of executive managers.[4] Gartner (experts in computer and technologies research) estimates that more than 70% of unauthorized access to information systems is committed by employees, as are more than 95% of intrusions that result in significant financial losses.[5] *All businesses must examine the risks associated with their own employees* in developing an effective protective system against cyberterrorist-type attacks.

There are three main categories of threats to computer systems:

1. Theft, including theft of assets, data, and programs
2. Manipulation, including the additions or deletions of information in data files or programs
3. Theft of computer time

Some examples of specific fraudulent activities that may be employed are:

- Adding, deleting, or changing input data, or entering fraudulent data
- Misposting or partially posting transactions
- Producing counterfeit output, or suppressing, destroying, or stealing output
- Tampering with programs; for example, to take money from many accounts in small amounts
- Altering or deleting master files, or holding them for ransom
- Overriding internal controls to gain access to confidential information
- Exploiting intersystem deficiencies
- Committing sabotage

- Stealing computer time
- Conducting electronic surveillance of data as it is transmitted
- Browsing or insider hacking, that is, probing into the database

Besides these and other threats, computerized accounting systems are vulnerable to all of the dangers inherent in any accounting system, whether computerized or manual.

PROFILING INTERNET FRAUDSTERS — *Solution/method of solving 9.C.*

Profiling is a common technique used by criminal investigators in locating criminals. Using whatever evidence is available, investigators compile what they know into a criminal profile. The profile aids in evaluating a suspect's probability of guilt and in the search for more evidence. Profiling is particularly necessary with Internet crime due to the invisibility, untraceability, and, often, lack of evidence.

According to the Commission on Critical Infrastructure Protection, an estimated 19 million people worldwide have the skills to engage in malicious hacking.[6] The profile of the authors of the typical malicious attack (and other Internet security incidents) is a male, 13 to 15 years old, with a lot of computer intelligence (neon hair and body piercing optional!). They usually begin malicious activities early. For example, Mixter (a self-proclaimed white hat hacker[7]) started learning computers at 6 and malicious activity at 14.

A host of other profile considerations can be relevant. Knowledge of the criminal's background, associations, tendencies, culture, strengths, and weaknesses aids greatly in investigations with predicting and confirming value. Criminal intent (motivation) is clearly a helpful determination. When coupled with the type of crime, the objective begins to build a portrait of the criminal on paper. "Knowing is half the battle." The other half of that sentence should be: "The other half is synthesizing and following through."

Criminal Intent

Intent can be used effectively in profiling computer fraudsters. Groups of criminals with shared objectives are, in technical terms, hackers, crackers, and script kiddies. Although hackers are the group most frequently mentioned, the term is not portrayed as it should be.

True hackers ("white hats"[8]) actually try to do a service for the Internet community. They look for vulnerabilities and weaknesses, then communicate the "hole" to the entity. These people enjoy the intellectual challenge of their activities.[9] Traditionally, the term *hacker* carried a positive connotation; it was a badge of honor regarding one's technical expertise.

People almost always refer to the "bad guys" as hackers because they are ignorant of the *technical* definitions. Bad guys are technically *crackers*[10] (sometimes referred to as "black hats") whose intent is to steal or destroy. Crackers in noncomputer terms are outlaws, armed and dangerous. Approach with caution.

The term *script kiddie* originated as a reference to young computer enthusiasts who download malicious code (e.g., viruses, denial of service[DoS]) generated by crackers, rather than author it, and conduct mischievous exploits. Kiddies are mostly not malicious, just bored. They are similar to street gangs who have created a way to tag the Internet (viral code) and invented their own form of graffiti (Web site defacements). They have gang wars online (using thousands of remote computers controlled by Internet relay chat {IRC} bots) and are immature.[11]

Steve Gibson's Web site (grc.com) was attacked by a vengeful teenage "script kiddie," and his system defended itself against hundreds of thousands of distributed denial of service (DDoS) attacks per day for several days. Finally, Steve wrote an open letter to the teen cyberterrorist and admitted that his Internet system could be brought down at any time by a sophisticated attacker. Shortly thereafter, the attacks stopped. This type of story has been played out over and over again. *Any entity on the Internet is subject to this kind of threat or risk.*

Another example is a female (rare among script kiddies) from Belgium who authored Sharpei, one of the first ".Net" viruses. She says writing these viruses and DDoS programs is "a form of art, just like other hobbies. Also, it's a fun way to practice programming."[12] This statement reflects the attitude, and demonstrates the problem, with attackers. They do not see any real harm to their victims, and are in it for the personal pleasure it brings.

Cybercrimes

The type of crime contributes to profiling. While Internet (cyber) crime can be blatantly apparent sometimes, at other times it is extremely difficult. Most fall under identity theft, blackmail, denial of service attacks, and various e-mail attacks: phishing, spoofing, sniffing, viruses, spyware, or steganography.

Identity Theft Criminals in the computer world, through various means discussed here, will try to commit the same crimes as in the physical world. Crimes often occur in multiples, and sometimes occur physically *and* digitally. In the case of identity theft, a criminal could physically and/or digitally vandalize, blackmail, or commit another, larger fraud, by gaining unauthorized access to targets.

Identity theft is more of a risk to an individual than to a firm, but it is not exclusively a personal issue. For instance, there was a widespread "phishing"[13] e-mail that pretended to be from eBay, asking customers who had not bought anything recently to provide some updated information, such as social security number, mother's maiden name, and driver's license number. It included a URL that, when accessed, looked like eBay but of course it was a criminal, seeking to steal the identity of the victim. Perpetrators use similar tactics to steal someone's access name, password, or other credentials and break into the targeted system.

Blackmail Thieves steal the typical physical items: credit cards or their data, financial accounts, or even someone's identity. Internet blackmail has actually been an area of high criminal activity, with targets such as online casinos, security and technology companies, and who knows what others, because they generally will not say. Ransoms with these attacks are known to be as high as millions of dollars. If this type of crime is encountered, one must seek the help of a technology specialist and a lawyer.

Denial of Service Attack A DoS attack is intended to harm victims in a different way. Like most attacks, variants of DoS exist and include distributed DoS and reflection DoS attacks. All of these malicious objects attempt to bring computer systems, specifically online web servers that provide e-commerce, to a rapid halt. When firms such as eBay.com, Amazon.com, and Yahoo.com are down, not only do those entities have no means of conducting business operations during that time, but they are high-profile businesses, and cyberterrorists will gain publicity from their acts.

E-mail Cyberterrorists might use a variety of nefarious e-mail attacks. Spam is unsolicited e-mail or junk e-mail. Spamming techniques can be used to clog an e-mail server to the point it locks up. One of the first so-called viruses was the Christmas Virus released into IBM's computers. A Christmas card message was sent that contained programming code to replicate the message to everyone in the recipient's address book, locking up IBM's systems for quite some time. Spamming the right system with the right code can work much like a DoS attack.

Spoofing is pretending to be someone else or some entity. The intent is to deceive the other party into taking action resulting in embarrassment or harm. Spoofing traditionally was associated with phishing, but now applies to the broader misrepresentation of self as someone else. Spoofing is often a gateway crime, opening up bigger and better fraud opportunities.

Viruses are a very significant threat to businesses in terms of resources lost. Experts estimate U.S. corporations spent about $12.3 billion to clean up damage from computer viruses in 2001, and many viruses cost over $1 million per virus. A virus can erase or disable system data, the operating system, or application software. One cybercriminal almost destroyed a business by erasing all data for existing projects. The business was a consulting firm that kept the project files on its network. The cybercriminal had inside information that the business did not have a current backup, and by sending a virus to erase key files and drives on the network, the firm lost all current information on projects and had a serious problem of reconstructing work performed to date. The business almost collapsed.

An emerging tool for cybercriminal and hackers is spyware. According to pcwebopedia.com, spyware, also called adware, is any software that covertly gathers information through the user's Internet connection without his knowledge, usually for advertising purposes.[14] Spyware ranges from harmless pop-up ads to the ability to record anything that happens on a computer and transmit that data to a remote site. For example, WinWhatWhere software can record all keystrokes on a personal computer and send them to some remote location on the Internet. [15] Spyware applications typically are bundled as a hidden component of freeware or shareware programs that can be downloaded from the Internet. Once installed, the spyware monitors user activity on the Internet and transmits that information in the background to someone else. Spyware can also gather information about e-mail addresses and even passwords and credit card numbers. During a recent consulting engagement, one author removed over 1,800 spyware objects on a single laptop computer!

Aside from the questions of ethics and privacy, spyware steals from the user by using the computer's memory resources and also by eating bandwidth as it sends information back to the spyware's home base via the user's Internet connection. Since spyware is using memory and system resources, the applications running in the background can lead to system crashes or general system instability. Because spyware exists as independent executable programs, they have the ability to monitor keystrokes; scan files on the hard drive; snoop other applications, such as chat programs or word processors; install other spyware programs; read cookies; and change the default home page on the Web browser, consistently relaying this information back to the spyware author who will either use it for advertising/marketing purposes or sell the information to another party.

Effective InfoSec Controls

Access control systems are the beginning layer of protection for systems and information. They are used to authenticate and verify, usually by using one of three basic approaches to security: (1) something you have, (2) something you know, and (3) something you are. [16] Specific controls range from access cards/readers (something you have), to passwords or PINs (something you know), to biometrics (something you are). The more risk that exists, the greater the need to consider a multifaceted access control system in order to maintain adequate security. That is, it takes more access security than just an ID and password.

The most general authentication, authorization, and verification controls are password systems, firewalls, and occasionally access cards or biometrics. The weakness of the first two security methods is that they have been compromised, and intruders have caused great harm and significant financial losses. The latter approach, biometrics, has the potential to provide the greatest level of security because it involves something you are, and because it can be more reliable than the passwords or firewalls, especially stand-alone password or firewall systems.

The difference between verification (authentication) and identification (authorization) needs to be emphasized. Authorization is the recognition of a specific individual from among all the individuals enrolled on the system. That is, the token or ID/Password are valid and that ID is authorized to have access to the system. Authentication, however, is the process of confirming that the person carrying the token (e.g., badge, card, password, etc., which is the claim of identity) is the rightful owner of the token. Ideally, access control systems would do both.

Passwords are the first line of defense in authenticating access to systems and data, and serve as a reasonably effective preventive system. One strategy is to create multifaceted passwords, especially where remote access is frequent or e-commerce is employed. One current sophisticated approach is to generate password PINs over very short time frames, sometimes less than a minute. When remote users log in, they check a beeper for the most recent PIN and can log in only with both their password and the dynamic PIN.

Although they appear to be much less expensive than biometric systems, password systems cost an organization. This cost usually happens in two ways: passwords that are forgotten and passwords that are stolen. The former requires time and resources to reset passwords. The latter is a security breach and can be much more costly, if the system is compromised. Since the human brain is not a perfect storage system when it comes to complicated and a long letter-number combination, the more sophisticated passwords might be forgotten. In such situations, the password needs to be reset and a new password must be created. According to Mandylion Research Labs, resetting a password security system of a company with 100 workers would cost $3,850 per year. If the company has 1,000 authorized personnel, the same process would cost up to $38,500 per year.[17]

For remote access, one control might be the use of call-back systems. If remote access is stationary (i.e., the same person always accesses the system from the same phone), this technique works well. Once a user logs in from remote location, the system hangs up the line and calls back on a predetermined phone number. Where call-back systems are impractical, multifaceted password systems should be employed—perhaps biometrics.

The most common biometric devices used for access control are fingerprint scanners, although facial and iris scanners and voice recognition systems are increasing in use.[18] Fingerprint scanners come in a variety of formats, from stand-alone devices to readers built into keyboards and mice. They are unobtrusive, inexpensive, and, essentially, they work. For example, the Public Benefits administrators in Texas and New York claim fingerprint identification has virtually eliminated fraud in their programs.[19] The obstacle to employing biometrics is no longer cost or variety of tools, but the problems in implementing biometrics into the system and organization.

Of special importance is the emerging trend toward integration of biometrics into networks and systems. More time is being spent on integrating biometrics into existing processes and applications, where feasible and applicable, and into network access control systems. Biometric systems are becoming a commodity item, and this progression leads to a potentially enhanced level of interoperability, something the biometric industry needs. Recently an increasing number of devices come with integral biometric fingerprint readers, such as notebook computers and computer keyboards; some come with smartcard readers as well, plus several variants of biometric mice.[20] This area provides a lot of promise for all concerned with InfoSec.

Careless information security procedures are a big problem. First there is the problem with accounts that remain in the firm's systems. IDC estimates that 30 to 60% of access files in large corporations are no longer valid.[21] These accounts serve as magnets to would-be insider employees and to outsider hackers, crackers, and intruders. Another problem is stale passwords: That is, there is either no password policy and procedure for changing passwords, or the policy goes unenforced, leaving passwords unchanged for long periods of time.

The integrity of a password is inversely related to the time it has been used; the longer a password is used without being changed, the weaker its integrity. "Strong passwords" is another best practice that is often overlooked. A strong password includes at least eight characters, at least one number, and is *not* a "real word." Finally, failure to actually enforce security policies is another common weakness in companies. Lax controls lead to easy access by cyberterrorists and other intruders.

SUMMARY

Computer frauds include a variety of things beyond the kinds of fraud schemes associated with internal frauds. Because computers are sometimes used to perpetrate a fraud, or track transactions for the fraudster, it is important to understand computers and systems can be used as a tool in a fraud. This chapter covers some of the basics in computer fraud and abuse, including some basic InfoSec and anti-fraud measures.

ENDNOTES

1. Cangemi, M. and Singleton, T. *Managing the Audit Function* 3e (Hoboken, NJ: John Wiley and Sons) p. 98.
2. "Survey: Hacking Often Unreported", MSNBC, April 7, 2002. See URL http://www.msnbc.com/news/735198.asp?0si=-&cp1=1
3. http://www.cert.org/present/cert-overview-trends/module-6.pdf
4. Cunningham, K. "Cyberterrorism: Are We Leaving the Keys Out?," *SC Magazine,* November 2002. Online at: http://www. scmagazine.com/scmagazine/sconline/2002/article/51/article.html
5. Ibid.
6. According to Computer Emergency Response Team. See "Combating Cyberthreats: Partnership Between Public and Private Entities," E. Lee, *Information Systems Control Journal,* Vol. 3, 2002.
7. A white-hat hacker is a hacker who works for an entity to improve its information security. A black-hat hacker would be a hacker who attacks computer systems without permission.
8. They are called white hats because (a) they have obtained prior permission to "hack," (b) hacking is a part of their job description and they are an employee, (c) they have a contract to conduct a pen test (specific domain, specific time frame), and (d) they have an engagement letter to conduct the pen test.
9. See technical definition of hacker at: http://pcwebopedia.com/TERM/h/hacker.html
10. See technical definition of cracker at: http://pcwebopedia.com/TERM/c/crack.html. Likely a reference to safe crackers.

11. According to ZDNet associate editor Robert Vamosi. See "Can We Stop Script Kiddies? Yes! Here's How," *ZDNet Reviews,* May 15, 2002, online at http://www.zdnet.com.

12. Singleton, T. "Managing Distributed Denial of Serivce Attacks," *EDPACS,* Volume XXX, Number 5 (November 2002), pp. 7, 9–20.

13. Phishing is a term used to describe social engineering, con artist, or plain old "fishing expedition" type activities. The perpetrator usually sends an e-mail and asks for information under the pretense of some official or legitimate cause. The purpose is usually to steal either your identity or access codes to a computer system.

14. This paragraph is taken from the definition of spyware provided by pcwebopedia at http://pcwebopedia.com/TERM/s/spyware.html.

15. Available from http://www.trueactive.com/default.asp.

16. Simon Liu & Mark Silverman, "A Practical Guide to Biometric Security Technology," IEEE Computer Society. Online at: http://www.computer.org/itpro/homepage/Jan_Feb/security3.htm

17. Singleton, T. "Biometric Security Systems: The Best InfoSec Solution?," EDPACS, Volume XXX, Number 9 (March 2003), pp. 1–20.

18. "The Lowdown on Biometrics," Government Computer News, 08/12/02. Online at: http://www.gcn.com/cgi-bin/udt/im.display.printable?client.id=gcn2&story.id=19567.

19. Mark Kellner, "Digital Security," *Government Computer News,* 08/12/02. Online at: http://www.gcn.com/cgi-bin/udt/im.display.printable?client.id=gcn2&story.id=19565.

20. Julian Ashbourn, "Biometrics: Making the Right Impression," *SC Magazine,* June 2002, pp. 58–63.

21. Ibid.

CHAPTER 11

Forensic Accountant as an Expert Witness

INTRODUCTION

Based on the definitions used in this book, one of the distinguishing differences between a true fraud auditor and a forensic accountant is the role played *after* the fraud investigation or audit is completed, competent and sufficient evidence has been gathered, the fraudster has been identified, and the fraudster is being prosecuted. Generally speaking, conducting the audit is the extent of the fraud auditor's work. A forensic accountant, however, is a specialist in providing expert testimony or serving as an expert witness in the subsequent trial. Regardless, the auditor involved in gathering the evidence is likely to be involved in the court case that follows, should one occur. This chapter provides information about the role of expert witness in a fraud case, the qualifications for the expert and his evidence, and some of the subtleties of the court processes, such as the strategies of the opposing attorney on cross-examination.

ROLE OF A FORENSIC ACCOUNTANT AS A WITNESS IN COURT

Lay witnesses in civil and criminal cases generally are restricted from giving legal testimony consisting of opinions, conclusions, and characterizations, although they may estimate the speed of a moving vehicle, approximate temperature and distances, identify common smells, and testify in matters of physical description such as age, height, and weight. However, qualified experts may give their professional opinions. Consider the Michigan Supreme Court Rules of Evidence on this point:

RULE 702: TESTIMONY BY EXPERTS

If the court determines that recognized scientific, technical, or other specialized knowledge will assist the trier of fact to understand the evidence or to determine a fact in issue, a witness qualified as an expert by knowledge, skill, experience, training, or education, may testify thereto in the form of an opinion or otherwise.

RULE 703: BASES OF OPINION TESTIMONY BY EXPERTS

The facts or data in the particular case upon which an expert bases an opinion or inference may be those perceived by or made known to him at or before the hearing. The court may require that underlying facts or data essential to an opinion or inference be in evidence.

RULE 704: OPINION ON ULTIMATE ISSUE

Testimony in the form of an opinion or inference otherwise admissible is not objectionable because it embraces an ultimate issue to be decided by the trier of fact.

RULE 705: DISCLOSURE OF FACTS OR DATA UNDERLYING EXPERT OPINION

The expert may testify in terms of opinion or inference and give his reasons therefore without prior disclosure of the underlying facts or data, unless the court requires otherwise. The expert may in any event be required to disclose the underlying facts or data on cross-examination.

RULE 706: COURT-APPOINTED EXPERTS

(a) Appointment
The court may on its own motion or on the motion of any party enter an order to show cause why expert witnesses should be appointed, and may request the parties to submit nominations. The

court may appoint any expert witnesses agreed upon by the parties, and may appoint expert witnesses of its own selection. An expert witness shall not be appointed by the court unless he consents to act. A witness so appointed shall be informed of his duties by the court in writing, a copy of which shall be filed with the clerk, or at a conference in which the parties shall have opportunity to participate. A witness so appointed shall advise the parties of his findings, if any, his deposition may be taken by any party, and he may be called to testify by the court or any party. He shall be subject to cross-examination by each party, including a party calling him as a witness.

(b) Compensation

Expert witnesses so appointed are entitled to reasonable compensation in whatever sum the court may allow. The compensation thus fixed is payable from funds which may be provided by law in criminal cases and civil actions and proceedings involving just compensation under the Fifth Amendment. In other civil actions and proceedings the compensation shall be paid by the parties in such proportion and at such time as the court directs, and thereafter charged in like manner as other costs.

(c) Disclosure of appointment

In the exercise of its discretion, the court may authorize disclosure to the jury of the fact that the court appointed the expert witness.

(d) Parties' experts of own selection

Nothing in this rule limits the parties in calling expert witnesses of their own selection.

RULE 707: USE OF LEARNED TREATISES FOR IMPEACHMENT

To the extent called to the attention of an expert witness upon cross-examination or relied upon by him in direct examination, statements contained in published treatises, periodicals, or pamphlets on a subject of history, medicine, or other science or art, established as a reliable authority by the testimony or admission of the witness or by other expert testimony or by judicial notice, are admissible for impeachment purposes only. Expert witnesses may be cross-examined as any other witness and especially as to qualifications, bases of opinions, and compensation for testifying.

Expert witnesses may express opinions in response to hypothetical questions, if the hypothesized facts in the questions are supported by the evidence of the case.

> *Accountants and auditors are often called upon to provide testimony in litigation support matters and criminal prosecutions in which their services are utilized to support investigations of such crimes as financial frauds, embezzlement, misapplication of funds, arson for profit, bankruptcy fraud, and tax evasion. Accountants and auditors may also be utilized as defense witnesses or as support to the defendant's counsel on matters that involve accounting or audit issues.*[1]

The last section is of particular importance in identifying both accountants/auditors and their role in fraud cases.

Daubert and Standards for Admissibility of Expert Witness Testimony

Over the years, the legal standards for acceptance of expert testimony have changed. The current U.S. standard is the *Daubert* case standards that were determined by the U.S. Supreme Court. These standards are critical in the determination of an expert's qualifications and, more important, her testimony.

Brief History of Legal Standards on Expert Testimony[2]   The courts used a "general acceptance" guideline for admitting expert testimony. This guideline was the result of *Frye v. United States*.[3] It stated that an expert opinion that was based on scientific technique is not admissible unless the technique is generally accepted as reliable within the relevant scientific community.

In 1975, the U.S. Congress adopted the Federal Rules of Evidence (Rule 702), establishing rules rather than common law as the basis for determining the acceptance of evidentiary issues. Rule 702 was designed so that more expert testimony would come before triers of fact.[4] The rule does not state that evidence is admissible only if it is generally accepted, and therefore it was in conflict with the previous standard established in *Frye*. Under Rule 702, trial judges rarely disqualified expert witnesses or testimony, but did limit the area where experts testimony could be offered.[5]

Daubert Ruling   In 1993, the U.S. Supreme Court empowered trial judges to be gatekeepers regarding expert witness testimony by making them specifically responsible for excluding unreliable expert witness testimony in *Daubert v. Merrell Dow Pharmaceuticals Inc.*[6] The Court also discussed limitations that Rule 702 placed on admissibility. One conclusion was that scientific evidence needed to be relevant and reliable. The Court also mandated a flexible approach in determining the admissibility of expert testimony. Four key factors to be considered are:

1. The credentials and/or experience that indicate an expert
2. The testimony's basis in fact
3. The testimony relevance and reliability
4. Other factors

In addition, the Court established five nonexhaustive factors to aid judges in assessing the reliability of expert testimony:

1. *Testing.* Can the theory or technique be tested, or has it been tested?
2. *Peer reviews.* Has the theory or technique been subjected to peer review or publication which aids in determining flaws in the method?
3. *Error rates.* Are there established standards to control the use of the technique? Is there a high rate of error or potential rate of error in the chosen method?
4. *Acceptability.* Is the theory or technique generally accepted in the relevant technical community?
5. *Time.* Did the theory or technique exist before litigation began?

While the *Daubert* ruling codified factors in evaluating the qualifications of expert witnesses, it also created some problems of its own. The most important to the topic of this book is the applicability of *Daubert* to nonscientific testimony, such as forensic accountants.

Cases That Amplified the *Daubert* Ruling Some courts applied the *Daubert* ruling only to scientific testimony, while other courts interpreted it more broadly. The U.S. Supreme Court resolved this predicament in *Kumho Tire Company, Ltd. v. Patrick Carmichael.*[7] The Court extended trial judges' exclusionary responsibility to the testimony of nonscientific, technical, and other specialized experts (e.g., forensic accountants). In the same case, the Court reasserted a critical finding from *General Electric Co. v. Joiner,*[8] that district courts hold the gate-keeper responsibility and circuit courts should overturn an admissibility decision only when there is clear abuse of discretion by a trial judge.

The second problem created in *Daubert* is that courts were inconsistent in the type of test employed in determining admissibility of an expert, which was the result of the flexibility in *Daubert*. Some judges interpret the *Daubert* ruling as close to the *Frye* test as possible, while others adopt the more liberal approach in Rule 702. Each judge is likely to employ his own criteria. Forensic accountants need to work closely with the attorneys to prepare testimony that will ultimately be considered appropriate and admissible in a specific court or by a specific judge.

Whether the *Daubert/Kumho/Joiner* principles extend to state courts is within the discretion of the various individual states.[9]

Implications for Forensic Accountants   The challenges allowed by *Daubert* apply to the expert testimony of forensic accountants. Because of *Daubert*, and the subsequent rulings in *Kumho* and *Joiner*, any errors leading to the exclusion of testimony by a forensic accountant have little hope of being reversed.

Forensic accountants must be careful to meet *Daubert* challenges successfully when being engaged as an expert witness. Since *Daubert*, an increasing number of testifying experts have been subjected to challenges by opposing counsel in an attempt to prevent the expert from testifying. In fact, several trial courts have applied the *Daubert* factors to exclude valuation-related expert testimony. For example, in *Andrew J. Whelan, et al. v. Tyler Adell, et al.*, the judge excluded the financial valuation expert testimony of a Big Four Certified Public Accountant (CPA).[10] The expert used only one valuation method, a discounted cash flow method that relied on speculative financial projections. In *Target Market Publishing, Inc. v. ADVO, Inc.*, the same thing happened: another Big Four CPA had his testimony excluded because he used only one method and speculative assumptions.[11]

Reilly provides these guidelines for forensic accountants serving as expert witnesses:

- Know the relevant professional standards.
- Apply the relevant professional standards.
- Know the relevant professional literature.

- Know the relevant professional organizations.
- Use generally accepted analytical methods.
- Use multiple analytical methods.
- Synthesize the conclusions of the multiple analytical methods.
- Disclose all significant analytical assumptions and variables.
- Subject the analysis to peer review.
- Test the analysis and the conclusion for reasonableness.[12]

Larry Crumbley, editor of *The Journal of Forensic Accounting* and a pioneer in forensic accounting, provided some helpful points for forensic accountants who are thinking about being expert witnesses. First, he suggests forensic accountants *review their qualifications*. They must make sure they have the competencies necessary to serve as an expert witness in a particular case. Second, they must *get their credentials in order*. Federal rules of civil procedures requires that experts disclose their identity, the issues their opinions will address, their professional qualifications (including their publications of the last 10 years and all cases in which they provided expert testimony in the last four years), and who is paying them. Also, they must *be realistic* about whether they are are the right expert for the job. Once a forensic accountant has been retained, she should *prepare in depth. Do not let the attorney mold conclusions.* The forensic expert must practice beforehand, possibly *recording one's own testimony and reviewing the audio recording.*

According to Parfitt, attorneys should do six things to assist in making sure the expert (forensic accountant) is *"Daubert*-proof."

1. Examine the forensic accountant's curriculum vitae (CV) for general qualifications, such as research in a relevant field, number of relevant publications, and publication bias.
2. Question the forensic accountant to ascertain whether there are any misrepresentations, inaccuracies, or significant omissions in the CV.
3. Examine positions the forensic accountant has taken in publications to identify consistent, or inconsistent, opinions.
4. Review copies of the forensic accountant's prior testimony on the subject to determine if opinions have been stricken in other trials.
5. Educate the forensic accountant fully on forensic accounting issues relevant to the case.

6. Prepare materials to support an argument to include your forensic accountant's testimony, including Rule 702 and *Daubert* case law, and relevant judicial opinions.[13]

FORENSIC ACCOUNTANT AS AN EXPERT WITNESS

When accountants and auditors are called by the prosecution, they generally testify about their investigative findings. When they are called by the defense, they may testify about the quality of the findings or the opinions expressed by the prosecution's accounting expert, in order to create doubt in the minds of jury members about the credibility or weight to give to the prosecution's expert.

Qualifications

Qualifying accountants and auditors as technical experts generally is not a difficult task. Questions are posed to them concerning their professional credentials—education, work experience, licensing or certification, technical training courses taken, technical books and journal articles written, offices held in professional associations, and awards and commendations received.

Defense lawyers usually are not prone to challenge the expertise of accountants and auditors, assuming they meet at least minimum standards of professional competence. To do so might give these experts an opportunity to fully highlight their professional credentials and perhaps make a greater impression on the jury or judge, thus adding more weight to their testimony. So defense attorneys often pass on the opportunity to challenge these expert witnesses.

The question of whether being a Certified Public Accountant or Chartered Accountant (CA) is sufficient to qualify oneself as an expert often arises. Generally, persons may be experts in their particular field of expertise if they have sufficient experience and are members of their institute. This situation does not mean that CPAs/CAs are automatically experts. However, this credential passes the first hurdle. To be considered an expert, it is helpful to have prior experience with litigation or criminal matters. This qualification is primarily a result of the knowledge and skills that are gained during the testifying experience.

Further, it is often beneficial to have been accepted as an expert in other matters, thereby easing current acceptance. A danger exists, however, of appearing to be an expert at being an expert witness.

Often, the counsel introducing the witness will read the expert's qualifications or ask specific questions of the witness to establish her credentials. On occasion, the qualifications of the expert witness are read directly into the court record. Although the expert's qualifications are not often contested, it is a distinct possibility. Over and above being accepted by both parties, it is most important that the expert witness be accepted by the court.

An extract reproduced from the proceedings in *Regina v. Scheel* shows how the accountant's qualifications as an expert witness can be established and how accounting exhibits might be introduced (see Appendix 11A).[14]

Effective Profile

Expert accounting witnesses must have a thorough knowledge not only of generally accepted accounting principles (GAAP) but also of the current promulgations of their institute. Often the expert's expertise may involve special knowledge of a specific industry, such as construction accounting or accounting in a stock market environment. In this case, the expert should be aware of recent developments and any important accounting issues within that area.

Experts must also be analytical and possess the ability to work with incomplete data; however, they may not always be able to recognize when data are incomplete. As a result, experts may make various assumptions that would then be open to interpretation or attack. If all data have not been made available, then it is quite possible that the opposing counsel may be able to offer alternate scenarios that are more plausible under the circumstances, thus discrediting the expert.

Experts must have the ability to simplify complex issues. It is helpful if they can communicate very directly and simply, keeping in mind that they are talking to nonaccountants and that the expert's role is to clarify complex issues so that everyone can understand them. In view of this, some background or experience in teaching often is helpful.

Being a Credible Witness

The goal of forensic accountants is to make their findings understandable to counsel, judges, and juries, and to avoid resorting to jargon and academic polemics about accounting rules and standards. The facts, stated simply and briefly, are all the audience needs or cares to hear. Anything beyond that only makes accounting and auditing more obscure.

To be a credible expert witness, accountants and auditors should be knowledgeable in their own fields by education and experience and members in good standing of the profession or of some specialized aspect of practice that would be pertinent to the case at hand. But there are other considerations as well to make an expert witness credible. Experts will appear credible when they follow these suggestions:

- Speak clearly and audibly.
- Refrain from using professional jargon.
- Use simple rather than complex terms to describe findings and opinions.
- Address the specific questions asked; do not go off on tangents or volunteer more than a question asks.
- Do not verbally fence with the defense attorney or prosecutor.
- Look directly at the question poser (prosecutor or defense counsel).
- Maintain a professional demeanor; do not smile gratuitously at the judge, the jury, the lawyer who hired you, or the opponent's counsel.
- Be calm and deliberate in responding to questions; speak neither too slowly nor too rapidly.
- Dress conservatively.
- Have neatly combed hair and newly shined shoes.
- Use graphs, charts, and other visual aids if they help to clarify a point.
- Do not read from notes if it can be avoided. (If the expert does read from notes, the opposition lawyer will probably demand to see them, and then the expert will appear to have rehearsed her testimony.)
- If you have documents to introduce, have them organized so that they can be retrieved quickly when asked to do so by the counsel for whose side you are testifying.

- Do not hem and haw or stammer. Retain your composure when a tough or complex question is posed.
- Ask for repetition or clarification if you do not fully understand the question.
- If you do not know the answer, say so—do not guess.
- In cross-examination, do not respond too quickly. Counsel for your side may wish to interpose an objection to the question.
- If the judge elects to ask a question, respond to it by looking at her.
- Do not stare off into space or at the floor or ceiling.
- Be friendly to all sides.
- Do not raise your voice in anger if the opponent's lawyer tries to bait you.
- Be honest. Do not invent. Do not inflate. Do not evade.

QUALIFICATION AND ADMISSIBILITY OF ACCOUNTING EVIDENCE

Documentary accounting evidence may be presented in a court of law in two forms: (1) primary, including original, individual accounting documents obtained from the parties concerned or other sources, and (2) secondary, including summaries and schedules based on the original documents. An accountant produces these secondary documents based on an examination of the primary evidence.

The admissibility of such evidence is well established in the United States. In *Hoyer v. United States*, the court held that in a prosecution for attempting to evade income taxes, summaries prepared from documentary and oral evidence were admissible to show the defendant's correct net income. In delivering the judgment of the court, Chief Judge Gardner said:

> . . . *these exhibits so compiled and prepared purported to show the correct net income of the defendant for the years covered by the indictment. They were prepared by experts from documentary evidence introduced and from oral testimony. As the documentary evidence had already been introduced, counsel for the defendant had ample opportunity to examine it and to cross-examine the expert as to the basic testimony and his calculations based thereon. The evidence was clearly admissible.*

The documentary evidence presented a complicated situation and required elaborate compilations which could not have been made by the jury. It is also to be noted in this connection that the Court advised the jury that the testimony of the experts was advisory and need not be accepted by them as a verity. [15]

In *Daniel v. United States*, District Judge Hunter, delivering the judgment of the court, said:

The rule is that a summary of books and records is admissible, provided cross-examination is allowed and the original records are available. Here the records of which the exhibits are summaries were in evidence, and the man who prepared them was available for cross-examination.

It is perfectly proper that litigants be permitted the use of illustrative charts to summarize varying computations and to thus make the primary proof upon which such charts must be based more enlightening to the jury. The district judge did not abuse his discretion by permitting the use of these summaries.

I would also observe that in the present case the summaries were helpful to the appellant, with respect to some of the counts.

The introduction of the summaries did not offend against the rule that requires the production of original documents, since the documents which were the primary source of the summaries were in evidence. It is accordingly unnecessary in this case to invoke the exception to the rule referred to by Wigmore in the following passage:

> *Where a fact could be ascertained only by the inspection of a large number of documents made up of very numerous detailed shipments . . . as the net balance resulting from a year's vouchers of a treasurer or a year's accounts in a bank ledger— it is obvious that it would often be practically out of the question to apply the present principle by requiring the production of the entire mass of documents and entries to be perused by the jury or read aloud to them. The convenience of trials demands that other evidence be allowed to be offered, in the shape of the testimony of a competent witness who has perused the entire mass and will state summarily the net result. Such a practice is well established to be proper.*

Most courts require, as a condition, that the mass thus summarily testified to shall, if the occasion seems to require it, be placed at hand in court, or at least be made accessible to the opposing party, in order that the correctness of the evidence may be tested by

*inspection if desired, or that the material for cross-examination
may be made available.*

*Accordingly, we were of the view that the learned trial judge
did not err in admitting the summaries previously described.*[16]

EXPERT'S ROLE IN THE LITIGATION TEAM

Generally, experts play an ongoing part in the litigation team. In particular, their involvement may be at various stages throughout the development of the case, most notably in:

- Case assessment
- Identification of documentation required to support the case, both additional and currently available
- Evaluation of the scope of work
- Preparation of initial financial assessment and analysis
- Consultation with counsel on legal issues and approach
- Preparation of report and accounting schedules and, if necessary, a document brief
- Negotiations between parties
- Assistance to counsel in court
- Expert evidence in court

The accountant may also be called on to give a different opinion from that reached by an equally credible expert accountant on the other side. This situation may arise because of different interpretations of the facts of the case or various alternative accounting techniques that might be available under the circumstances. In some cases, given equally plausible alternatives, the case often is decided on based on whichever side has the most credible expert witness.

PRETESTIMONY ACTIVITIES

Pretestimony activities generally encompass preparing the report of the expert witness to a final stage. Without stating that the list is all-inclusive or appropriate in all circumstances, reports should include a discussion of these financial aspects:

- Issues
- Reliance on data to achieve conclusion
- Assumptions made in arriving at conclusion
- Restriction on assumptions
- Date of information cut-off
- Opinion and conclusion based on the available documentation
- Limitations of opinion and sensitivity to assumptions
- Detailed schedules and documents supporting the opinion and conclusion

One important problem in preparing reports and accounting summaries arises from the delegation of tasks to junior accountants. If the person giving evidence has not had direct knowledge or has not examined the specific documents or prepared the accounting summaries, it may be possible that the expert will be trapped under the hearsay rule. If tasks are delegated, it is important that the review process entail review of all work to original documentation on a 100% basis.

It is also important to know the effect of other assumptions on the conclusion or opinion reached in the report. It is often possible to trap an expert into giving alternate opinions, based on other assumptions that had not been considered. Generally, working papers supporting the report and accounting schedules should not show contradictory conclusions to the report, as they are producible in court. This suggestion does not advocate that working papers should be deleted or amended subsequent to preparation; rather, it is a caution that these papers should be prepared with the precept that they could ultimately be submitted to the court and, as such, should take the appropriate form when they are prepared.

Another aspect of pretrial preparation relates to the availability of all notes that the witness intends to use or rely on. These notes may be requested in evidence for the court or may be producible during examination.

Further activities could consist of determining whether sufficient material is present to support the report. It may be necessary to derive information from other witnesses to support the expert's conclusions. This information normally is communicated by reference to discoveries or earlier will-says. Unfortunately, the witness cannot refer to these unless he has direct knowledge of their contents. If the accountant has relied on opinions or information presented by other witnesses, then he must either hear that evidence in court or have the transcript or agreed statement of facts available. Otherwise, that information and any opinions drawn from it would not be allowable.

It often is useful to have a list of all other witnesses including the witnesses for the other side. This information is important so that the expert is not surprised by the existence of other experts or reports. The expert can then determine if it is necessary that he be present for the testimony of those witnesses and obtain the related court approval. If another expert will be present, then it is incumbent on the expert witness to examine the alternate reports and assess whether reasonable points are brought by the other side that may affect the credibility of the expert's report.

Other pretestimony activities encompass ensuring that any required graphic displays are ready and available, that all important discussions with the lawyer have been held as part of the pretestimony meetings, and that the expert completely understands the report and all other relevant issues in the trial, whether accounting related or not. Most important, experts must ensure that they agree with counsel as to the sequence of the experts' evidence and the strategy for presenting it. It is often useful to have a dry run at the direct testimony, with counsel posing all the questions to the expert witness in order to avoid surprises during trial.

At pretestimony meetings, it is often appropriate to discuss the witness's qualifications again to assure that they are current, to discuss the strengths and weaknesses of the case, and to discuss and agree on which parts of the expert's reports, if not all, are to be entered into court as exhibits.

TRIAL AND TESTIMONY

On the Stand

Judges and juries often base their assessments of expert witnesses at least in part on how the witnesses look. Therefore, it is important that witnesses be well groomed and neatly dressed. In the case of an accountant, a dark business suit is the expected image. This appearance may enhance the image to psychological advantage. In the witness box, the witness should maintain a poised, alert appearance, stand still, and be ready to take the oath. It is important to control the hands, avoid fidgeting, and maintain eye contact with the questioner. As the judge will be taking notes, the witness should speak slowly enough to ensure that the judge does not fall behind. The voice should be strong and directed to the questioner. The witness should enunciate clearly.

Several things should be avoided in giving evidence. These range from drinking five cups of coffee immediately before testifying or chewing bubble gum while giving evidence, to small physical mannerisms that may affect one's appearance. These physical mannerisms, which might be as simple as rubbing the hands together continually, looking down at one's hands, continually moving in the stand, or jingling coins in a pocket, could quickly become irritating to the judge.

Direct Examination

The purpose of direct examination is to enable counsel for the side the expert represents to draw out the financial evidence to prove the case. Most likely, this examination will be only a reiteration of what has been discussed previously with counsel outside of the courtroom. It is still very important, however, for the expert to refresh her memory by reference to anything she may have read, written, or given in evidence on the case beforehand.

Direct examination is the most organized aspect of the trial; it is the stage in which the expert's credibility must be established with the judge or jury. According to the concept of the primary memory feature, people remember best what they hear first and last. This fact is often a useful idea to employ in giving or structuring evidence. A further noteworthy point is that the jury often has a limited attention span in a long trial; thus, it is often useful to use a "grab/give/conclude" method of presenting evidence.

For a witness, the interpretation of questions and the ability to listen are crucial skills. Even though the witness already may have gone through a mock direct examination, it is critical that each question be evaluated carefully again; the witness should reflect on the questions asked and not anticipate them. (They may have been changed since the time of rehearsal.) Throughout, it is useful to remember that this aspect of testimony was rehearsed in advance and so is the easiest part of examination.

It is necessary to be honest in answering questions. Less obvious, however, is the need to avoid bias and prejudice when answering. The answers to all questions should be clear and concise, and when complex terms are used, they should be clarified. Use of notes should be limited as much as possible in order to maintain eye contact with both the judge and the rest of the court.

Accounting schedules should be described accurately and succinctly in layperson's terms. Schedules are by their nature concise documents and should be described in that manner. If opinions are given, they should be given with conviction once the appropriate groundwork has been laid.

Cross-Examination

Cross-examination is truly the highlight of the adversarial court system; it is geared to allow counsel either to clarify or to make points at the witness's expense. As such, it is generally the most difficult part of the trial process for any witness. Anything unexpected can turn up that might refute or embarrass the witness, whose credibility is constantly called into question.

The goals of the opposing counsel during cross-examination are threefold. The first is to diminish the importance of the expert testimony just presented. The second might be to have the expert testify in support of the opposing position by providing a series of assumptions. The third is to attack the opinion itself or to show the inadequacies of the expert's work in arriving at her opinion, thereby discrediting the opinion, the report, and the witness in the eyes of the court.

The opposing counsel can attack or question anything that was said or entered into court. This cross-examination includes notes, working papers, affidavits, will-says, reports, and preliminary trial or discovery transcripts. Often cross-examination is conducted in an atmosphere of confrontation and contradiction. At all times, financial expert witnesses must remember that, however crucial to the case they may be, they are merely a piece of the puzzle. Most important, witnesses must not take attacks or attempts to discredit them personally. There are many ways to discredit an expert witness. Throughout the process, it is important for the witness to maintain pride and professional integrity. An adage to remember is that "even mud can be worn well."

In general, proper attitude and demeanor during direct examination are also applicable to cross-examination, except that opposing counsel wants to reduce or limit the impact of the witness's evidence. It is natural to feel a certain amount of apprehension at this stage, and this stress does a great deal to keep the witness alert.

The jury often watches the judge, and therefore the expert often can take a clue as to the tempo and reaction of the jury and the judge to the evidence being presented. Slight changes in style and presentation can be made accordingly.

The opposing counsel usually has a plan of cross-examination in mind, and an expert witness should be able to establish this direction to prevent falling into a trap or erring. A danger of this mental logic, of course, is that the witness will spend as much time planning ahead as answering the questions and may not be giving appropriate weight to the immediate questions. Further, in attempting to anticipate questions, the witness may misunderstand the one being asked.

When asked questions, the expert should evaluate them carefully and take time to consider the answers. The witness should be calm and pause before answering, and tread very carefully toward the answer, knowing exactly how it relates to both the question and the issues before the court.

When answering, it is important to be honest and to avoid the appearance of bias and prejudice. It is equally important not to exaggerate, ramble, allow oneself to be baited, or attempt to be humorous. One of the most devastating blows to a litigation or defendant is having expert witnesses make a transparent attempt to hide errors or lose their temper.

Generally, it is a rule of thumb for expert witnesses not to give away or volunteer information. Further, during their responses, often it may be extremely difficult to avoid being trapped in various assumptions, what-if scenarios, and generalities presented by counsel during cross-examination. If this entrapment attempt occurs, the expert should retrench by asking for the question to be rephrased in smaller components.

It is critical *never* to underestimate the accounting expertise of the opposing counsel. Often opposing counsel underplay their understanding of the issues in order to lull the expert into a sense of security. Obviously, this tactic can lead the expert into a difficult situation.

In general terms, opposing counsel's golden rule is to cross-examine only if the cross-examination would benefit a case. In questioning the witness, opposing counsel will generally ask either simply worded short questions or leading questions. Usually counsel knows the answers to their questions in order to eliminate any surprises and to allow them to lead the witness along. Several techniques are also available to destroy witnesses without touching their evidence.

Opposing counsel generally will evaluate answers and then take a specific approach that furthers their arguments. Usually witnesses will not be allowed to explain or elaborate on answers at that time as that would allow a witness to alter the thrust of the carefully orchestrated cross-examination. Opposing counsel is also continually questioning or evaluating how its last question and answer could be used against the witness. If the question has raised new ground, can it be developed and used to enhance the opposing counsel's position?

Opposing counsel will often prepare by reading all of the witness's earlier testimony and publications. Opposing counsel might also speak to other lawyers about the witness's earlier performance in court. This preparation may indicate specific weaknesses a witness may have. If any are discovered, the questioning of the witness will probably be directed to that area.

Opposing counsel may also attempt to take psychological control of a witness by:

- Using their physical presence to intimidate
- Maintaining nonstop eye contact
- Challenging the space of the witness
- Posing fast-paced questions to confuse the witness
- Not allowing the expert to explain or deviate from the exact question

Opposing counsel often uses physical domination. Opposing counsel will quickly discover the expert's response pattern and might take an aggressive stance to lead the expert to the point where he or she is unsure, with devastating results.

Opposing counsel might use these strategic methods to discredit witnesses or to diminish the importance of their testimony. These methods could be used singly or in conjunction with one another, and are not an all-encompassing list. In cross-examination, a good counsel will quickly discover the witness's weak areas and employ any possible techniques to achieve his or her goal. Thus, it is often useful to have an overall understanding of some of the more common methods employed, which include:

- Myopic vision
- Safety/good guy
- Contradiction
- New information
- Support opposing sides theory
- Bias
- Confrontation
- Sounding board
- Fees
- Terms of engagement
- Discrediting the witness

Myopic Vision   Myopic vision entails getting the expert to admit to excessive time being spent in the investigation of a matter, then highlighting an area of which the expert is unsure or in which he or she has not done much work. This area may not be central to the issues in the case but must be relevant to conclusions reached. Then the opposing counsel will make a large issue of it and prove that the expert's vision is myopic in that the work was limited in extent or scope and, as such, substandard. At the same time, the question of fees could be drawn in to show that large sums were expended to have this "obviously incomplete" work done.

Safety/Good Guy   Often opposing counsel will begin a cross-examination gently, not attacking the expert and so lulling her into a feeling of false security. Then opposing counsel might find a small hole that could be enlarged quickly. Many times opposing counsel appears friendly and conciliatory, so that the jury becomes sympathetic to their cause. Opposing counsel may also attempt to achieve a rapport with the witness that will make her want to help the opposition to bring out information in the matter. Doing so might result in the witness giving information that otherwise would not have been given. With this additional information, it might be possible for opposing counsel to find a chink or hole in the evidence and develop it further.

Contradiction   Opposing counsel might use leading questions to force the witness into a hard or contradictory position. Alternately, counsel can establish in court the credibility of a potentially contradicting document or quote from other articles written by other experts in the field. If these documents or articles contradict the expert, then the expert might admit to that contradiction. If the contradiction exists, the expert might be drawn into an argument as to who is the most appropriate or experienced expert in the circumstances. Instances also have occurred when witnesses have contradicted themselves or their own articles written several years earlier merely because they have forgotten or have become confused by the attack.

New Information   Opposing counsel may introduce new information of which the expert might not be aware, or refer to a specific relevance in the conclusions the expert witness reaches. This tactic is normally done to confuse witnesses so that they might contradict themselves or develop a series of alternate scenarios, given the new information that shows that their report and opinions are no longer of value.

Support Opposing Sides Theory   This approach establishes and recognizes an expert's qualifications and evidence. The same information the expert uses is then used and interpreted by opposing counsel in a different way to support an alternate theory. By getting the expert to agree to the alternate interpretation of the facts and theory, opposing counsel has in effect made the expert a witness for the other side. This technique is useful to obtain concessions from witnesses that would damage their conclusions and, ultimately, their credibility.

Bias   This method draws the expert's counsel and the expert together to show possible collusion in the evidence being presented in testimony, and hence show bias. This bias can be shown if opposing counsel determines that the expert's counsel had instructed the witness about what to say or by limiting the expert's scope and hence conclusions. This approach can also focus on the question of whether the expert was told by the client what to do and look for. With this approach, opposing counsel can attempt to show that the expert overlooked important documentation in an effort to assist their client.

Confrontation This very simple method is the continued use of a confrontation of wills to put witnesses into a situation in which they might lose control and become angry. Once a witness has exploded, credibility disappears.

Sounding Board This method uses the witness as a sounding board to reacquaint the jury with the favorable aspects (to opposing counsel) of the case. This technique often uses the "Is it not true" and "Would you agree with me" approach. Constant nonstop agreement is useful to browbeat the expert. To the judge and jury, agreement with various questions the opposing counsel raises may also be interpreted as a general concurrence with the opposing counsel's position. This tactic is often a valuable psychological tool.

Fees This method attacks the witness for taking an inordinate amount of time to achieve the result. Further, the attack may indicate incomplete work and may be correlated to the fees charged. This method is often related to "bias" and "myopic vision." Because of high fees or reoccurring engagements with a client, it may be suggested that the witness and his opinion are biased for the client. This technique often builds to a conclusion in which opposing counsel shows that the work was superficial and unprofessional, but the expert received a great deal of money for this and other areas of service to the client; the direct implication is that the testimony was purchased or that the expert was paid to overlook facts contradictory to his or her conclusions.

Terms of Engagement This technique normally starts by opposing counsel obtaining the original engagement letter and examining the terms of engagement, then showing that the expert intended to examine only items in support of his or her client and glossed over any alternative theories, generally to the detriment of the opposition. Therefore, the witness could be portrayed as partial.

Discrediting the Witness   Discrediting the witness is the concept of proving that the expert is unworthy to be a credible witness. This strategy often is accomplished by showing that the expert currently is, or has previously been, grossly biased, prejudiced, corrupt, convicted of criminal activities, shown to engage in immoral activities, made inconsistent statements, acquired a reputation for a lack of veracity, and/or exaggerated his qualifications. Discrediting might also look at the quality of the experts' educational background to reveal any other unusual activities that might bias them or exclude them from the court as experts.

Survival Techniques

Larry Crumbley makes these suggestions to forensic accountants regarding their testifying.[17]

Use Visual Aids   Simplify the presentation of accounting matters that are often difficult for the general public even when they are simple to the accountant, but also can be sophisticated in the case of testimony in court. Use PowerPoint charts, graphs, or related illustrations.

Do Not Answer an Ambiguous Question   If you are unable to respond to a question, say so and request clarification.

Maintain Your Composure   Opposing counsel will attempt to discredit you and destroy your self-confidence if your testimony could have a detrimental impact on their client's case. The more effective your testimony is for your side, the more intense the attack from opposing counsel is likely to be.

Be Patient   There will be many delays, motions, recesses, sidebars, and so forth. On the stand, you must remain calm in demeanor in what will sometimes feel like a chaotic or turbulent scene. Your client, the judge, and the jury will expect you to be professional at all times.

Maintain a Careful Sense of Humor   Well-timed, natural humor is fine, in the right circumstances. It actually can help an expert witness to appear natural and spontaneous. However, a joke can backfire. Make sure not to use cruel jokes, and do not force one.

Know Your Limitations   Do not try to bluff when you do not know an answer. Successful expert witnesses claim expertise only in those areas where they are justified in doing so. The other side has access to its own accounting experts who can validate or refute your testimony. Opposing counsel will normally try to build a case around its own experts rather than attack a witness who is poised and objective.

Do Not Become Argumentative or Defensive   Avoid displays of negative behavior, even though it may be hard to hide your feelings at times. If the opposing attorney appears to have gained the upper hand during cross, remember that your attorney has the option to "redirect" testimony to examine the points necessary.

Do Not Forget Who Is Deciding the Case   Direct your replies to the judge and jury. You are speaking to people who will base their understanding and acceptance of your testimony on your professionalism. They must trust you in order for you to be effective. Much of what you say will be accepted or rejected according to whether you speak clearly, project self-confidence, and communicate a strong sense of ethics, a positive attitude, and enthusiasm. These factors may have a greater influence on the outcome than the actual testimony.

Summary: 10 Points   Here are 10 points for the expert witness to remember both in preparing for and in giving evidence at trial. Remember to:

1. Prepare your material completely.
2. Know your material thoroughly.
3. Plan your testimony in advance.
4. Be alert.
5. Listen carefully.
6. Carefully consider each answer, and pause before answering.
7. Be honest and avoid bias.
8. Clarify—use simple words.
9. Keep your cool.
10. Maintain professional pride and integrity throughout.

SUMMARY

There is much about being an expert witness in a fraud investigation that most auditors would not know. This chapter details the role of the expert witness, and the rules that will be used to admit expert testimony. It is likely that if an auditor serves as an expert witness that the opposing counsel will challenge that person's qualifications using *Daubert*. Therefore, it is extremely important to understand the *Daubert* challenge and to be prepared for one from the beginning of the case.

Once the auditor is on the witness stand, the protocol for successful testimony goes far beyond telling the truth or having good forensic evidence. The auditor must convince a judge or jury, who are laymen in terms of accounting, and put forth a good image socially. This chapter conveys best practices to perform well on the witness stand, which many consider to be more important than the evidence itself.

APPENDIX 11A

Extract from the proceedings in Regina v. Scheel:[18] *Illustration of how the accountant's qualifications as an expert witness can be established and how accounting exhibits might be introduced.*

Robert John Lindquist: Sworn Examination-in-Chief by Mr. Hunt (Crown):

Q. Mr. Lindquist, where do you reside, sir?

A. I live in Toronto, Ontario.

Q. And what is your occupation?

A. I am a chartered accountant.

Q. And do you practice on your own or with someone else?

A. I practice in partnership with other chartered accountants under the firm name of Lindquist, Holmes, and Company.

Q. And how long have you been operating the partnership as a chartered accountant?

A. Close to six years now.

Q. And prior to that were you associated with any other firm?

A. Yes, prior to that I worked for a period of six years with a national accounting firm where I studied after my graduation from University.

Q. And in what year did you qualify as a chartered accountant?

A. In 1972.

Q. And since that date have you had occasion to testify in court with respect to accounting matters?

A. I have.

Q. And on approximately how many occasions would that have occurred?

A. An estimate of some 50 occasions.

Q. Your Honor, I tender Mr. Lindquist as a witness who should be classified as an expert witness on the basis of his qualifications that I have elicited.

Mr. Hermiston:

I am content with the qualifications, Your Honor.

His Honor:

Thank you.

Mr. Hunt:

Mr. Lindquist, I understand that you have prepared a number of documents relating to various transactions dealing with Metro Pallet Repair?

A. Yes, I have.

Q. Could I see Exhibit A? I am presenting to you a document, a rather large document, marked Exhibit A on the Voir Dire. I would ask you to look at that document and tell me if you recognize that?

A. Yes, I do.

Q. And did you prepare that document yourself?

A. Yes, I did.

Q. And I wonder if, so the jury can see it, you would hold it in such a way that the jury will be able to see the structure of the document. It appears to consist of a number of columns, vertical columns; am I correct?

A. That's correct.

Q. And the document is headed what?

A. It's headed "Analysis of Sales for the Period August 1, 1973, to October 3, 1973."

ENDNOTES

1. Michigan Supreme Court Rules of Evidence: Rules 702, 703, 704, 705, 706, 707.
2. R. F. Figlewicz and H. D. Sprobge, "The CPA's Expert Witness Role in Litigation Services: A Maze of Legal and Accounting Standards," *Ohio CPA Journal* (July–September 2002), pp. 33–38.
3. *Frye v. U.S.*, 293 F. 1013 (D.C. Cir 1923).
4. V. M. Hansen, "Rule of Evidence 702: The Supreme Court Provides a Framework for Reliability Determinations," *Military Law Review* 162 (1999).
5. R. F. Reilly, "Accountants Consideration of Daubert-Related Decisions in Expert Testimony," *National Public Accountant* 45, No. 8 (2000), p. 12f.
6. 509 U. S. 579 (1993).
7. 526 U. S. 137 (1999).

8. 522 U. S. 136 (1997).

9. L. L. Kruschke, 2000. "Expert Opinion Testimony in State Courts," *Judges & Lawyers Business Valuation Update* 2, No. 6 (June 2000).

10. D.C., U.S. District Court, civil action nos. 87-442 and 87-1763.

11. 136 F. 3d 1139, U.S. App. Lexis (1998).

12. Reilly, "Accountants Consideration of Daubert-Related Decisions in Expert Testimony."

13. M. A. Parfitt, "Daubert-Proof Your Expert," *Trial* (July 2005), p. 88.

14. Ontario Court of Appeals, *Regina v. Scheel*, May 12, 1978.

15. *Hoyer v. U.S.*, 8 Cir. 223 F.2d 134, 1955, p. 138.

16. *Daniel v. U.S.*, 5 Cir. 343 F.2d 785, 1965, Hunter District Judge, p. 789.

17. D. L. Crumbley and K. A. Russell, "So You Want to Be an Expert Witness," *Journal of Accountancy* (October 2004), pp. 23–30.

18. Ontario Court of Appeals, *Regina v. Scheel*.

CHAPTER 12

General Criteria and Standards for Evaluating an Expert's Qualifications[1]

INTRODUCTION

Determining that a given person is sufficiently knowledgeable and capable of serving as an expert depends on two factors. First, does the candidate possess the objective qualifications for the job? Does he have the appropriate credentials, relevant prior experience, and critical information that bears on successful resolution of the case?

Second, does the expert, even if sufficiently qualified, have the personal characteristics to function effectively as part of the investigative team? Is the individual a team player? Does her professional reputation and the quality of previous work recommend using her in the case at hand? Can the expert explain technical complexities in such a way that both the criminal justice practitioners—investigators, prosecutors, and judges—and the jury can clearly understand their meaning and importance? Does the expert project a professional manner? Can he build and keep rapport with others? The sections that follow address in detail both the requisite formal credentials and the essential personal characteristics that effective consultants and expert witnesses must display.

CREDENTIALS

Credentials and standards vary for assessing the knowledgeability of out-of-court experts, depending on the area of expertise. Even with regard to laying the foundation at trial for the court to accept a witness as an expert, the criteria, although generally standardized between fields of expertise in the eyes of the law, are not inflexible and are subject to some variation. With these caveats in mind, there are several broad areas in which experts are expected to have credentials and qualifications that distinguish them from laypeople.

These include:

- Professional licensure, certification, or registration by a recognized professional body in the field of expertise in question
- Undergraduate, graduate, and postgraduate academic degrees that are either in the field of expertise or serve as a suitable background to it
- Specialized training and/or continuing professional education beyond academic degrees that indicate up-to-date familiarity with the latest technical developments in the subject area
- Writings and publications that display technical opinions and are available as part of the general body of knowledge in the subject area
- Relevant teaching, lecturing, and/or other consultancies that indicate that one is held in high professional esteem in the subject area
- Affiliation with professional associations
- Directly relevant prior experience gained through similar assignments, whether as technical advisor or expert witness, in the subject area
- Special status, or access to privileged information, peculiar to the case at hand, which renders the individual an expert

Professional Licensure, Certification, or Registration

Most professional organizations, to some degree, regulate their members and feature mechanisms for reviewing a practitioner's qualifications—often at periodic intervals. Endorsements about competence—a license to practice the profession, a certification in a specialty area, or registration at a central professional regulatory authority in the jurisdiction—are all common practices. A professional license, certification, or registration is an important factor in assessing the level of basic competence for technical advisors in most areas of expertise useful in financial and computer-related crime investigations. Establishing an individual has a license or certification in the profession, and/or is registered in the jurisdiction as a practitioner of that profession, is a standard step in laying the foundation at trial for the court to accept the testimony of such a person as an expert.

Standards used to qualify a practitioner in a given profession can easily be determined by inquiring of the professional licensing or certifying body in question. In addition, many jurisdictions require practitioners in a wide variety of professions, who may have acquired their credentials elsewhere, to register with a central government authority if they want to practice their profession locally. The central registering authority can be a useful source of information on professional licensing standards locally and perhaps a source of expert referrals.

Many of the more traditional professional organizations supply experts in crime cases. Those include lawyers, engineers, and forensic chemists. Most states have laws that dictate the criteria for professional licensing in these broader professions.

Academic Degrees

Traditionally, the academic degrees professionals hold have been a key to determining whether they will qualify as expert witnesses.[2] Even when experts are used only behind the scenes in the investigation of computer-related crimes, their backgrounds can be investigated by the defense and their credentials will be considered. This consideration is particularly true because as technical advisors they become potential expert witnesses.

Despite the strategic importance of appropriate academic credential for experts whose credibility the defense may challenge, it is important not to rely too heavily on academic qualifications alone. Many universities do not have well-developed courses about computer-related crime, especially on the postgraduate level, and because the field is changing so rapidly, the courses they do have may not be current. Therefore, knowledgeable sources agree that when an expert witness's academic credentials are considered, how recently the degrees were awarded and whether she has continued to take courses in the field should be considered as well.

Training and Continuing Education

Developments in computer programming, electronics, telecommunications engineering, information technology auditing, computer security, and other specializations are increasing rapidly. Training and continuing education in these areas, and such fields as combating white-collar crime, economic crime, and computer crime, are being offered widely. Professional associations and regulatory bodies frequently offer certificates of completion and other objective indicators of ungraded skills for attending such courses.

How many current, relevant training courses and continuing education courses has the prospective technical expert attended? How up to date is he on the state of the art in this technical field? A showing of such currency is generally a corollary to the presentation of academic credentials to the court when an expert witness's qualifications are reviewed. The absence of such current educational updates would not only have a strong effect on the quality of the expert advice given to the government, but it can lead to the government's expert witness being impeached on cross-examination and the technical accuracy of aspects of the government's case being challenged.

Writings and Publications

Whether prospective expert witnesses have published in the field of their purported expertise is traditionally an important factor to review when laying the foundation at trial for the technical advisor to take the stand as an expert witness. Prior publications may be less relevant when experts are used as technical advisors to the investigative or prosecutive team during the case preparation stages. However, this situation is not necessarily the case. The prior publications of computer-related crime scholars/researchers retained to assist in profiling the computer felon(s) and determining the modus operandi in complex computer fraud cases will be directly relevant. Their availability could greatly assist the team by providing them with an orientation, and such published views could be challenged if the technical advisor's identity is discoverable during pretrial.

What books or articles has the technical advisor written on the subject in question? Were they published, and if so, how recently?

How were the expert's works received by professional peers? Are the expert's works considered authoritative? Do other published works in the same field challenge or contradict the expert's published views? Are the experts' published views consistent in all of their writings? Are their published views, while consistent among themselves, congruent with their current views on the case at hand? These are all critical questions to be addressed when selecting an expert. Especially if there is to be an established or prolonged professional relationship with the expert, the consultant's published works must be analyzed and monitored during pretrial preparation to avoid significant discrepancies that may arise between the expert's present planned testimony and past, possibly contradictory, positions taken.

Teaching and Other Consultancies

Activities that show a consultant's prior acceptance as an expert advisor or instructor go to the issue of her reliability and credibility as part of the government's team. Teaching or consulting in a given field traditionally is considered when an expert's credentials are presented to the court before the person takes the stand as an expert witness. Because of the newness and rapid evolution of computer-related technology, such credentials may hold more weight in a computer-related crime case than academic degrees or publications. A careful check with past users of the prospective experts' service—trainees or clients for whom they have consulted—can be an excellent way to assess their reliability and stature, plus the currency and nature of their views before retaining them in a given case.

Government experts' extensive prior teaching and/or consultancies, if they have been retained for a fee, sometimes can work to the detriment of the prosecution. For example, experts who for a fee have done extensive training of investigators and prosecutors of computer crime, and/or who have for a fee testified frequently for the prosecution in such cases, but not for the defense, could be impeached for bias and/or financial interest if the government calls them as expert witnesses.[3] Especially when a substantial part of an expert's income derives from such services to law enforcement, his comparative usefulness as an expert witness may be compromised.

Even if such experts are not potential expert witnesses, their identity and involvement in preparing the case may prove discoverable by the defense and lead to allegations of bias in the technical advice rendered at the investigatory stage. These considerations aside, retention of an expert who has extensively trained and consulted for only one side in such cases can lessen the fundamental value of having an outside expert on the investigative team in the first place.

Professional Associations

As in the case of professional licensure, prospective experts' certification or membership in professional associations adds to a presumption of competence and is routinely included in the proffering of an expert's credentials to the court before presenting expert testimony. As with the matters of licensure, academic degrees, continuing education, and prior consultancies, membership in professional associations is subject to verification checks and to the gathering of references from the expert's professional peers. This verification is an important and useful quality-control check.

Previous Similar Experience

Because the various computer technology fields are new and new developments in computer technology occur so quickly, formal credentials are less important in computer-related crime cases than direct prior experience with the victim company's computer operations, the brands of hardware or software the victim used, and the software applications involved. In addition, prior experience in investigating computer-related crimes, providing computer security, or computer-related crime research can be the critical element that renders a particular party an expert advisor. Identifying trustworthy and objective advisors who have such direct prior experience can be the most important factor in selecting an expert. Despite traditional criteria, such as formal credentials, by which a proffered expert's qualifications to testify as an expert witness are normally assessed, the trial judge has broad discretion to base a decision that an individual is an expert qualified to testify on a given subject primarily—or even solely—on that person's prior relevant experience.

There are pitfalls in overreliance on technical advisors with extensive prior experience in a subject area. Maintaining control over the overall management and direction of the case can be difficult. Susceptibility to defense charges of partisanship and bias against experts with extensive prior experience disproportionately on the government's side only is another hazard. Regardless, past experience remains the single most important qualification of experts in computer-related crime.

Sole Access to Privileged Information or Facts

Employees of the victimized agency or of the manufacturer, vendor, or service organization whose computer products the victims used can be among the most useful technical advisors when investigating a computer-related crime case or preparing one for trial. The background, education, and other credentials of such people can vary tremendously; this group can include top management at the victim organization, in-house computer technologists, data providers, equipment operators, and others who handle relevant data or are in sole possession of facts about the victim's operations. As a result, these people's qualifications in their own fields, while important, will prove secondary to their familiarity with aspects of the victim's operations and equipment. For the narrow purpose of laying out what such operational practices routinely were or what equipment capabilities and vulnerabilities are, courts can be expected to admit expert testimony from such people, if the prosecution is able to demonstrate their familiarity with such factors and their general competence.

The greatest pitfalls in using such individuals as pretrial technical advisors or as expert witnesses at trial are: (1) distinguishing the true area of competence and (2) bias. Employees or service personnel may be qualified to speak authoritatively on only very narrow points and be completely unqualified on other related points. In addition, loyalty to the employer, job security considerations, or a grudge against the employer or another employee may taint the individual's objectivity and hence her utility. And, of course, the investigative team must be especially circumspect about bringing such persons in as technical advisors, unless and until their possible complicity in the crime is completely ruled out.

PERSONAL QUALITIES OF THE EXPERT

The other standards in deciding whether to use a particular person as a technical advisor or expert witness are the personal qualities of the prospective expert. Because this area is primarily subjective, as distinguished from the relative objectiveness of credentials, it is difficult to say what the key factors are and how they should be assessed. However, eight considerations hold true for the use of technical advisors or expert witnesses in any major case, whether it is computer related or not. The sections that follow present these considerations.

Ability to Work as Part of a Team

Regardless of the area of their professional competence, many individuals are not temperamentally or attitudinally geared to working as part of a team. Doubtless this problem is more prevalent with certain professions than with others because of the nature of the work and other factors. Assessing whether a prospective expert will be a team player is a critical decision that must be made very early in the relationship, before the expert is retained. Reference checks and personal interviews help in making this determination. Effective management of the expert in the case, the security of sensitive investigative data, and the effectiveness of the expert as a witness on the stand are only a few of the overriding considerations that dictate using only team players in expert roles.

Trustworthiness and Integrity

Despite the advisability of limiting a technical advisor's access to casework on a need-to-know basis, the expert invariably will be exposed to sensitive information during the course of the case. At the very least, this exposure will extend to a knowledge of her own role in the case, of those aspects of the investigation where she has been providing input, and the identities of others on the investigative team. The trustworthiness and discretion of the expert must be assured and maintained. Similar to the problem of ensuring that the expert is a team player, detailed reference checks and personal interviews must be used to check the expert's trustworthiness and integrity.

Professional Reputation and Recognition

An expert's stature and reputation among his peers are as important as academic degrees and publications, while this reputation will be partly a product of the authoritativeness of his views and credentials and experience in the field, it will also be reflective of his qualities. Many of the qualities will be directly relevant to whether the expert will be able to establish a harmonious working relationship with others on the case.

Experts' reputations can cut both ways with regard to their credibility as expert witnesses on the stand: If their views are controversial or even contested, the greater the experts' fame, the more likely the defense will be able to identify counterexperts familiar with the views and at odds with them. However, increased fame can go to the issue of stature and authoritativeness, by which opposing expert opinion can be overshadowed.

Reference checks and a review of the literature in the field to accurately gauge experts' professional stature and reputation are important steps to take before retaining them. Even if they are not retained as potential expert witnesses, the nature of their role in the case or the nature of the retainer agreement can make experts' identities discoverable by the defense at the pretrial stage, and thus their reputations are open to attack.

Quality and Timeliness of Previous Work

It is critically important to assess the quality of experts' work before retaining them. Most directly, the quality of their prior consultancies and service as expert witnesses must be checked out in great detail. The professional community's perception of the quality of the experts' work, publication, teaching, or lectures should be determined. If the government's expert is a potential expert witness, assume that the defense will make a thorough assessment in this area and will attempt to impeach the witness. The investigative and prosecutive team cannot afford surprises on cross-examination in this regard. Employers, prior clients, professional references, and professional and regulatory agencies, among others, should be contacted for an assessment of the quality and timeliness of the prospective experts' work.

Professional Bearing and Demeanor

Perhaps subtle, but always significant, is the professional bearing and demeanor of the technical advisor. The ability to speak authoritatively, to sustain composure under vigorous cross-examination, to avoid argumentativeness with opposing counsel, and to simplify for the judge and jury without condescension are essential characteristics. The absence of any of these should exclude the admitted expert from consideration as an expert witness. Moreover, the behind-the-scenes technical advisor must also possess these qualities, because she must work closely with the other members of the investigative team, often under pressure.

Determining professional bearing and demeanor can be complicated. Initial impressions during interviews and preliminary discussions about the case are important, as are assessments by references and other outsiders. However, all of these observations are of limited utility. Engaging in role-play early in the process with other investigators or prosecutors simulating an interrogation or cross-examination will provide useful information about the experts' reactions under pressure and in response to challenges to their expertise. Playing devil's advocate in a discussion with experts about their views or opinions on technical issues, or asking them to discuss the weaknesses in their own positions, or probing them on subjects beyond their area of expertise to assess the degree to which they are opinionated by nature are also useful techniques. In short, stress interviews for experts, whether they are viewed as potential expert witnesses are not, are essential tools to gauge bearing and demeanor.

"Presence" Before a Group

The ability to present ideas effectively to a group is a learned skill. However, many individuals in all areas of endeavor lack this skill. An expert whose knowledge of a technical area is sound and who can effectively advise investigators behind the scenes may or may not possess an effective presence before a group. This skill is critical in any expert witness; for potential expert witnesses, advance screening for the presence of this skill and practice sessions to enhance it for trial are a must. However, the ability to make effective presentations to groups may also be a necessary attribute of the behind-the-scenes technical advisor; this situation should be considered when retaining any expert.

Advisors at the investigative or pretrial stages of complex cases may be called on to give orientation sessions on technical aspects of the case to a large group of investigators and other technical advisors. This circumstance requires experts to be effective at group presentation. In addition, should the identity of the technical advisors become known to the defense at the pretrial stage, depending on the nature of their relationship with the government and their role in the case, they may be subpoenaed to testify. This case would require them to have the same ability to effectively command the attention of a group as if they had been designated by the government as potential expert witnesses.

Ability to Explain Technical Issues in Lay Terms

A thorough grounding in their field of expertise and the ability to make an effective group presentation are undercut if technical advisors are unable to simplify complex technical matters so that intelligent laypeople can understand them. Indeed, this ability is the most fundamental skill technical advisors or expert witnesses must possess. The ability to make technical points understandable to the members of the investigative or prosecutorial team is critical to their ability to erect a sound theory of the case and to implement an effective strategy to break the case and/or obtain a conviction. Similarly, the ability to bring important technical points home to the judge and jury, without confusion or condescension, will have a direct impact on the likelihood of a favorable verdict.

If the experts have performed other consultancies in the past or served previously as expert witnesses, it should be easy to determine whether they have this skill by performing a thorough reference check. However, in the absence of these prior experiences, an effective technique would be to have prospective experts explain to a group of lay office staff the meaning of a few technical terms or concepts the interviewer selects. If the office staff cannot grasp the expert's explanation, chances are that other laypeople on the investigative team or the jury will not readily understand either. The presence or absence of strong interpersonal communications skills in experts is universally acknowledged as a key factor in the advisability of retaining them.

Mannerisms and Idiosyncrasies

Distinctions distract. Peculiar mannerisms, unusual modes of dress, and other aspects of experts' personalities tend to deflect attention from their message. The use of vulgarity or excessive humor at inappropriate times and derogatory remarks about professional rivals alienates listeners and turns them against the speaker and thus against the message. Such distractions must be eliminated at all costs in the case of potential expert witnesses, by either modifying their behavior or replacing them. Again, because behind-the-scenes technical advisors can under certain circumstances be subpoenaed to testify, these caveats are not limited solely to designated expert witnesses.

SOURCES FOR LOCATING EXPERT WITNESSES

Technical advisors for use in crime cases can be selected or drawn from a number of sources. These include:

- In-house sources
- Other law enforcement agencies
- Other agencies of state or local government
- State and local licensing, certifying, and registering bodies
- Law enforcement professional associations

EXHIBIT 12.1   Likely Sources of Technical Advisors in Computer-Related Crime Cases, by Type of Experience

Technical Advisors	In-House Resources	Other Agencies of Government	Licensing Bodies	Professional Associations in Subject Area	Law Enforcement Professional Associations	Victim Company or Organization	HW/SW Manufacturer Vendor/Servicers	Other Organizations in Victim's Industry	Area Universities, Research Centers	Private Consulting Firms	Other Law Enforcement Agencies
Computer scientists		X	X	X		X	X	X	X	X	
Electronic engineers		X	X	X		X	X	X	X	X	
Telecommunications engineers		X	X	X		X	X	X	X	X	
Computer crimes scholars			X	X	X				X	X	X
Subject matter experts from victim's industry				X		X	X	X			
Computer users						X	X	X			
Data providers						X	X	X			
Computer operators						X	X	X			
Non–computer personnel who interface in victim's operation						X	X	X			
Computer programmers	X	X	X	X	X	X	X	X	X	X	X
Systems analysts	X	X	X	X	X	X	X	X	X	X	X
Database managers				X		X	X	X			
IT auditors	X	X	X	X	X	X	X	X	X	X	X
Computer security specialists	X	X	X	X	X	X	X	X	X	X	X
Experienced computer-related crime investigators	X	X	X	X	X		X		X		
Forensic scientists	X	X	X	X	X		X		X		X

- Professional associations in the subject area of expert knowledge sought
- The victimized organization
- Manufacturers/vendors and serving organizations that supply equipment or interface services to the victim

- Other organizations in the victim's field of activity or industry
- Area universities and research centers
- Private consulting firms specializing in the subject area
- Prior experience at obtaining experts
- Preexisting relationships with other agencies and referral sources
- Facts and circumstances of each case

Determining which source(s) to use for a particular sort of expert will be dictated by a mix of factors (see Exhibit 12.1).

DISTINGUISHING THE ACTUAL AREA OF COMPETENCE

A concluding consideration when selecting an expert is offered as a caveat: Be certain of precisely for which area(s) of expertise the investigative team needs other advisors, and carefully distinguish between these various areas of technical expertise when selecting a given consultant. For example, the decision to retain a computer programmer, an information technology (IT) auditor, and a computer security specialist as a core team of outside technical advisors when undertaking a complex computer-related crime case will be a common decision. However, selecting a programmer who is proficient in the programming language of the victimized company will be equally essential. Selecting a programmer and an IT auditor who are familiar with business applications of computer technology within the victim's field or industry will be necessary. When selecting a computer security consultant, one must decide whether a physical security specialist or a data security specialist is needed, or both. (Most computer security consultants are not expert in both.) These examples could be expanded almost infinitely.

Distinguishing the area(s) of specialized expertise needed must be coupled with distinguishing the true area(s) of a given consultant's expert competence from other areas in which he is not truly expert. This process is made more difficult because experts in one area are often unaware, or unwilling to admit, the limitations of their expertise. In such situations, representatives of the victimized organization or the manufacturers or vendors of the computer hardware or software equipment involved in the crime may be the best sources of guidance as to precisely what outside expertise is needed and what types of people would be likely to have the requisite capabilities. Consultation with experienced computer crime investigators or prosecutors, whether local or from other jurisdictions, can provide helpful information about the legal ramifications of securing outside technical advice.

SUMMARY

What constitutes a qualified expert witness in a fraud case? One must be more than an auditor or accountant. This chapter covers the best practices of assessing qualifications for an expert witness and identifying those credentials deemed indicative of an expert in this field. Although written 25 years ago, the content of the original government document is just as valid today as it was then in determining the qualifications of an expert witness in a fraud case.

ENDNOTES

1. Excerpted from the Bureau of Justice Statistics and Koba Associates, Inc., *Computer Crime Expert Witness Manual* (Washington, DC: Bureau of Justice Statistics, 1980). Reprinted with permission of the Bureau of Justice Statistics, U.S. Department of Justice. This document was written before the *Daubert* case and the resulting legal rules and guidelines for evaluating experts, their methodologies, and their conclusions. *Daubert*, therefore, supersedes the information in this chapter, as it is a ruling of the U.S. Supreme Court on how lower courts are to be gatekeepers in that evaluation, and provides legal guidance for that process. See Chapter 11 for an explanation of *Daubert* and its ramifications on the *legal* standards for evaluating an expert's qualifications and testimony.
2. J. D. Kogan, "On Being a Good Expert Witness in a Criminal Case," *Journal of Forensic Science* (January 1978), p. 195.
3. Michael H. Graham, "Impeaching the Professional Expert Witness by a Showing of Financial Interest," 53 *Indiana Law Journal*. 35, 44-47 (Winter 1977), p. 198.

CHAPTER 13

Gathering Evidence

INTRODUCTION

Knowledge of the rules of court, the legal system, and especially evidence are necessary for the effective completion of a fraud investigation by a forensic accountant or fraud auditor. The forensic accountant in particular is normally involved with the final phase of a fraud investigation—prosecution. Forensic accountants also often work with lawyers on cases. Either way, the forensic accountant must know the basic rules of the justice system regarding evidence. As was said earlier in the book, every fraud investigation should *assume* it is going to end up in court from the start. Then if it does, evidence will be "forensic"—effective for purposes in court. Ignorance on the front end could easily compromise evidence, impairing the ability of a victim to obtain the best outcome from a civil case, or a successful prosecution in a criminal case.

RULES OF EVIDENCE

A court trial is intended to deduce the truth of a given proposition. In a criminal case, the proposition is the guilt or innocence of an accused person. The evidence introduced to and received by the court to prove the charge must be beyond a reasonable doubt—not necessarily to a moral certainty—and the quantity and quality of evidence must convince an honest and reasonable layperson that the defendant is guilty after it is all considered and weighed impartially.

But what is evidence and how can it be weighed and introduced? In a broad sense, evidence is anything perceptible by the five senses and any species of proof such as testimony of witnesses, records, documents, facts, data, or concrete objects, legally presented at a trial to prove a contention and induce a belief in the minds of the court or jury. In weighing evidence, the court or jury may consider such things as the demeanor of witnesses, their bias for or against an accused, and any relationship to the accused. Thus, evidence can be testimonial, circumstantial, demonstrative, inferential, and even theoretical when given by a qualified expert. Evidence is simply anything that proves or disproves any matter in question.

To be legally acceptable as evidence, however, testimony, documents, objects, or facts must be relevant, material, and competent to the issues being litigated, and gathered lawfully. Otherwise, on motion by the opposite side, the evidence may be excluded. Now perhaps we should elaborate on relevancy, materiality, and competency:

Relevant

Relevancy of evidence does not depend on the conclusiveness of the testimony offered, but on its legitimate tendency to establish a controverted fact.[1]

Some of the evidentiary matters considered relevant and therefore admissible are:

- Motive for the crime
- Defendant's ability to commit the crime
- Defendant's opportunity to commit the crime
- Threats or expressions of ill will by the accused
- Means of committing the offense (possession of a weapon, tool, or skills used in committing the crime)
- Physical evidence at the scene linking the accused to the crime
- Suspect's conduct and comments at the time of arrest
- Attempt to conceal identity
- Attempt to destroy evidence
- Valid confessions

Material

The materiality rule requires that evidence must have an important value to a case or prove a point at issue. Unimportant details extend only the period of time for trial. Accordingly, a trial court judge may rule against the introduction of evidence that is repetitive or additive (that merely proves the same point in another way), or evidence that tends to be remote even though it is relevant. Materiality, then, is the degree of relevancy. The court cannot become preoccupied with trifles or unnecessary details. For example, the physical presence of a suspect in the computer room or tape library or near a terminal on a day when a spurious transaction was generated may be relevant and material. One's presence in a noncomputer-related area of the building may be relevant, but immaterial.

Competent

Competency of evidence means that which is adequately sufficient, reliable, and relevant to the case and presented by a qualified and capable (and sane) witness. The presence of those characteristics or the absence of those disabilities that render a witness legally fit and qualified to give testimony in a court applies in the same sense to documents or other forms of written evidence. But competency differs from credibility. Competency is a question that arises before a witness's testimony can be considered; credibility is that witness's veracity. Competency is for the judge to determine; credibility is for the jury to decide.

The competency rule also dictates that conclusions or opinions of a nonexpert witness on matters that require technical expertise be excluded. For example, testimony by an investigating officer on the cause of death may not be appropriate or competent in a trial for murder or wrongful death, because the officer is not qualified by education, study, or experience to make such an assessment. The officer testifying that there were "no visible signs of life" when the body was found may be acceptable, however.

When an expert witness is called on to testify, a foundation must be laid before testimony is accepted or allowed. Laying a foundation means that the witness's expertise must be established before a professional opinion is rendered. Qualifying a witness as an expert means demonstrating to the judge's satisfaction that by formal education, advanced study, and experience, the witness is knowledgeable about the topic on which his testimony will bear. The testimony of experts is an exception to the hearsay rule.

Hearsay Rule

The hearsay rule is based on the theory that testimony that merely repeats what some other person said should not be admitted because of the possibility of distortion or misunderstanding. Furthermore, the person who made the actual statement is unavailable for cross-examination and has not been sworn in as a witness. Generally speaking, witnesses can testify only to those things of which they have personal and direct knowledge, and not give conclusions or opinions.

But there are occasions—exceptions—when hearsay evidence is admissible. Some examples are:

- Dying declarations, either verbal or written
- Valid confessions
- Tacit admissions
- Public records that do not require an opinion but speak for themselves
- *Res gestae* statements—spontaneous explanations, if spoken as part of the criminal act or immediately following the commission of a criminal act
- Earlier testimony given under oath
- Business entries made in the normal course of business

Primary Evidence

Photocopies of original business documents and other writings and printed matter are often made to preserve evidence. Investigators use these so that the original records needed to run a business are not removed and to ensure that in the event of an inadvertent destruction of such originals, a certified true copy of the document is still available as proof. Investigators may also use the certified copy to document their case reports. At the trial, however, the original document—if still available—is the best evidence and must be presented. The best evidence in this context means primary evidence, not secondary; original as distinguished from substitutionary; the highest evidence of which the nature of the case is susceptible: "A written instrument is itself always regarded as the primary or best possible evidence of its existence and contents; a copy, or the recollection of a witness, would be secondary evidence."[2] Further, "Contents of a document must be proved by producing the document itself."[3]

HEARSAY EXCEPTIONS

In an idealistic sense, a court trial is a quest to determine the truth. However, the means of acquiring evidence vary. Some means are legal, others are illegal; for example, they may violate constitutional guarantees against unreasonable search and seizure, forced confessions, or failure to be represented by counsel. Realistically, therefore, a court trial can result only in a measure of truth and not in absolute truth in the philosophical sense.

Yet and In the Anglo-American tradition, witnesses other than experts cannot generally testify as to probabilities, opinions, assumptions, impressions, generalizations, or conclusions, but only as to things, people, and events they have seen, felt, tasted, smelled, or heard firsthand. Even those things must be legally and logically relevant. *Logical relevancy* means that the evidence being offered must tend to prove or disprove a fact of consequence. Even if it is logically relevant, a court may exclude evidence if it is likely to inflame or confuse a jury or consume too much time. Testimony as to the statistical probability of guilt is considered too prejudicial and unreliable to be accepted.

Testimony as to the character and reputation of an accused may be admissible under certain conditions, even though it would seem to violate the hearsay rule. Such testimony may be admitted when character is an element of the action; that is, when the mental condition or legal competency of the accused is in question.

Evidence of other crimes an accused committed is not generally admissible to prove character. It may be admitted for other purposes, however, such as proof of motive, opportunity, or intent to commit an act.

A witness's credibility may also be attacked by a showing that she was convicted of a serious crime (punishable by death or imprisonment for more than a year) or for such crimes as theft, dishonesty, or false statement. Such conviction should have occurred in recent years—usually within the last 10 years.

Evidence can be direct or circumstantial. Direct evidence proves a fact directly; if the evidence is believed, the fact is established. Circumstantial evidence proves the desired fact indirectly and depends on the strength of the inferences the evidence raises. For example, a letter properly addressed, stamped, and mailed is assumed (inferred) to have been received by the addressee. Testimony that a letter was so addressed, stamped, and mailed raises an inference that it was received. The inference may be rebutted by testimony that is was not in fact received.

The best evidence rule deals with written documents proffered as evidence. The rule requires that the original, if available, and not a copy thereof, be presented at a trial. If the original was destroyed or is in the hands of an opposite party and not subject to legal process by search warrant or subpoena, an authenticated copy may be substituted. Business records and documents kept in the ordinary course of business may be presented as evidence too, even if the person who made the entries or prepared the documents is unavailable.

OTHER RULES OF EVIDENCE

Chain of Custody

When evidence in the form of document or object (means or instrument) is seized at a crime scene, or as a result of subpoena *duces tecum* (for documents), or discovered in the course of audit and investigation, it should be marked, identified, inventoried, and preserved to maintain it in its original condition and to establish a clear chain of custody until it is introduced at the trial. If gaps in possession or custody occur, the evidence may be challenged at the trial on the theory that the writing or object introduced may not be the original or is not in its original condition and therefore is of doubtful authenticity.

For a seized document to be admissible as evidence, it is necessary to prove it is the same document seized and is in the same condition as it was when seized. Because several people may handle it in the interval between seizure and trial, it should be adequately marked at the time of seizure for later identification, and its custody must be shown from that time until it is introduced in court.

Investigators or auditors who seize or secure documents should quickly identify them by some marking, so they can later testify that they are the documents seized and that they are in the same condition as they were when seized. Investigators might, for instance, write their initials and the date of seizure on the margin, in a corner, or at some other inconspicuous place on the front or back of each document. If circumstances suggest that such marking might render the document subject to attack on the grounds that it has been defaced or it is not in the same condition as when seized, the investigators or auditors can, after making a copy for comparison or for use as an exhibit to the report, put the document into an envelope, write a description and any other identifying information on the front of the envelope, and seal it.

These techniques should be applied any time investigators or auditors come into possession of original documents that might be used as evidence in a trial. If auditors make copies of documentary evidence, they should take steps to preserve their authenticity in case they are needed as secondary evidence if the original documents are not available for the trial.

Special Circumstances for Computers and Technology

There are some critical issues related to digital evidence that every fraud auditor and forensic accountant should know. Basically, there are three steps involved in acquiring digital evidence:

1. Acquire the digital evidence without altering or damaging the original.
2. Authenticate the digital evidence for analysis (duplicate it where feasible).
3. Analyze the digital evidence without modifying it.

There are special tools to perform these steps (e.g., EnCase and hashing software).

Many things that the average fraud auditor and forensic accountant might not know about digital evidence need to be addressed. Some examples will illustrate the scope of digital evidence and how difficult it would be to have an adequate level of knowledge:

- "Fingerprints" on modern printed documents can be traced back to the printer that printed them.
- E-mail "fingerprints" in the header and so forth exist that can be used to authenticate the sender and usually even the computer used to send it.
- Cookie data.
- Hidden data found on storage devices can be retrieved and examined as possible evidence.

This retrieval process includes the use of "undelete" to retrieve deleted files, the end of the block that holds a file that probably has unrelated data, unused space that has data, temporary files, random access memory (RAM), logs, and the possibility of retrieving data that were overwritten. A host of standard cyberforensic means and tools exists to extract these "hidden" data. Acquiring digital data is not so simple. A bit-streaming (bit-by-bit) backup is necessary, not a conventional backup.

A specialist familiar with cyberforensics knowledge and with the training and tools to investigate properly is required when investigating a fraud with digital evidence. It is a good idea for a fraud investigator or forensic firm to prepare for digital evidence collection and examination before an applicable fraud occurs. This preparation could mean simply knowing and retaining a cyberforensics consultant or firm to be employed when necessary, or it may mean permanently hiring a specialist. If that preparation is not done, the resulting investigation will be subject to time and cost pressures, and may possibly be less effective than it could have been. For instance, it will take days to examine the digital evidence, and victim organizations will not allow their systems to be set aside for days. Thus forethought and preparation are essential to obtaining the appropriate evidence within the constraints which the fraud investigator will be working.

Rich digital sources of information and evidence are available. Fraud auditors and forensic accountants should be familiar with all of the available different storage devices. Fraudsters can hide data in many ways by moving it from organizational systems, including their own computer, and placing it on a removable, portable device. Such devices include:

- Flash drives (thumb drives) that are small enough to hide in a pocket or the palm of one's hand and can be disguised as a normal fountain pen
- Digital watches
- Digital cameras
- Memory chips for digital cameras that are small enough to hide under a postage stamp
- Personal digital assistants (PDAs)
- Cell phones

There are some U.S. Secret Service agents and FBI agents who do nothing but collect and analyze information from cell phones. Cell phones contain voice mail, text messages, notes entered in the contacts file, phone numbers and addresses, and a log of phone numbers missed, received, and made. That is a lot of potential evidence for a fraud investigation. It should be noted that people tend to let their guard down when doing e-mail, text messaging, instant messaging, and other informal communications. Those communications are digital, and digital files exist someplace that contain the content of those communications. These two facts combined make these digital sources rich in terms of a source for evidence.

Regarding the issue of legal prosecution and "forensic" evidence, in the beginning of an investigation, it may not clear that the case is going to end up in litigation or legal prosecution. However, it is quite easy for evidence to get tainted. So fraud auditors or forensic accountants should *assume* that *every* investigation is going to end up in court. That assumption will ensure the investigative process is successful either way. In 2000, a cracker stole credit card information from online retailer CD Universe. Supposedly, the three security groups hired as consultants and the FBI made some mistakes in their initial steps that compromised the evidence and thus hampered any subsequent prosecution.[4]

Custody of evidence is linked to authenticating evidence. Forensic evidence by definition means it will stand up in a court of law. As we all have seen or know, evidence can be tainted because of improper custody of it. In the case of fraud and digital evidence, that compromise can happen at the very beginning. Fraudsters sometimes put Trojan horses on their computers that will automatically destroy digital evidence. It is also true that if a computer is off and an investigator turns it on and begins to look through the computer files for evidence, that investigator and his activities will automatically taint the evidence. Windows changes date-time stamps, and booting a system and browsing computer files will do a number of things that cause the digital evidence to be different from what it was before the boot. Thus that digital evidence is no longer admissible in court, because it is no longer in its state at the point of the capture of the evidence or as it existed when the fraud was being perpetrated. Therefore, it is *critically important* that the fraud investigation initially take the correct steps in capturing the digital evidence. For example, one should not turn a computer on, off, or pull the plug until and unless an expert in cyberforensics has directed the action. Certain tools allow a technician to capture the digital information from RAM and the hard drives without disturbing the original state of the computer. One example is EnCase. But regardless, an expert in cyberforensics is needed to properly acquire the digital evidence up front, and that person's expertise will be critical in the ongoing analysis of that digital evidence.

Then there is the custody from that point forward. A log (see Exhibit 13.1) should be kept that shows the unique identification of the evidence (e.g., drive serial number), the physical location, what was done, who did it, when, what tool was used, and so on. Documentation is critical to making evidence "forensic" for presentation in court.

Evidence	Physical Location	Tests	Person	Date	Tool
Drv #411-651-66	ABC Corp. / Rm 214	Picked up computer	T. Jones, CFE	06-01-06	n.a.
Drv #411-651-66	Secure lab #114	Backup of drive	J. Smith	06-01-06	Encase

EXHIBIT 13.1   Custody Log

Secondary Evidence

To introduce secondary evidence, one must explain satisfactorily to the court the absence of the original document. Secondary evidence is not restricted to photocopies of the document; it may be the testimony of witnesses or transcripts of the document's contents. Whereas the federal courts give no preference to the type of secondary evidence, most other jurisdictions do. Under the majority rule, testimony (parol evidence) will not be allowed to prove the contents of a document if there is secondary documentary evidence available to prove its contents. However, before secondary evidence of the original document may be introduced, the party offering the contents of the substitute must have used all reasonable and diligent means to obtain the original. Again, this is a matter for the court to determine.

When the original document has been destroyed by the party attempting to prove its contents, secondary evidence will be admitted if the destruction was in the ordinary course of business, or by mistake, or even intentional, provided it was not done for any fraudulent purpose.

Privileged Communications

The rule supporting privileged communications is based on the belief that it is necessary to maintain the confidentiality of certain communications. It covers only those communications that are a unique product of the protected relationship. The basic reason behind these protected communications is the belief that the protection of certain relationships is more important to society than the possible harm resulting from the loss of such evidence. Legal jurisdictions vary as to what communications are protected. Some of the more prevalent privileged relationships are:

- Attorney–client
- Husband–wife
- Physician–patient
- Clergy–congregant
- Law enforcement officer–informant

When dealing with privileged communications, consider these basic principles:

- Only the holder of a privilege, or someone authorized by the holder, can assert the privilege.
- If the holder fails to assert it after having notice and an opportunity to assert it, the privilege is waived.
- The privilege may also be waived if the holder discloses a significant part of the communication to a party not within the protected relationship.
- The communication, to be within the privilege, must be sufficiently related to the relationship protected (e.g., communications between an attorney and client must be related to legal consultation).

Under common law, a person cannot testify against his spouse in a criminal trial. While they are married, neither may waive this testimonial incompetency.

Conversations in the known presence of third parties are not protected. Protected communications are those that are in fact confidential or induced by the marriage or other relationship. Ordinary conversations relating to matters not deemed to be confidential are not within the purview of the privilege.

The laws of different states vary widely in the application of the principles of privileged communications. Depending on what protected relationship is involved, different rules may apply regarding what communications are protected, the methods of waiver, and the duration of the privilege.

Whenever an auditor/investigator is confronted with the need to use evidence that consists of communications between parties in one of these relationships, she should consult with an attorney, especially if the evidence is crucial to the case.

Admissions and Confessions

The goal of a forensic accountant in a fraud investigation is to eventually obtain a written confession by the fraudster, if a fraud did indeed occur. That goal is why the processes of a fraud investigation deliberately avoid confronting the suspect until the last phase of the gathering of evidence. The last phases include interviews, and the last round of interviews is to interview the fraudster. By then the forensic accountant has gathered sufficient evidence to identify the fraudster. So the step of gathering evidence by the forensic accountant includes interviewing people, beginning far away from the "target," and gradually interviewing people closer to the suspect. When it finally comes time to interview the target, the purpose of that interview is to obtain a signed confession and is thus referred to as an admission-seeking interview.

Criminal phenomena occur as a result of four factors:

1. The criminal's motivations
2. Opportunities to commit crimes, presented by weaknesses in people, internal controls, safeguards, or protection measures
3. Means to commit crimes—resources (knowledge of weaknesses), skill in exploiting them, and a mental disposition to do so (confederates and tools)
4. Methods—the plans to execute crimes while minimizing the risk of capture

Crime is a risk for both victim and victimizer. The victim's risk is the loss of something valuable—life, limb, or property. The victimizer's risk is the loss of freedom, social status, and possibly of life, limb, and property too. But criminals intend to gain something as a result of a crime, something to which they are not legally entitled. So criminals, rational ones at least, must concern themselves with weighing the risk of discovery, apprehension, and conviction against the intended gain.

If the risk of discovery and the amount of the possible gain are great, then more time and thought must be spent on planning, disguising, surprising, escaping, and possibly covering up the crime. Fortunately for police authorities, criminals tend to act in haste. Their plans often go awry. They do not anticipate everything that can happen. They usually add to their arsenal of defenses rationalizations for their misconduct, or alibis. "It wasn't me; I was elsewhere." "The devil made me do it." "I am poor and misunderstood, a victim of oppression." "He [the victim] had it coming." "I must have been crazy for doing what I did."

These rationalizations are what police interrogations are intended to sort through. Here again, intuition may play an important role. Criminals usually offer an excuse or justification for what they do. Sometimes they feign ignorance or illness. Sometimes they even feign amnesia. Interrogation cuts through these defenses, excuses, and rationalizations.

During an interrogation, it is important to remain sensitive not only to what the suspect is saying but to the manner in which it is being said, and to observe facial expressions, body and eye movements, word choices, and posture. Verbal fencing with the suspect does not help. Challenging the suspect's comments on the basis of pure logic and rationality does not persuade most criminals to confess. Suspects can stay with a lame excuse forever and almost come to believe it after a while. The reason they persist in lying is that their crimes were not committed out of a sense of logic but mainly for emotional reasons, such as lust, greed, anger, or envy. So in interrogating suspects, one must be prepared to deal with their emotions. "Why did you do it?" is not a very good question early on. It calls for intellectualizing by the suspect, or rationalizing, rather than an emotional response.

The better choice is to ask questions that do not get to the *gravamen* (main issue) of the crime at all—questions about a suspect's feelings and emotions:

- How are you feeling?
- Can I get anything for you?
- Do you feel like talking?
- Can I call anyone for you?

The purpose of these innocuous questions is to build rapport, first at the emotional level and later at a rational level. Not all criminal suspects feel compelled to talk about their crimes, but most do, if an interrogator can establish rapport with them. And rapport can be established even after they are advised of their right to remain silent.

An apprehended suspect, or one merely being informally interviewed before arrest, is under great emotional strain. Fears of conviction and incarceration are exacerbated. These fears must be overcome before intelligent conversation can be achieved. The tone and demeanor of the interrogator/interviewer must be reassuring, if not friendly. Intuition enters this process only if the investigator remains calm, dispassionate, and sensitive to the emotional needs and concerns of the suspect or witness. Intuition does not work when the investigator's mind is cluttered with isolated facts or a list of questions about the details of a crime.

Once investigators have learned something about the suspect's history, family, friends, and feelings, they can discern the most appropriate interrogation technique. If the suspect remains cold, aloof, and noncommunicative while innocuous questions are posed, he will be the same when the questions get more serious. In such a case, the investigator needs a command of all the known facts of the crime to gain a confession.

If the suspect responds openly to the investigator's offers of kindness and civility, the latter can lead by general questioning. The investigator will let the suspect describe the crime and not get in the way by verbal bantering, accusation, or sparring. The suspect should be allowed to tell the story in his own way, even if the investigator knows that some of the facts are being distorted. The investigator can always come back and ask for clarification and then compare the conflicts with the testimony of witnesses or confederates.

The importance of confessions and admissions in resolving crime should not be understated. Without such confessions and admissions, many crimes would never be solved. In some fraud cases, accounting books and records do not provide enough evidence to convict a suspect. So a confession from a thief, defrauder, or embezzler makes fraud prosecutions easier. A freely given confession often details the scheme, the accounts manipulated, and the uses to which the purloined funds were applied. The evidence gathered after a confession may corroborate the crime. A confession alone will not support a criminal conviction, however, so the auditor will have to retrieve from the data available within the accounting system and from third-party sources enough corroborating evidence to support the confession.

ENDNOTES

1. *ICC v. Baird,* 24 S. C.T. 563, 194, U.S. 25, 48 L. Ed. 860.
2. *Manhattan Malting Co. v. Swetland,* 14 Mont. 269, 36, p. 84.
3. *Nunan v. Timberlake,* 85F. 2d 407, 66 App. D.C. 150.
4. Kruse II, Warren G. and Jay G Heiser. 2002. *Computer Forensics: Incident Response Essentials* (Boston: Addison-Wesley, 2001), pp. 8–9. Taken from MSNBC, June 8, 2000.

Index